55° 50° 40°

5°

N

SURINAM   FRENCH
          GUYANA

ATLANTIC OCEAN

0°

Amapó

Trombetas

Pará

Jari

Amazonas

Marajó
Island

Belém

Xingú

Guupi

Santarém

Fordlândia

São Luís

Itaituba

Iriri

Pará

Tocantins

King Ranch

Maranhão

Tapajós

Marabá

Paragominas

Jamanxim

Fresco

Tocantinópolis

Menkranoti

Cachimbo

Araguacema

Xingu

Mira
Norte

BRAZIL

45°   40°

Araguaia

Xingú National Park

Goiás

15°

Mato Grosso

Main Map Area

Cuiabá

Brasília

Trans-Amazon Highway

55°   50°

South America

aries   Parks and Reserves

         Rivers

0   300   Miles

0   500   Kilometers

Scale

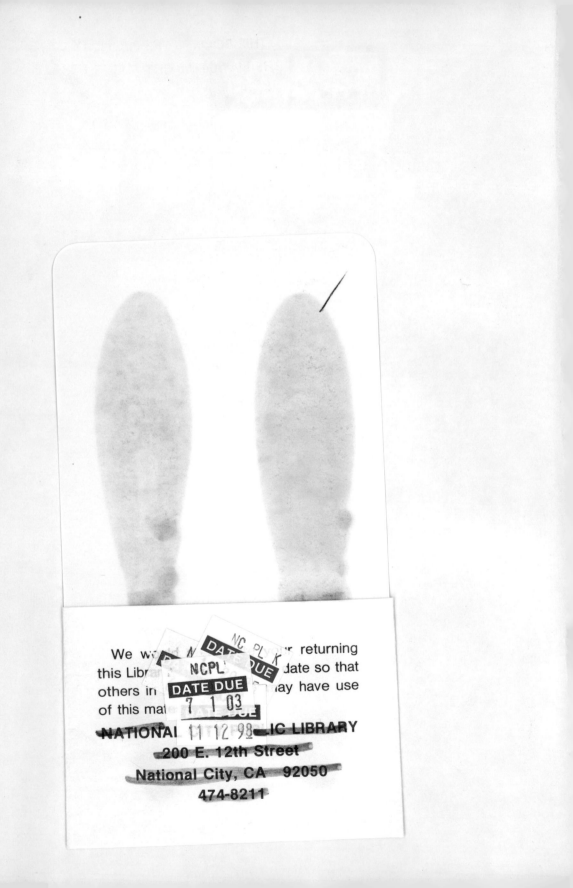

 *The Rivers Amazon*

Winnifred
E. Short
Memorial

J. Morehouse

The Rivers Amazon

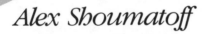

Alex Shoumatoff

Sierra Club Books
San Francisco

Library of Congress Cataloging in Publication Data

Shoumatoff, Alex.
    The Rivers Amazon.

    Bibliography: p.
    Includes index.
    1. Amazon Valley—Description and travel.
2. Shoumatoff, Alex. 3. Natural history—Amazon Valley.
I. Title.
F2546.S535   918.1'1'046   78-8585
ISBN 0-87156-210-3

Jacket design by Paul Bacon

Book design by Marjorie Spiegelman

First Edition

Printed in the United States of America

*To my father, whose love of nature, and
my mother, whose love of literature,
have largely shaped the path I have chosen*

Table of Contents

Preface   1

Chapter 1   Contact   7
Chapter 2   The King Ranch   19
Chapter 3   The Planalto   33
Chapter 4   The Indians   39
Chapter 5   Menkranoti   55
Chapter 6   On the River   91
Chapter 7   The Capital of the Jungle   99
Chapter 8   The Economy of Light   111
Chapter 9   Fish Stories   125
Chapter 10   Peruano's River   141
Chapter 11   Out of Time   163
Chapter 12   Vanishing Animals   187
Chapter 13   A Gringo in Quechualand   203
Chapter 14   Recovery   223

Bibliography   233
Selected Index   247

Photographs follow page   86
        and page   150

Preface

Several years ago I resolved to celebrate my thirtieth birthday in the Amazon. I would leave my civilization for a while, get lost in jungle, and taste the world pure and uncorrupted by its influence. I would find people whom it had not yet reached, living in a simpler time, in natural harmony with their surroundings. I would see if life as it is presented in the United States is the way it has to be, or if there are alternatives. And I would study in the greatest biological laboratory on earth.

I submitted a proposal to explore the Amazon valley and to report on the current state of our knowledge about it. I proposed to spend eight months in research and preparation, eight months in the field, and eight months analyzing and writing up my findings. The proposal was accepted and I started to work immediately.

Many people, I soon discovered as I began my research, had been drawn by the lure of the Amazon. Among them was John Muir, who, because he reasoned that his lung condition would only worsen in the tropics, ended up going to Yosemite Valley instead. Mark Twain, too, was "fired with a longing to ascend the Amazon" after reading Lieutenant William Herndon's *Exploration of the Valley of the Amazon* (1851–2). He found fifty dollars in the street in Cincinnati and took off immediately to New Orleans to find a boat for Pará, as Belém was then called. But there was none. In a few days he was out of money, and he ran into a Mississippi river pilot whom he begged to teach him the river.

As letters from scientists at work on various aspects of Amazonia began to come in, I discovered how much of the valley is still unknown and unexplored. In almost every area of natural science there are tremendous gaps: the flora is only half identified, and only ten percent of its pharmacological potential analyzed; only two thirds of the fish have names, and a uniform system for classifying them has yet to be agreed upon; the habits of such conspicuous Amazonian animals as the river turtle, the jaguar, and the giant otter are largely unknown; and the same holds for the ecology and social behavior of the primates. Knowledge of the bird fauna was thought to have been complete until the discovery in 1976, in Chiclayo, Peru, of the *pava de tombes,* thought to have been extinct. Only a dozen people know the birds of lowland Amazonia, and none is willing to say that there are no important finds still to be made. Indian groups whose existence was not even suspected are still being run into, and there are probably a few who will hold out against contact through the century. Meanwhile the list of known villages in which outsiders have never set foot remains at least a hundred.

My discovery of the *lack* of knowledge about Amazonia in turn influenced my conception of the sort of book I could write. I finally decided to use the travel format because it is the most truthful and probably the most effective way of getting across my impressions—for they *are* only impressions—and to let the contents stand for whatever the book is worth. At the same time I was aware that in choosing the travel genre, I was harking back to the great nineteenth-century naturalist-explorers of the Amazon, Spruce, Wallace, and Bates. Their combined work remains vital today because of its scope. Forging into unknown territory, these men were intrigued by *everything*—a quality that, in this age of increasing specialization, is not much encouraged. My own approach to nature is closer to the wide-eyed curiosity of these men than it is to the statistics and systematics of today.

The book, then, follows my journey. It starts at the mouth of the river and proceeds gradually deeper into the interior, to two forest tribes, with intelligence-gathering stops at the few outposts of civilization along the way; and finally ends (with my near death) at the alleged source of the Amazon. Anything encountered in the course of my travels—a spectacular sunset, a random bit of song, or an unidentified sound in the night—was fair game, as far as I was concerned; it revealed something about and was in itself part of the *nature* of the Amazon. With this open-ended approach, I did not lack for material. It was the final process of selection that was difficult.

I was very fortunate in having Danny Delaney, a friend from my hometown, to go with me. He had just gotten out of the army, where his training as a medic would prove invaluable for me and the many people we would meet who needed attention. He was twenty-two and the idea of a South American adventure was far more appealing to him than staying in Westchester County and accumulating the twelve credits he needed for his college degree.

As the hour of departure drew near, we put a lot of thought into what to take along. Much of our tropical kit—the tent, the space blanket, the Vietnam jungle boots, the fishing rod—would prove useless baggage and be unloaded along the way. But certain things were essential: a hammock, a good pair of sneakers, and a well-stocked medicine chest with antibiotics, anti-malaria, -amoeba, and -worm tablets, and rubbing alcohol to cleanse and soothe insect bites. I also took along a small nylon-string guitar which would hold dozens of Indians spellbound, and a battery-powered cassette tape-recorder. Nothing was more fascinating for them than to hear their own voices played back. The tweezers on my Swiss Army knife would come in handy for rooting out maggots nesting in my legs. We carried no guns. It would have been a great mistake to have done so.

At last the great day came. A small crowd of loved ones grew smaller as the train pulled out of our hometown station and took us to the city and the plane to Belém. "Lots of luck," the man who sold cigarettes and newspapers shouted. "I hope they don't put you in a pot down there."

Acknowledgments

Besides the people named in the text, the following were of invaluable help. I emphasize that I am fully responsible for the use to which I have put their information, and for any misrepresentations that may have resulted. Fernando Costa-Novaes, Jesco von Puttkamer, Loren McIntyre, John Cohen, Timothy Plowman, Ramon Ferreyra, Francis Huxley, Anna Roosevelt, Hilgard O'Reilly Sternberg, Daniel Gross, Betty J. Meggers, Robert Carneiro, Jean H. Langenheim, H. W. Irwin, Nigel Smith, Ann Prance, Will Stubblebeim, Diane Schwartz, Garard Lamas, J. Calvin Giddings, Homer Vergil Pinkley, G. Marlier, J. J. Wardack, Julio de la Torre, and Ben Bradlee, Al Horne, and Harry Rosenfield of the Washington *Post*. I would also like to thank the Marsh Memorial Sanctuary, Mount Kisco, New York, for allowing me a leave of absence and for their grant.

5

It is impossible to behold such immense masses of water in the centre of a vast continent, rolling onwards to the ocean, without feeling the highest admiration.

—*Richard Spruce*

1

Contact

The attention is fixed upon so many objects that one can hardly give an account of the impressions he receives.

> —*Alexander von Humboldt,*
> *on first looking at the*
> *Amazonian rain forest.*

Some said it had been a chapel. Others were convinced that it had been a distillery where the padres brewed *cachaça*. But that had been two hundred years ago, and now only a skeleton of outer brick walls, with arching doorways and windows, was left. A strangler fig had sprouted on one of the walls, sending down its roots to smother the building like wax from a melted candle.

Two centuries ago, the building had been surrounded by sugar cane. Now it was thick jungle, trees a hundred feet tall, dripping with vines, ferns, and air plants. The air beneath them was stifling. Every leaf in the vicinity was giving off moisture, and I was bathed in a sweat which refused to evaporate, but stung my eyes and streamed down my body.

I reached down and ran my fingers along the midribs of a little plant called *Mimosa pudica*. The leaves folded up like a woman shrinking from someone's advances. Beneath the mimosa a lone black ant an inch and a half long was making its way among the dead leaves in search of a cricket, a beetle, or a wasp to drag back to its hole. The sting of one of these *Tocandeira* ants could put a man into anaphylactic shock.

A few feet from my head the slender body of a sapphire hummingbird hung in the air for several moments, then buzzed on, leaving a little beyond it a brown and white butterfly resting at eye

7

level on the side of a tree. The butterfly appeared to be facing up but on closer inspection what I had thought was its head turned out to be an extension of its folded wing. It was mimicking itself to fool the birds into striking at a part of its body that it could afford to lose.

A shadow passed over the vegetation as a hook-billed kite coasted into the adjacent palm and banana swamp, and landed on a dead limb where he stayed for the next half hour. A red-ruffed fruit-crow flew into a cecropia tree and stood with a long green caterpillar in its beak among the splayed, drooping leaves. At least ten kinds of birds were singing and it sounded as if there were also someone nearby whistling briskly to himself. Somebody, I thought, must be gathering fruit in the jungle. Afterwards I learned that the remarkably human whistler was a parasitic cuckoo.

A troop of monkeys came crashing through the trees. I couldn't see them, but they were probably *macacos de cheiro,* squirrel monkeys, the only simians still common around Belém. One of them knocked the dead brown leaf of an aroid, as big as an elephant's ear, out of the crotch in which it had been growing, and it came floating down and got caught in some vines.

Danny and I could hear foliage being splattered in the distance. The sound was coming our way, and before long we were caught in a warm, driving rain. After twenty minutes it stopped. The air, cleared, was suddenly breathable. We stepped out of a doorway of the ruin and made our way back into Belém. It was our first contact with the Amazonian rain forest.

As the only port of entry to Amazonia, Belém had been riding tides of prosperity and decline for four centuries. Lately it had received a boost from the building of the fifteen hundred-mile-long Belém-Brasília highway. The road had soon become the most important way of delivering goods into the interior, and Belém had revived as a center of commerce, having been in a slump since 1964 when the military coup d'état, in its campaign against communism and corruption, took away its free port status. In those days Belém had been a racy place, with a constant flow of hot diamonds, jaguar and otter hides, and other contraband coming down from upriver, and a flourishing black market of American cars, Japanese radios, and French perfumes.

With revenues from the highway, Belém had sown a quick crop of high-rise buildings, giving the city an impressive aerial view for its travel posters. But down in the streets below, the sleepy tropical atmosphere and the famous easygoing Brazilian graciousness pre-

vailed. The sun at noon was enough to paralyze even the most ambitious. All civilized effort ground to a halt. Shopkeepers pulled
down their metal blinds and went home for lunch and a siesta. The
tourists went down to the fort and sat at tables that looked out
across miles of swirling muddy Amazon to a long green island
wobbling in the heat. Behind that island was another island, Marajó,
which is bigger than Switzerland.

The city was back on its feet by three. Children of assorted
colors came out and played soccer on the winding, cobbled side-
streets that led down to the big open-air market by the docks. Every
once in a while the street would converge on a plaza dominated by
an old church with a weathered, Alamo-type front, small trees growing out of the bell towers, and maybe two or three men lying in the
doorway. Down at the market the stalls were filled with many kinds
of fish and fruit, jute, bell peppers, and other vegetables grown a
hundred miles away in the Japanese community of Tomeasu. Having
come in on an earlier tide, the shrimp boats were stranded in the
grey mud, and their crews, with the day's catch delivered, had the
rest of the day to swing in hammocks. An ancient, peg-leg man
beckoned and opening a basket held up a small tan and copper boa
that tied itself into knots and glided around his arm in a spiral. The
market was attended by hundreds of *urubús*, black vultures with
grey heads, perched on the peaks of the buildings, walking along
the wooden frames of the stalls, and devouring the garbage.

Shortly after we arrived, we entered the restaurant of the Hotel
Central, and sat at one of the tables with greasy white cloths that
looked on the main boulevard. Long-bladed fans turned overhead.
It was the sort of place where you expected Humphrey Bogart, Sid-
ney Greenstreet, and Peter Lorre to walk in at any second. A bald,
bespectacled man in his seventies, who had been nursing a beer a
few tables away, noticed the trouble we were having with the
Portuguese menu and came over to help us. His name was Johnny.
"Johnny Shaves, sir, at your service." He had been around the world
seven times, made and lost a number of fortunes, dropped out of
Cambridge University at nineteen to prospect for gold in Man-
churia; moving on to South Africa to be the head engineer for the
De Beers diamond mine; going into business in Guyana with Jimmy
Angel, the flying ace; getting swindled by a crooked lawyer out of a
sugar plantation in India; and finally ending up in Belém eight years

ago. "I know plenty of better places," he told us philosophically, "and I know plenty of worse places." He lived by special arrangement in a garret above the elevator shaft of the King Hotel amid stacks of paperbacks in English, all of which he had read several times, sitting at a table with nothing but a towel around him, his thick reading glasses secured with string. Occasionally he would try his own hand at fiction, preferring the O'Henry-type short story with the bang ending. Most of his characters were secret agents in Her Majesty's service. At seven p.m. he would descend to his table at the Central, and the waiter would bring him his beer. He had cut living expenses down to three dollars a day, he told us. To keep going he worked as a tourist guide for the Booth Line, the Liverpool-based steamship company that has been running cruises up the Amazon since the days of the rubber boom. "I make a dishonest living any way I can," he said.

Johnny was a gold mine of information about Amazonia. Shaves on piranhas: "The piranhas make a growling noise like a dog and can clean a bullock in thirty minutes. The water boils and the fish bite each other in the frenzy. Piranha, in Amazonian slang, means a hooker, and it is also the name of the best brand of *cachaça* (white rum)." Shaves on diamonds: "A diamond lives because it's properly faceted. A well-cut diamond has sixty-two facets. It must have a caulet, a flat bottom. The finest stones are called Brazilian first water diamonds. They are the standard by which other diamonds are measured. You might find one anywhere in the Amazon: in Roraima, on the Tocantins, in Goiás. They're oily and don't look like anything when you pick them up. The brightest diamonds are blue-white. Why? Look, if you have a white shirt and you send it to the laundry, how do you make it whiter? Add a little blue."

"Embora," he snapped at an urchin who had approached our table with a bunch of lottery tickets. "That means bugger off." Johnny took a sip of his beer and watched the crowd stream out of the cinema across the street, stunned, after a violent American movie that had managed to pass the censors. "Eight years ago they had no lights in the street and you took your life in your hands crossing it. An unshaven policeman would come up to you and say, 'Give me a pack of cigarettes and I'll take you across.'"

During the next few days we sought out information for our expedition from several valuable resources in Belém. We spent an informative afternoon at the Belém headquarters of Projeto RADAM. The title of almost every Brazilian organization is an acronym, and

RADAM gets its name from the radar-photographic survey it has been conducting of the Brazilian Amazon. Amazonia Legal, Otto Bittencourt Netto, the number three man at RADAM told us, is made up of the states of Pará, Amapá, Amazonas, and Acre, the northern parts of Mato Grosso and Goiás, the northeastern corner of Maranhão, and the territories of Roraima and Rondônia. It takes up five million square kilometers, which is more than half of Brazil and almost as large as the entire continental United States. Still largely uncharted and unknown, it is the last vast wooded wilderness on earth. "The idea of the government is to know the Amazon," Netto said. "We do not know its real potentiality."

In 1971, in collaboration with the United States Air Force, RADAM began to make high-altitude photographs of Amazonia; these were more revealing than satellite pictures, which are unable to penetrate clouds. The photographs were taken at a scale of one to four hundred thousand and blown up to one to two hundred and fifty thousand. Netto took us to a conference room whose walls were papered with the blow-ups that had been pieced together to give an aerial picture of the entire region.

A number of interesting things showed up in the pictures: a new four-hundred-mile river in western Amazônas, undiscovered because it is completely hidden by vegetation; some two hundred circular structures in northern Pará that Netto suspected were extinct volcanic cones. "We soon found out that Amazonia isn't as flat as we had thought it was," he told us. "It has more topography over two hundred meters than anyone had realized."

The next phase of the project was to send out teams of geologists, agronomists, forest engineers, geographers, cartographers, geomorphologists, and ecologists. They went up rivers that had never been explored and descended from helicopters into places where white men had never been. Fifty men died in rapids and helicopter crashes. In Rondônia one of the teams made the first contact with an unknown tribe of Indians, and the survey was suspended while *sertanistas,* or trained contact-men, from FUNAI, the National Foundation for the Indians, went in to do the delicate job of winning their confidence and preparing them to cope with the civilization that had suddenly come into their lives. Netto explained how a helicopter team operated: men lowered from the hovering craft would first open a clearing with chainsaws, then the helicopter would land, and the team would go to work. After five days or so it would pull out and return to Manaus to analyze the various soil, mineral, and wood samples. Some three to four thousand of these clearings had already been opened, Netto estimated, and others were being opened up at the rate of four or five a day.

The reports the teams began to send in were impressive—five billion dollars worth of timber, mostly mahogany and cedar; eighteen billion tons of iron in the Carajas Mountains between the Tocantins and the Xingú rivers; tin, cassiterite, and manganese in Rondônia, Pará, and Roraima; kaolin in Pará; gold on the Rio Tapajós; bauxite in the Amazon's floodplain. On the slopes of one of the extinct volcanoes in Pará, a team found six lakes, each at a different level, and each a different color. "We hope to find titanium," Netto told us, "copper, lead, zinc, uranium, and phosphates. We are also exploring for oil." Perhaps they would find some at the mouth of the Amazon; off Marajó Island, the depth of the sediments is twelve thousand feet. The rich oil deposits in Peruvian and Ecuadorian Amazonia at the foot of the Andes are already being tapped. Some geologists claim that the organic debris accumulated there because it is the site of an ancient river delta. They explain that the Amazon used to run the other way, emptying into the Pacific. One hundred and eighty million years ago, the theory goes, when Africa and South America were joined, the Niger and the Amazon were the same river, rising in the deserts of Morocco. Then the continents moved apart, and the sunken Pacific plate began to grind into the western edge of South America, heaving up the Andes and causing the Amazon to reverse its direction. From the topographical standpoint the Amazon could easily have run west at one time. Its floodplain is almost perfectly flat for thousands of miles, and the only thing that keeps the water moving is the pressure of the rain and the snowmelt at its sources.

The ultimate purpose of the six-year, thirty-million-dollar RADAM, Netto told us, was to present a comprehensive zoning map for the utilization of Amazonia. It would show which areas to mine, which to farm, which to preserve as national parks, where the natural pastures are, and where new settlements of people could best be accommodated. But RADAM is really only a blueprint. How much of the structure will get built, and when, remains to be seen. With less than two people per square kilometer, Amazonia is one of the least populated places in the world. Once you get off the major tributaries, there are only scattered families of *caboclos,* rural Amazonians of mixed white and Indian blood. They are rugged people, leading the isolated, self-sufficient life of pioneers. And deep in the forest, in the headwater areas, semi-nomadic groups of Indians are living a hunting and gathering and rudimentary agricultural existence that hasn't changed much in the last ten thousand

years. The problems of "conquest"—the tremendous distances involved and the forbidding nature of the environment—have enabled most of the valley to resist development and integration with
the rest of Brazil right up to the present.

Some twenty-five miles out of Belém, an observation tower of metal
pipes had been built up into the crowns of the trees, some one
hundred and twenty feet up. From the top we looked over four
hundred hectares of virgin rain forest, with the Amazon in the distance. The first thing we noticed was how many different shades of
green there were. While the forest is evergreen, each species has a
different periodicity, blooming and flushing new leaves at different
intervals. Some of the leaves had just come out and were light
green or reddish, with a velvet sheen. Many were a deeper, richer
green, and a few were beginning to turn dull and brown. Only one
species, *Ceiba pentandra* of the *Bombaceae* family, was in flower, a
lone lavender dome in the bobbing sea of green. Most of the trees
before us were of even height, although other trees of varying size
were staggered below them, and a few trees called emergents had
thrust out of the canopy. Next to the tower the breezes played in the
twice-compound, feather-like foliage of an emergent *Fabaceae* in
the legume family; it seemed strange that such a giant should have
such diminutive leaves. Three green parrots, raucous but in tight
formation, flew by, but otherwise it was very quiet; by midmorning
few of the birds were singing any more and there was only one
tattered white swallowtail to represent Belém's butterfly population.
You wouldn't have thought Belém is one of the most species-rich
spots in the world for birds and butterflies—five and seven
hundred respectively.

The dark floor of the forest was even quieter. Little was growing except low patches of selaginella, similar in habit and appearance to our clubmosses, and pennant-like clusters of *Araceae* and
Maranteceae. In the struggle to find nourishment from the poor
and periodically inundated soil, the roots of the trees had spread
laterally, forming huge buttresses called *sapopoemas,* and some had
developed pneumatophores to breathe with, like the cypress knees
of Florida swamps. Lianas ran up the straight, limbless trunks like
cables. There was a noticeable lack of dead wood on the ground,
only a tidy mat of tan and ochre leaves, and the fumes of their clean,
rapid disintegration, combined with the penicillinlike aromas of
moulds, seared our nostrils.

After our preliminary view of the jungle we were about to enter, we stopped at the Museo Goeldi, Belém's charming natural history museum, to thank Dr. João Murça Pires, the curator of botany, for providing us with the truck and the *mateiro,* or woodsman, who had taken us to the tower. A quiet man with an ironic smile, Dr. Murça Pires is Brazil's foremost authority on the vegetation of low-land Amazonia. He has spent the last few years identifying the trees in three undisturbed jungle stands—one in the *várzea,* or season-ally flooded forest, one in the *igapó,* or swamp forest, and one in the *terra firme,* or upland forest. We had visited the three sites, but since it was the dry season, could see little difference in the three communities, which are the basic forest types of Amazonia. The difference, Dr. Murça Pires told us, is mainly in composition, and since most of the species look the same, it was not surprising that we should be confused. "In the tropics the trees don't need to specialize as much as they do in dry or cold areas," he explained. Then he made one helpful distinction—in the *várzea* and the *igapó* the trees tend to have more prominent buttresses.*

Most of the trees can only be told apart by the minute charac-teristics of their flowers, and since they often have no flowers

---

*On the fifteen hectares which Dr. Murça Pires examined, he found 8,996 trees whose circumference at breast height was thirty centimeters or more. They belonged to three hundred and forty-five species, each of which con-stituted less than 1% of the total number of trees, except for *Eschweilera,* which took up nine percent of the *várzea* and *Euterpe oleracea,* which composed 23% of the *igapó.* Eighty-three species were common to the three areas, 73 were exclusive to the *terra firme,* 26 to the *igapó,* and 48 to the *várzea.* The six most common trees in the *terra firme* were *Eschweilera odora, Eschweilera amara, Tetragastris trifoliata, Vouacapoua americana,* and *Goupia glabra;* in the *igapó: Buterpa oleracea, Caraipa grandiflora, Virola surinamensis, Symphonia globulifera,* and *Tapirira guianensis;* in the *várzea: Euterpe oleracea, Pentaclethra macroloba, Carapa guianensis, Theobroma subincanum,* and *Pterocarpus officinalis.*

Dr. Murça Pires learned that as their size and height increased, the number of trees diminished, and that each species tended to have a favorite height, to be filling, in other words, a particular ecological niche. He found, however, that the growth curve of the trees was continuous, and that there were therefore no strata, or concentrations of trees at one height, which the rain forest is commonly represented as having. "The gaps are all filled," he reported.

below a hundred feet, identifying them is no easy matter. The *mateiros* who work for Dr. Murça Pires shoot the flowers out of the tree with a shotgun when he only wants it identified, and when he wants a good specimen for his herbarium, they "swarm" it, slipping a cloth belt around their feet, grabbing the tree in their hands, pulling their feet up to their hands, and repeating the process until, inchwormlike, they reach the flowers. But only relatively small trees, less than two feet in diameter, can be swarmed. The *mateiros* climb the big ones with nail-studded boots and a metal loop around the trunk and their waists, leaning into the tree and flipping the loop to get higher.

The tallest tree found in Amazonia so far, Dr. Murça Pires told us, was a *Dinizia excelsa*, sixty-seven meters, in northern Pará. The biggest circumferences, fourteen meters at breast height, belonged to a Brazil-nut tree, *Bertholletia excelsa*, also in Pará. The trees around Belém with the greatest number of individuals were *Lecythidaceae*, legumes, and *Burseraceae*; with the greatest number of species, legumes with about a thousand, and *Burseraceae*, with about a hundred. "Nobody knows what plants are in there," Dr. Murça Pires said in answer to my question about the total number of species in Amazonia. "Only the margins of the rivers are at all studied. About twenty-five thousand species have been named so far, but the total number is probably twice that."

The real danger in Amazonia is not from the wild beasts or the headhunters, but from the diseases, most of which are insect-borne. The swarming microbial life of the region is still poorly understood. To get some idea of it we visited the Evandro Chagas Institute, a tropical disease research center on the edge of Belém, and talked with the director, a woman named Dr. Gilberto.

The most widespread health problem in the Amazon, she told us, is malaria, which came over from Africa on slave ships some time early in the nineteenth century. In 1859 Henry Walter Bates, a British naturalist who had been working in the Amazon for eleven years, came down with *sizoens*, "the ague of the country," which was malaria. This was years before drugs like sulfa and perenatomine would be developed, and the only remedy available was quinine, made from the bark of the cinchona tree. "I always carried a stock of medicine with me," Bates wrote in his journal, "and a small phial of quinine, which I had bought at Pará in 1851 but never yet had use for, now came in useful. I took for each dose as much as would lie on the tip of a penknife blade, mixing it with warm chamomile tea.

"The first few days after my first attack I could not stir, and was delirious with paroxysms of fever; but the worst being over, I made an effort to rouse myself, knowing that incurable disorders of the liver and spleen follow ague in this country if the feeling of lassitude is too much indulged."

Bates did not realize that his ague had been transmitted by the bite of the *Anopheles* mosquito. There are actually three species of *Anopheles*, Dr. Gilberto told us, which transmit several different strains of malaria. The two common strains, one of which is a much more serious proposition than the other, can now be cured by simple pill treatment, but many rural Amazonians are suspicious of pills or ignorant that the treatment exists. There are also a few resistant strains which are incurable. Little is known about them except that they are particularly virulent and usually fatal.

In 1968, one person out of every hundred thousand in Amazonia was tested for tuberculosis, and 14.4 percent had a positive reaction. In 1970, 21.5 percent of those tested were positive. Hepatitis, Types A and B, is another growing problem, wherever new settlements of people are established. Venereal diseases are an established fact of city life. Typhoid can be picked up wherever there is contaminated water, but the typhoid levels in Amazonia are about the same as in most places. Pneumonia, measles, and influenza are a problem for the Indians, who have no resistance to them. Since the century began the three diseases have wiped out well over half of the indigenous population of Amazonia.

Leprosy is active throughout western Amazonia, particularly in Acre, a state in the western part of the basin, where 10.1 people in every thousand have it. There are two basic kinds of leprosy with several intermediate varieties. One tends to be chronic and the other of shorter duration and more amenable to treatment by sulfa drugs. The disease is often contracted when there is a marriage between two genetically susceptible families, and is probably passed on by skin contact or by the handling of shared objects, although exactly how leprosy is transmitted remains a mystery.

One of the most grotesque diseases in Amazonia is leishmaniasis, in which a protozoa produces chronic subcutaneous ulcers. In advanced stages of the disease the nose and palate disintegrate. Leishmaniasis is transmitted by a mosquito whose habits and life cycle are not well understood. Five new cases a day enter the Hospital for Tropical Diseases in Manaus to be treated with chemicals which are for some people as debilitating as the disease itself.

Yellow fever, which carried off many of Bates's friends in Belém in 1850, is no longer an urban problem, but can still be contracted in the jungle. Smallpox, another nineteenth-century plague, has been eradicated from Amazonia; in fact there are only a few foci, or active centers, left in the world. Bubonic plague itself, cholera, and diphtheria are not serious problems, although they do occasionally break out. Beriberi was a big problem during the rubber boom at the beginning of the twentieth century for the gatherers who drank too much *cachaça* and didn't eat enough fresh vegetables, but is no longer widespread. Schistosomiasis, a liver disease which attacks children bathing in water where there are plenopid snails, is common in Northeastern Brazil, but in Amazonia there are only two foci: one near Belém, the other on the Rio Tapajós, at Fordlândia, where Henry Ford tried to grow rubber trees in a row in the nineteen-thirties and learned that he was only setting them up for their natural enemies.

Most people in Amazonia have intestinal worms. It is something they live with, although the worms can cause a number of parasitical diseases — trichocephaliasis, ancilostomiasis, strongiloidiasis, belhausia. Some of the worms enter through the soles of their feet, others in the food they eat. There are also various protozoa which parasitize the intestines. The most common is the amoeba, which is acquired by drinking water or eating vegetables contaminated with feces. Some amoebas are benign, others abscess the liver. Still other protozoa inhabit the bloodstream; one, *Triponozoma crusii,* causes Chagas' disease, which Darwin apparently picked up during his brief tour of central Brazil. This protozoon is transmitted by the hissing beetle, which bites its victims on the face while they are sleeping and then defecates next to the bite. By scratching, the sleeper unconsciously rubs the dung into the wound, and the protozoa that infest the dung are introduced into the bloodstream. Twenty years later the symptoms of Chagas' disease — cardiac and digestive dysfunction — appear. Fortunately, Chagas' disease is under control in most of Amazonia.

Certain worms called microfilaria also travel in the bloodstream. One of them causes onchocerciasis, or African river blindness. Like elephantiasis, this disease is transmitted by the black fly. A certain number of the injected microfilaria migrate to the eye, where they die and cause blindness. Two thirds of the Yanomamo nation, who live on the Venezuela border and are the largest native group in the Amazon basin, were recently discovered to be victims of the disease. At the moment onchocerciasis is only a problem for still isolated Indians, but the Brazilian government is concerned about its transmission to the national society, and a medical team is now studying the disease, about which little is known, in the Yanomamo village of Tototobi.

There are a number of ectoparasites that can attach themselves to you as you are walking through the jungle—chiggers, ticks, scabies, *bichus de pe,* which are gravid female insects of the species *Tunga penetrans* who bore through the skin to lay their eggs, causing sharp pain. Another insect whose larvae fatten themselves on human flesh is the botfly, *Dermatobia hominis.* The botfly lays its eggs on the long proboscis of a biting insect called the *mutuca,* which injects them as it is feeding. In such a favorable environment the botfly larvae grow many times their normal size into spiny, inch-long maggots that break the skin after forty days. The botfly can cause a disease called miiasis, and secondary infections can result from the activities of all the ectoparasites, not to mention the bites of the numerous kinds of mosquitoes and the sandflies, which are also vectors of arboriviruses like equine encephalitis.

Finally there are various fevers like Oripush fever, transmitted by the *acuticordes* mosquito. It comes in cycles of seven years and lays you out for about three days. Dr. Gilberto could tell me little about *febre negra de Lábrea,* blackwater fever, a jungle sickness which causes liver dysfunction but whose etiology is not known.

And nothing is known about the mysterious *febre* that erupted in the state of Pará several years back, killing seventy-one people, including the research unit sent in to identify it. SUCAM, the Superintendency for Public Health Campaigns, had no alternative but to close off the area in which the fever had broken out, and within several weeks the epidemic died of its own accord.

Most of the diseases we stood a chance of contracting in the jungle could be treated with pills or injections, except for the ones whose first symptoms appeared only years afterward. I was especially eager to learn how the jungle people diagnosed and treated diseases.

The following day, we left the city.

2

The King Ranch

Twenty years ago there were no highways in Amazonia to speak of. The roads went a little way out of Belém, Manaus, and Santarém, then stopped. If one wanted to go somewhere one took a boat or flew.

Then, in 1955, the Belém-Brasília highway was begun. "Crossing regions formerly unknown to man," as a government booklet boasted, the highway started at the mouth of the Amazon, headed due south in an almost dead straight line, cutting through virgin rain forest, then entered a land of rolling hills clothed with grass and low, twisted trees, and finally, more than two thousand kilometers later, reached the site that had been chosen for Brazil's new capital. The road was ready by 1960 and its impact was profound. In the next decade the population between Belém and Brasília jumped from a hundred thousand to two million, and the number of villages and towns from ten to 120. Before the road, cattle ranching in Amazonia had been limited to Marajó Island, at the river's mouth and the natural savannahs along the Rio Branco in Roraima Territory; and some of the *várzea* along the main river had been cleared for pasture. When the floods came, the steers were herded on great rafts called *marombas,* and fed with the vast islands of grass that drift down the Amazon at floodtime. But now large properties along the Belém-Brasília highway were bought up by ranchers, and clearing was begun. By 1970 five million head of cattle were grazing along the highway.

The *fazendeiros,* or ranchers, had assumed there would be no trouble converting the rain forest into a grassland. This was a reasonable assumption since it had been widely believed that Amazonian soils are among the richest in the world. Any soil that produced such a staggering vegetation must be prodigiously fertile. Almost every naturalist who went into the Amazon had accepted this—even Henry Walter Bates, the nineteenth-century British naturalist who spent fourteen years in the Amazon and was not ordinarily one to jump to conclusions.

The *fazendeiros* soon found, however, that the depth of their soil was no more than three inches in most places. Beneath it was usually a thin layer of white sand, then an impermeable zone of red clay. The soil was very poor.* Heavy rains robbed it of its mineral richness. How, then, did you explain the forest? The answer was that the nutrients are all in the soil and are quickly recycled. Constant high temperature and humidity make up for the lack of minerals in the soil. The tropical climate speeds up plant growth, but also hastens the decomposition of dead vegetation by microorganisms that return the minerals to the soil. Billions of fungal filaments called mycorrhizae creep along the floor, forming a web which catches whatever nutrients there are and feeds them back to the plants before they can leach down into the sand. The forest makes up for its small mineral capital by circulating it rapidly. The system is called a closed nutrient cycle. The forces of growth and decomposition are in equilibrium. "This balance," José de Castro and Arthur Fereira Reis wrote, "is the result of the furiously destructive life of the forest, with plants being born and dying at the same time, killing and being killed in a terrible fight for life, each anxious to appropriate its share of the mineral salts."

But once the trees are taken down the system collapses like a punctured tire. The mycorrizhae shrivel, rain washes away the soil, wind blows away the sand, and the red clay hardens into a brick-solid hard-pan called laterite, in which few seeds can germinate. The process, which a group of scientists describes as "green hell to red desert," is irreversible. In five to ten years most of the cleared land will be no good, for pasture or anything else.

The poverty of the soil is understood by the Indians; that is why they are semi-nomadic, moving their villages as soon as the gardens cease to be productive. The *caboclos,* much of whose cul-

---

*According to RADAM, only 4.02% of the Amazon has medium to high fertility soil, and of that 79.89% is *várzea* and under water for part of the year. There are two rich crescents of limey-Carboniferous soil between Manaus and Gurupa. Brazil-nut trees and palms are concentrated in them. The best *terra firme* soils are in the state of Acre. Mr. Netto estimated that 100,000 square kilometers in Acre had high agricultural potential, but "the relief," he said, "is not so flat. Rain is heavy, and erosion might be a problem."

tural ecology is derived from the Indians, know about the soil, too; they also practice a shifting, slash-and-burn agriculture. The ranching in Pará was based on a fundamental misconception about the suitability of the soil for long-term, sedentary use. Amazonia's fertility is an illusion; it is a "counterfeit paradise," as Betty J. Meggers, a cultural ecologist at the Smithsonian Institution, has put it.

But still the clearing along the Belém-Brasília highway continues. The people need protein: most Amazonians live in a chronic state of undernourishment, and as their standard of living rises and they can afford an alternative to rice and beans, more of them will become meat-eaters. And there is money to be made in ranching, even if it proves to be a short-term, hit-and-run operation. The Brazilian government, eager to encourage any productive use of Amazonian land, has done nothing to stop the clearing except to pass a law enjoining the *fazendeiros* to leave intact half of the jungle on their property. The *fazendeiros* get around this by selling their uncleared patches to other *fazendeiros,* who, as new owners, can cut fifty percent and sell the remnant to someone else. Large multinational corporations like Volkswagen and Swift-Armour have bought up Pará and are burning off the jungle.

Instead of going directly to Brasília, I wanted to see the ranching in Pará, which is the biggest thing happening in the Amazon. As we headed south on the Belém-Brasília highway, all the land in sight of the bus window had been reduced to a burnt-out wasteland, broken only by the occasional blackened pole of a dead tree. Flames swept the horizon, smouldered on the charred red ground, and licked the apron of the highway. Half of Pará must have been on fire. There was no sign of any ranching. The grass near the highway had already been killed by overgrazing, and the cattle moved back, deeper into the jungle.

Leafing through my two-way pocket dictionary I made dismal attempts to communicate with the man sitting next to me. He was getting off at Paragominas, the capital of the cattle country. He owned and operated a small *fazenda* — five hundred hectares outside of town. Most of the ranches were hundreds of thousands of hectares. The biggest and best-run one was the King Ranch. A "Meester Charles" was the manager.

At about nine p.m. the bus pulled into the moonlit square of Paragominas. We crossed a sewage ditch on a plank and checked into the pink Hotel Minogerais, then went for a stroll down one of the long empty streets that led from the square. The wind was howling and the white sand flying. A man on a mule rode by, holding his crop out to one side. The mule was moving at a pace between a walk and a trot, scurrying along briskly but hardly lifting its feet from the ground. Man and mule disappeared into the swirls of sand. We passed a row of pick-up trucks parked in front of a bar. Within, a rowdy crew wearing finely tooled cowboy boots, Stetson hats, and revolvers on their hips was crowded around a pool table. A big black pig rooted in the marketplace. In one of the stalls a kerosene lamp illuminated the face of an ancient woman tending pots of beans and *farinha*. Paragominas resembled a town in the Nevada desert. There was no trace of the jungle.

That night we had our first encounter with the *Culex* mosquito. The insect is called by its Indian name, *carapana,* in the rural Amazonia, and *perne-longo,* long-foot, in Brazil at large. All it takes is two or three of them in your room to leave you a sleepless wreck in the morning. What possible survival value could the incessant high whine have, I wondered, as I lay listening to a few of them flying above my bed. Wouldn't it be much better for them if they could approach and bite in silence? Maybe they couldn't help it. Maybe the whine was a by-product of their flight mechanism which they hadn't yet succeeded in de-selecting. Maybe, since the *carapanas* must number in the trillions and the insects are in no danger of extinction, there has been no pressure on them to evolve a quieter flight mechanism. Maybe, I conjectured, approaching hysteria, they whine to give their predators a chance. But I didn't think animals did that sort of thing. Maybe, though, it was in the overall interests of the organism that some of them die. Finally, with the pillow wrapped around my ears, I managed to drop off from sheer exhaustion. It was only later that I learned from an entomologist the real reason for the *carapana*'s whine: the female *carapana* attracts the male with the sound, much as a female firefly lights up her abdomen. The whining sound is a by-product of its wingbeat frequency of 500 cycles per second, and is within the octave of middle C, usually the note G. It can only be heard when the insect is three or four feet from your ear. After a meal of blood, which is the best time for copulation, the whine goes up slightly, and the males receive the signal with sound receptors on their antennae. But only sexually mature males have their antennae in tune and are capable of receiving the signal. Some opera singers in outdoor theaters, the entomologist went on, complain of insects which converge upon their open mouths as they hit the insects' wingbeat frequency. Mosquitoes evolved their whine without humans in mind. Most of their hosts don't have the ability to swat.

In the morning we sat out on a red dirt road waiting for a ride to São João, forty kilometers away. The arrival at noon of two gringos in a battered "pickoppy" brought everyone in São João to the windows of their board-and-batten *barracas* or shacks. People took our gear and we followed them into one of the houses. In the front room were some tables, with rows of beer and *cachaça* bottles along the back wall. The next room was the living quarters, with colorful hammocks strung from post to post, and a beautiful mulatto woman sitting in one of them and nursing a baby, while chickens ran around and pecked the dirt floor. In the back yard were a stand with a washbasin, strings of clothes drying in the sun, an outhouse, and a few papaya and tattered banana trees.

We ordered eggs and were served a banquet which half the village watched us eat. I managed to get it across that we were trying to get to the King Ranch. There was an agent for the ranch here, our host told us, but he was out of town and his radio was broken. It looked as if we would have to barge in unannounced.

A car took us several miles and left us at the beginning of the road to the ranch. For the next six hours we sat on a split-rail fence playing checkers with our portable set. The new grassland was unnaturally quiet. It was a dry, alien habitat into which few of the animals of the rain forest, which we could see in the distance, would come. A few pallid skinks scuttled along the dusty ground. A small blue butterfly that must have been related to our spring azure landed on the swaying kernels of some nut sedge. A flock of small, voiceless finches, the male blue and the female black and gold, seemed at home among the dense clumps of introduced African grasses. The only noisemakers were grasshoppers that sounded like tinkling bells and yellow-bellied kiskadee flycatchers called *"bem-ti-vis,"* the uninhibited songsters who are the mockingbirds of Amazonia.

It grew dark. In the distant jungle a frightening chorus of birds, insects, frogs, and monkeys raged against the dying of the light. A big red planet, Jupiter, appeared low in the western sky, and red veins of heat lightning broke out in the east. The lights of a *fazenda* several miles away went on, and we could hear the purr of its generator. We were beginning to feel very unimportant.

Several hours later, just as we were crawling into our sleeping bags, a "pickoppy" full of *macheteiros,* the drifters who are hired to cut down the jungle, pulled up. As we packed up and loaded our gear on the truck, the *macheteiros,* who had been drinking and were singing several songs at the same time, got out and urinated on the hubcaps. Soon the dark shape of a lone, cone-shaped monadnock rose out of the flatness on our left, then the countryside on our right was blazing in the night. "It's been burning for three days now," the driver told me as we raced along the flames.

A few hours later we rode under arching stick letters that said FAZENDA URAEM, and then we found ourselves standing on the manager's porch. If Meester Charles was at all puzzled by our sudden appearance, he kept it to himself. Shaking our hands warmly he brought us chairs and called to someone inside, *"Oi Rufina, trage-me dois cafezinhos, por favor,"* (Oh Rufina, bring me two cups of coffee, please.). The accent was unmistakably British. He was, in fact, South African. His full name was Charles Rowcliff. He was in his late forties and wore a handlebar moustache that gave him the appearance of an affable walrus.

After an amiable chat in which we managed to establish a mutual friend, Johnny Shaves of the Hotel Central, he brought up in a very tactful way, not wishing to seem too curious, the subject of what we were doing here. I produced a letter that explained I was making a study for an organization concerned with "preserving the integrity of ecosystems."

"Ah," he said with a slow nod. "So you've come to see how we are raping the environment. Normally visits to the ranch must be cleared in Belém, but since you're here, you're here."

He took us to the guest bungalow, where we met a medical chemist from Texas named Jimmie R. Tullis, who had been brought in to do something about the malaria. The year before, he told us, the malaria rate among the *macheteiros* had reached thirty-three percent. Half a dozen men had died and the *fazenda* had been on the verge of folding.

The next morning Tullis took us to the clinic he had set up with help from the Chagas Institute in Belém. Here the *macheteiros* had their teeth worked on with a foot-powered drill and were treated for the secondary infections which, because they often go untreated, are a major cause of death in Amazonia. We looked into a room where half a dozen men down with malaria were sweating it out on cots.

"Malaria," Tullis explained, "is an insect-borne parasite that attacks the oxygen-producing red blood cells. An untreated victim can die within eight days of being bitten. It goes for the liver. Once the parasite gets into your liver, the malaria can linger for years." We thought of Rowcliff, who still hadn't gotten over the malaria he had picked up in Haiti years before. "I know when the fever's coming because my knees start to ache," he had told us.

"There are several species of *Anopheles* mosquito whose bite will give you malaria," Tullis went on: *"darlingii,* which breeds in swamps throughout Amazonia; *aquasalis,* which breeds in salt water along the coast; and *cruzii,* which breeds in the pools of water that collect in bromeliads and is the major transmitter in southern Brazil. The one here is the so-called whitefoot mosquito, *Anopheles darlingii.* It has a territory of about five hundred yards and comes out at about six p.m., flying on a horizontal plane and biting any warm-blooded animal in its path. It bites between six and seven, when many of the *macheteiros* are bathing in the river, and then again at eleven.

"Three to eight days after the mosquito has injected the parasite, the victim starts vomiting, running a fever of a hundred and two to a hundred and four degrees, sweating like a pig, and shaking uncontrollably. Then the fever subsides for about a day, as the parasites, metamorphosing into their gamete or non-pathogenic phase, multiply and spread. When the fever comes back red blood cells are ruptured like crazy and it's at this point that you can die unless you are treated. Whether you die or not depends on how many parasites you have in you. In an extremely severe case there are eighty to a hundred per microscopic field.

"When we got here a year ago we found one of the *macheteiros* in a coma, hardly able to breathe. We gave him mouth to mouth resuscitation, brought him in from the *mato* (the jungle), and drew his blood. The poor guy was averaging 380 parasites per field. We shot him up with cloroquine, plasma, and vitamin B. Three days later his count dropped to a hundred. Now he's back to work. But he would have died, no question."

Tullis took us into his small lab and put a blood smear taken from one of the patients in the next room under a microscope. Two dark purple dots had punctured the larger, paler circles of the red blood cells. They were *Malaria vivax* parasites, one of the two strains Tullis had identified at the *fazenda.* In a corner of the slide he pointed out several liver flukes that were still unknown to science.

The *macheteiros,* who came mostly from Maranhão, the poverty-ridden state to the east of Pará, brought the parasite with them. The whitefoot mosquitoes, which breed whenever there is standing water, spread them around. "Malaria," Tullis pronounced, "is a marriage between the strain and the vector." The strain was easier to control. Nighthawks, flycatchers, frogs, fish, snakes, and several other species of insects including the praying mantis, eat whitefoot larvae, and Tullis was planning to start hanging DDT bombs around the huts of the *macheteiros,* to intercept the mosquitoes on their feeding runs. But there was no way he was going to wipe out all the whitefoots on the *fazenda.* So the main thrust of his program was to break the chain at the people stage. All new *macheteiros* were screened at the gate. No one with a positive count was allowed in. Once every two weeks everybody on the *fazenda* had his blood drawn. All positive cases were treated at the clinic until cured. This seemed to be working. The previous month's malaria rate had been 6.6 percent.

"Some of the men are superstitious and refuse to be treated," Tullis told us. "If they refuse, we throw them off the *fazenda.* Others will spit the pill out when your back is turned. You have to keep an eye on them."

Rowcliff joined us for lunch at the guest bungalow and we sipped gin and tonic helplessly as a fire swept acres of prime grassland below us. The fire had spread from a pile of burning rubbish at the gate, and now a topaz wall of flame shooting up to thirty feet was moving slowly toward the bungalow. Luckily there was a stream between it and us.

"Damn," Rowcliff muttered. "Whenever I want to start a fire, it rains." We got into his pickup for the grand tour. The first problem for someone in his position, he explained, was motivating the men. "If you want to get people to do things around here," he said, "you have to be some kind of a character. Put on a big act." And so Rowcliff spoke with a rich drawl that captured the men's attention, and chose his words with humor and relish. He was an entertaining man for whom the men could bring themselves to work. At the same time, there was no question who was in charge. "They get used to me," he said. "I don't get used to them. When grandmother visits, it's the grandchildren who get used to her." He walked with authority, and had never had to draw the .38-caliber revolver he wore on his hip.

He had started on a plantation in Haiti, then gone to work on the river Jari in northern Pará, clearing jungle for a reclusive American billionaire named Daniel K. Ludwig. Ludwig's property is bigger than Connecticut, and few visitors have been allowed to see what he is doing there. According to his head forester, with whom I spoke in the United States, he is growing Caribbean pine, a fast-growing Asian tree called *Gmelina,* and rice, and is also mining the kaolin on the property. Kaolin is a rare clay used in the manufacture of china. People in Manaus who had been there told me he is having great success with his rice, and the other crops aren't working out as well.

Four years before Rowcliff had been hired by a corporation that included the King Ranch of Texas, the Swift-Armour Meat Packing Company, and a consortium of Brazilian interests, to develop land it had bought in southern Pará. "The first thing we had to find out was where our property is. We're still not completely sure. We came down the Gurupi River. It took two weeks. There was no road of course. We put that in."

The only people Meester Charles encountered on the river was a village of some sixty Urubú and Tambés Indians. I had read about the Urubú in a book called *Affable Savages* by Francis Huxley, of the famous British scientific family, who had lived among them in the nineteen fifties. To them the *urubú,* the vulture, was a symbol of universality because, like fire, it consumed everything. Like most Amazonian tribes the Urubú raided other Indians and took captives, especially women. The captive was allowed to marry and treated as a full Urubú, except that at any moment, whenever a *rite de passage* required the live sacrifice of an enemy, he could be put to death. Urubú women were renowned for their feather work. They denuded parrots of their feathers, then rubbed the birds' skin with an irritant extracted from a frog which made the feathers grow back in different colors. Urubú women wore long blue skirts. Among the tribe's superstitions was a belief that if a man ever saw menstrual blood or a certain blood-colored fungus that sometimes appeared in tubs of manioc meal, he would soon grow sick and die. Their word for making love was *suruk,* and as in most societies, *suruk*ing was a favorite pastime, and the subject of most Urubú jokes and myths.

I did not know it at the time, but read later in a British magazine, *The Economist,* that the Urubú had been dispossessed when officials from FUNAI, the National Indian Foundation, "testified that there were no Indians living there so as to grant land title to a large cattle ranch." The ranch in question was undoubtedly the one we were now riding around.

Rowcliff's next step was to start clearing. He experimented with tractors that dragged chains behind them and were supposed to mow down everything in their path. But the wood of the trees proved too hard, and he ended up hiring the work out to Brazilian contractors or *empreteiros,* and paying so much for every hectare they cleared. The contractors brought in teams of *macheteiros, peões,* or *braçóes,* as they were variously called. They tended to be a pretty rough bunch. Rowcliff preferred them between eighteen and thirty-five, in good graces with the law, and free of malaria, but a few who did not meet these criteria always managed to slip through. He thought, but was not sure, that there were now about seven hundred *macheteiros* on the *fazenda.*

"There are several of my highly energetic men now," he said, indicating a lean-to on the right in which several sullen-looking individuals were swinging in hammocks.

The *macheteiros* lived in *barracas* or *boccas,* wall-less lean-tos with clear plastic roofing, and bought their food at exorbitant prices from the *empreteiros,* who bought it at cost from the *fazenda.* "They eat rice, beans, and farinha, hunt game and tortoises in the forest, and get a lot of fish from the river," Meester Charles said. "We supply them with meat." Movies were occasionally projected on the wall of the storehouse.

The *macheteiros* usually worked for thirty to sixty days, then moved on, or if they were deeply in debt to their *empreteiro,* they disappeared in the middle of the night. They received the Brazilian minimum wage, 605 cruzeiros, or about $66.50, a month. "I go up to the States and they talk to me about poverty," Rowcliff said with feeling.

"The first thing they do," he went on, "is to go into the jungle with brush hooks and machetes and slash down the small stuff. Then they go in with axes. A few of the *empreteiros* are rich enough to have a chain saw."

Knocking down the trees was no easy task. The biggest ones were a hundred and fifty feet high and fifteen feet in diameter at breast height. A forester had identified a hundred and fifty of the more common Amazonian species on the *fazenda,* and no one knew how many more there were. Most of them wouldn't accept a nail. Rowcliff let the *macheteiros* leave standing three of the biggest or hardest trees per hectare. Once it had been knocked down the forest sat and dried for ninety days.

"Then we use the match," Rowcliff continued. Most of the burning was done in the dry season. The heat of a burning 125-hectare lot could get so intense that it created a "firestorm" complete with thunder and lightning, small tornadoes which tore the bark from the trees, and violent explosions. We passed an enormous tree which had been sandblasted into the air and had landed upside down with its root buttresses sticking up like the fins of a crashed rocket ship.

Rowcliff took us to a place where the *macheteiros* had only just begun to slash down the small stuff. I waded in through the prostrate brush to the edge of a winding, pea-green stream. On the other side the exuberance of plant and animal life had not yet been disturbed. I caught a whiff of something very pleasant, not unlike the smell of olives, and made out among the braided lianas the speckled orange tongues of a spider orchid. All sorts of sounds traveled through the dark galleries, woodpeckers' screams, towhee and screaming pia whistles, the thin quaking of frogs, the monotonous drone of cicadas, the sawing and rasping and rattling of crickets and grasshoppers. The din grew so loud that I almost had to cover my ears; then it fell off. I looked hard but couldn't see a single animal. They were all hidden among infinite sizes, shapes, and shades of green.

"It's alive in there, isn't it?" Rowcliff said, giving me an understanding look when I had come back to the road. "And we are tearing it all down." He eyed my notebook. "Write that down."

We drove on in silence. Finally he said, "I can't afford to be one of these ecological purists who doesn't believe in cutting down a single tree. I have to get things done. This is the frontier. You forge ahead and pick up the pieces afterwards."

After the forest has been burned Meester Charles waits for the rains to soften the soil and work in the ashes, then plants fast-growing grasses and nutritious legumes. "We plant as soon as possible," he said, before the irreversible process of erosion and laterization, or hardening, claims the land. "We plant colonial or guinea grass. It gets to be three feet high, but the trouble is that it clumps and doesn't spread. We are also trying out an Australian grass, which has a piney smell, and the African *Brachiaria,* and putting *canarana,* the native aquatic grass, in the wetlands. For creeping legumes, we have *Pueraria* and *Centrosema.* The *Pueraria* is very aggressive. It smothers everything in sight, like kudzu in your South. After planting we put out the cattle to spread the seed through the stamping of their feet."

Rowcliff believed that laterization could be prevented by generous seeding of legumes and a policy of grazing no more than eight head per acre, and that with proper management the land could remain productive much longer than five years. Much of the land along the Belém-Brasília highway, he said, had been ruined because of overgrazing and insufficient legumes.

Late in the afternoon we stopped at a corral in the middle of a five-thousand-hectare piece in which the grasses were coming in strong. Rowcliff pointed with pride to a pen of brown calves which were his own breed—a cross between *Melore-zebus,* which are descended from the white, hump-backed Brahma cow of India, and Santa Gertrudis from the King Ranch, Texas. "They're docile, hardy, and adapted to dryness," he told us. "I don't think there's a better cattle for this climate." Meester Charles had 7600 head on the *fazenda,* and was just beginning to ship them to Belém. He sent them in at 460 kilos.

Two *macheteiros* who had been boarding up a new bunkhouse shouldered shotguns and headed for the jungle in the hopes of shooting a monkey, a tapir, or a deer. We were standing in the middle of about 10,300 acres of cleared land. The black trunks of the dead trees that peppered the pastures did not seem so ugly or conspicuous, as the new grass beneath them gleamed in the weakening sunlight. "You have to feel this out from moment to moment," Meester Charles remarked vaguely, as if he were almost talking to himself, and for a moment we forgot ourselves and were drawn into the sphere of his ambitions. Right or wrong, the ranch was a monumental endeavor.

Fazenda Uraem had 70,000 hectares, of which about 20,000 had been cleared. All over southern Pará the jungle was being pushed back westward across the Araguaya River; in some places the land had already been cleared to the banks of the Xingú. At that moment, several hundred kilometers to the south, on an enormous *fazenda* belonging to the Volkswagen Corporation, a fire bigger than Belgium was raging out of control. A lot of good wood was just being burned, and it seemed like a terrible waste. But then that's exactly what the North American settlers had done with their forest. There had been more wood than anyone had known what to do with. It had stood in the way of civilization, and the easiest way to contend with it had been to burn it.

Here in Amazonia the problem was magnified. There were many more species of trees, few of which had recognized commercial value. A few kinds could be converted to planks and fenceposts at Meester Charles's sawmill. But most of them were of such incredible density that they could only be used for parquet floors and tobacco pipes. Brazilian law required that the *fazendeiros* do something with the wood, but there was no market for it, so it just went up in flames.

The next morning we tried to persuade Rowcliff to let us visit the Urubú Indians. Most of them lived several hours by motorboat down the Gurupi River and on the opposite bank, but one group, we had learned, had moved back across the river and were living on land deeded to the *fazenda,* about a day's walk through the jungle. The *empreteiros* had poached a few Urubú men, who had worked on the clearing crews for a month, paid them with tools and clothing, and then returned them to the village.

"Nothing doing," Meester Charles pronounced emphatically. "Our policy is a sort of apartheid. We don't have anything to do with the Indians and they don't have anything to do with us." To appease us he sent for the gatekeeper, who had started the fire which was still going strong around the guest bungalow. He had two names, Amazônas and Jennings, and had lived with the Mundurucu Indians on the Tapajós River. He had visited the Urubú four times. "They are very savage," he said, "and one of the hardest tribes to domesticate. They live in villages with the Tambés Indians and number about two thousand. There are about five hundred warriors. They have a few rifles and do most of their hunting with bows and their fighting with clubs. They raid each other's villages a lot. They all wear shirts and speak Portuguese. They have malaria and some die. The village on the *fazenda* has thirteen or fourteen houses, with a family in each one. Their *tuxaua,* or head man, is called Zaponeras. I traded some machetes with him."

"So long," I yelled to Meester Charles. "I'll be checking my meat patties from now on to see where they came from." The pickup pulled away from the guest bungalow, passed Amazônas' fire, then Amazônas himself, who was holding open the gate and giving us the thumbs-up sign. Further down the road there were fires on both sides and the driver gunned the truck through twenty-foot flames only a few yards away.

Back in Paragominas with a five-hour wait for the bus on our hands we sat in the dispatcher's shed with two big *jaboti* tortoises on their backs. No one seemed to know or care that they were a protected species. They would fetch a good price in Belém. The dispatcher had hung up the epauleted khaki shirt in which he greeted the buses and flopped into his hammock with a movie magazine. Two boys were picking on a twenty-two-year-old mulatto dwarf named Sebastiano. Sebastiano seemed to be the main source of comic relief in Paragominas, but he didn't seem to mind, chasing after the boys with wild *capoeira* kicks while his pants kept falling down. *Capoeira* is a martial art-form which was brought to Brazil by slaves from Angola and looks a lot like karate.

It was Saturday night and the whorehouse next door was getting a lot of business. The girls were lush and heavily painted, and they looked about fourteen. After several hours we realized that the boy next to us was not sleeping, but in a coma. His friend, a young black in a hard hat, told us that he had malaria. He had got it working at Fazenda Uraem but had refused to be treated. "He just wants to go home," the friend told us. The boy was about sixteen. His friend tried to force a cigarette in his mouth, then a cookie. The boy revived just enough to spit out both. His friend looked at us desperately. We took out one of our cloroquine pills and after many attempts finally got it down him. But Danny suspected that it was probably too late.

☙ 3 ❧

The Planalto

Two days later the white towers and gleaming lake of Brasília appeared like a mirage on the Planalto, Brazil's high central plateau. Here we would spend a month waiting for permission from the National Indian Foundation (FUNAI) to visit a remote Amazonian tribe. Brasília had started from scratch in 1960. It had not grown organically but had been catapulted into being by the determination of one man, Joscelino Kubitschek, who died in a car accident the week we arrived and was given a hero's funeral attended by millions in the city's sunken glass cathedral. Kubitschek's motto had been "fifty years in five," and to realize his goal of getting Brazil caught up with the technologically advanced countries as soon as possible, he knew the nation's northern half had to be developed. By relocating the capital, he gave the region new importance. People migrated *en masse* from the arid Northeast, whose thirty million inhabitants have an average annual per capita income of less than $800 and form Latin America's greatest concentration of poverty, and settled in the Distrito Federal. In only seventeen years the population of Brasília and its satellite cities had passed four million.

The capital itself is called the Plano Piloto because it is shaped like an airplane, with two wings radiating from a central shaft. It was designed by Oscar Niemeyer, a disciple of le Corbusier, and consists mainly of independent towers separated by green spaces. The Brazilians have had no trouble relating to their capital's cold glass modernity, or melting its impersonality with their famous *calor humano,* or human warmth. Brasília's success is marred only by a few environmental problems: its attractive lake is badly polluted, and its highway system is already inadequate for the volume of traffic that uses it.

The best things about Brasília are its situation and its climate, which is about like that of San Diego. Few cities are so open to the sky. On clear days the air is sharp and clean, and the sky's blueness diffuses into infinity. On overcast days monumental cloudscapes gather over the Planalto; black curtains of rain sift down, and the light breaks through in shafts. At sunset every pane of glass in the city that faces west is tinted rose. Then the moon comes up, huge and orange. The horizon rumbles, lightning cracks and pulses behind the clouds.

Fifteen minutes out of Brasília, civilization gives way to the *cerrado,* a grassland flecked with low, twisted trees with stiff, broad leaves. In the gullies, along the streams that cut the Planalto, are the gallery forests, miniature versions of the rain forest that takes over five hundred miles to the north. Some of the springs that bubble up along the scarps of the plateau head south, providing water to the capital. Others head north, feeding the Araguaya River, a tributary of the Tocantins, which flows into the Amazon.

One Sunday afternoon we got on a bus that said Água Mineral, and was going to the spring at the Parque Nacional do Brasília. I took a dip in the spring along with several other people, picking up a low-grade virus whose symptoms—nasal congestion and chills— appeared almost immediately and took several days to get over. We walked half a mile, entered a gallery forest, and sat on the bank of a clear, rippling stream. A morpho, one of the world's largest and most spectacular butterflies, sailed past us with lazy flaps of its metallic blue wings, and headed for a bamboo thicket. Another large butterfly, *Napeocles jucunda,* skipped along on the muddy ground, and when it rested it looked no different from a dead leaf. Above us a pair of yellow and black siskins called *pintassilgos* were flying in and out of a small sock of grass and twigs that dangled from a branch.

Walking along a dirt road we were stopped by two patrolmen and spent the rest of the afternoon riding with them around the ninety-thousand-acre park. They were down-home country boys from Goiás, and proud of their wildlife. The one driving stopped the truck and pointed to a huge flightless *ema* or rhea, which looked like an ostrich, bounding through the grass. We stopped again below a dead tree in which an exquisite bird of prey, a caracara, was crouching with spread wings, about to take off. The men got out and showed us where a wolf* had rubbed against a barbed-wire fence, leaving some of its red hair tangled in the tines. They

---

*The maned wolf, a threatened species, is extremely rare in Brasília Park.

pointed to a hole in the red ground which belonged to a *coruja* or burrowing owl. The bird popped out and swiveling its head around a hundred and eighty degrees inspected us curiously. We saw two sizes of deer: the *campeiro** and the *catingueiro*. The *cateingueiro* was almost as small as the key deer of Florida. It stood its ground fearlessly until we got within ten feet of it, then bolted into the trees with high, gazellelike leaps. *"Tranquilidade,"* one of the patrolmen sighed.

A few days later we joined Dr. George Eiten's botany class on a field trip. A native of Bronx, New York, Dr. Eiten is now a professor at the University of Brasília and the world expert on the vegetation of the *cerrado*. "The *cerrado* is the only semi-deciduous savannah in the world," he told us. "The nearest to it is the woodland of Katanga in the Congo. Its twisted or leaning trunks are a characteristic which it shares only with the elfin cloud forest of the Andes. Ecologically, it is the equivalent of the tall grass prairie in the central United States, but it is woodier, and, as in the coastal pine forest of the United States, the trees are fire-adapted. The roots reach to deep, always moist layers in the soil and every species sheds its leaves every year, but not at the same time."

Dr. Eiten stopped the bus along road DF-6, two kilometers east of Lake Paranoa, one of Brasília's artificial lakes. The students got out and waded with stakes, twine, and plastic bags into the dense *cerrado*. He helped them mark off twenty- by fifty-meter study plots and explained Whittaker's method for determining species richness, in which the center strip in a larger grid is closely examined. Then he told us that the *cerrado* had about three hundred and thirty species of vascular plants per hectare, which was pretty good for a non-forest flora. There were about one hundred and fifty kinds of trees—nothing compared with the rain forest, but then, he pointed out, the *cerrado* was much richer in non-woody plants. He showed us a strange shrub called *Vellozia flavicans* on which leaves like wisps of grass had sprouted at the tips of long, branchless stalks. The paucity of foliage was a xeromorphism: the plant looked as if it were adapted to dryness, but it really wasn't, since its deep roots gave it constant access to water. Most of the *cerrado* was xeromorphic, as opposed to the true xerophytic plants that grow in completely arid places. Next to a three-foot bell jar of baked red clay

---

*The *campeiro*, known in English as the pampas deer, is becoming rare; reserves in which it occurs are even rarer.

made by soldier termites we found some bracken. "Just like the ferns at home," I said.

"The same species grows all over the world," Dr. Eiten explained. He crushed the aromatic leaves of some false quinine and held them up for us to smell. The laughter of a campo flicker erupted in the pounding, dry silence. Behind us we could hear the high, steady squawking of a plush-crested jay and the single loud whistle of a tinamou.

There are three kinds of *cerrado: campo limpo,* or "clean savannah," has few trees; *campo sujo,* or "dirty savannah," is almost a forest; and the *cerradão,* the thickest community, *is* a forest. In about the middle of Mato Grosso the *cerrado* and the riverine gallery forests give way to the semi-deciduous *mata de transição,* which is lower, denser, and more filled with palms than the actual rain forest. In some places the *mata de transição* is replaced by *babaçuzai,* or palm forest, named after the *babaçu* palm, the dominant species. Then the rain forest proper takes over. It is called the *mata* in Brazil and the *selva* in Bolivia, Peru, Ecuador, Colombia, and Venezuela. Within the *mata* are the *terra firme, várzea,* and *igapó* forests, already encountered in Belém. Dr. Murça Pires defined the *várzea* and *igapó* as the seasonally and permanently flooded forests respectively, but other botanists define *várzea* as *either* seasonally or permanently flooded forest along the white-water rivers, while *igapó* is either seasonally or permanently flooded forest along black-water rivers. Further confusion arises around the Amazon's mouth because there is both *seasonal várzea,* which is under water several times out of the year, and *tidal várzea,* which is flooded twice daily as pressure from the rising tides of the Atlantic backs up the river. The *tidal várzea* zone ends about a hundred miles upstream. An effort is being made to standardize the terminology.

In southern Amazonia, between the Rios Tocantins and Tapajós, and particularly between the Rios Xingú and Tapajós, there occur patches of almost impenetrable, vine-infested forest called *mata de cipó;* why there, and only there, is not known—the soil does not seem to provide an explanation. The mountains of Rondônia, Roraima, and Acre and the eastern slopes of the Andes host a low, thick woodland called the *montane forest.* Unlike the lowland *mata,* it is often dominated by one or two tree species and is rich in orchids and epiphytic mosses. And the shrubs and low trees that grow on rock outcrops like the ironstone of the Serra de Carajas in Pará, are yet another community.

In white sandy places the *mata* sometimes gives way to a community of low bushes called *campina,* or to *campinarana,* a dry, depauperate forest, rich in orchids and bromeliads, with a floor of sedges. In the upper Rio Negro valley there is a large area of forest on white sand called *caatinga.* It is similar to *campinarana* but it gets more rain and is denser and richer in tree species and ground flora. In northern Roraima there is a lot of *campo* or savannah; when a savannah is subject to flooding, as on Marajó Island, it is called *campo de várzea.* The dry sand dunes along the rivers are often taken over by a low, shrubby community called *restinga,* and yet another type of forest occurs along small rivers that are subject to flash floods. It is called the *flash floodplain forest.* And finally, on much of the Atlantic Coast, mangroves, whose buoyant seed-pods drifted over from Africa, have sprouted. These are the main plant communities of the Amazon basin.

One afternoon I asked Dr. Paolo Nogueiro Neto, Brazil's Minister of the Environment, how much of the Amazonian rain forest had been taken down. He said about one tenth. To judge from what I had seen in Pará, it seemed more like one third, the estimate made by FAO, the United Nations' Food and Agricultural Organization. But to judge from later flights over the Amazon, during which I would see nothing but trees stretching for hundreds of miles in every direction, it seemed closer to the three percent for the valley as a whole proposed by Jonathan Kandell of the *New York Times.* The size of the Amazon basin is not something that is easily conceived.

If the deforestation of Amazonia continues at its present rate, there may be serious global repercussions. In a recent *Scientific American* article, George Woodwell estimated that .5 to 1.5 percent of the world's rain forests is being cut annually, about two thirds of which grows in the Amazon valley. If the rate is taken to be 1 percent, then 4.5×10^5 grams of carbon are being released annually. Half the figure is from the burning of fossil fuel, half from the burning of our forests. If this trend continues, by the year 2020 the atmospheric carbon levels will double. Carbon dioxide is a critical determinant of climate because it absorbs radiant energy at infrared wavelengths. Woodwell predicts a warming in the world's climate over the next few decades that will severely disrupt agriculture, fisheries, and almost every other biological activity of man.

The concern voiced widely a few years ago, that cutting the

Amazon rain forest would deprive the world of its major producer of oxygen (the most common figure is that two thirds of our oxygen is produced in the Amazon valley) is no longer taken seriously by most scientists. Most of our oxygen, they have found, is produced by algae floating in the oceans. The Amazon is a mature forest in photosynthetic equilibrium: it requires as much oxygen as it releases.

But another concern *is* being taken seriously: when an area is stripped of its forest, it is stripped, by ecological feedback, of its rainfall. There is no information on what would happen to the world's weather patterns if the Amazon valley became a desert, but the consequences would undoubtedly be grave.

The thought of losing the greatest genetic repository on earth is equally distressing. A few years ago, the World Wildlife Fund calculated that if the Amazonian rain forest continues to be cut over at its present rate, a million species of plants and animals will become extinct, many before they have even been discovered. In Washington, Tom Lovejoy, the Fund's Amazon expert, explained how the figure had been arrived at: "About one and a half million species of organisms have been described on earth—a million animals, and half a million plants. There are probably three to four to ten million species in all. If you cut over all the primary forest in Amazonia ten percent of the total biota on earth would go. Taking the highest estimate, that would be one million."

During our month in Brasília we talked with many people who were concerned about the future of Amazonia. Some were in the government, some were scientists. Some were anthropologists who had just come in from the field with tales of what the Indians were going through as they were meeting the modern world for the first time. At FUNAI's library we learned a great deal about the native people of Amazonia with whom we would soon be coming face to face.

4

The Indians

The Indians of the Amazon valley, like all Native Americans, are descended from Paleo-Mongoloids who migrated from the Far East during the last Ice Age, somewhere between seventy and thirty thousand years ago, crossing from Siberia to Alaska on a temporary land bridge over the frozen Bering Strait. Their features are clearly Mongoloid: high cheekbones, black eyes and epicanthic fold of the eyelid, and lack of beard, eyebrows, or eyelashes. And many of the elements in their cultures—the blowgun, the penis sheath, the chewing of lime or ashes with a narcotic, and the pan-pipe, are also found in the indigenous cultures of Asia. Some of the parallels are striking. Peruvian pan-pipes from 500 B.C., for instance, have the same scale as the ones now being blown in Oceania.

To judge from the refinement of their projectile points, the people who entered the New World were already accomplished hunters. They stalked the big game of the period—mastodons, mammoths, ground sloths, giant cats, camels—and were probably as big a factor in the extinction of these creatures as the warming climate and the spread of the forests which favor smaller mammals.

The Indians moved slowly, about sixteen kilometers a year; more slowly when they had to adapt to the conditions of a new ecological zone. By 40,000 years ago they were in North America. Some stayed. Others continued by way of the intermontane valley of California into Central and South America. Some found the Andes to their liking. In Ayacucho, Peru, twenty thousand years ago, a hunting party stormed a cave inhabited by a ten- to fifteen-foot-tall giant sloth, killed and ate it, and were then buried alive in the cave by a landslide, not to be discovered until 1968 by archaeologist Richard MacNeish. The descendants of this party created the fabulous Inca civilization which was at its peak in the sixteenth century when the Conquistadores came and, in their blind lust for gold, annihilated it. Today the survivors of the conquest are scattered over the bleak steppes of Ecuador, Peru, and Bolivia, still herding llamas, growing the same crops their ancestors did, and speaking Quechua, the Inca tongue.

Other Indians descended into the Amazon valley and learned to live in the rain forest. They began as nomadic hunters and gatherers, gradually evolving into agriculturists. As they fanned out and became isolated from each other, four major linguistic groups developed: Tupi-Guarani, Jê, Karib, and Aruak. A few of the remotest tribes like the Trumai and the Yanomami invented languages that have no relation to the other ones spoken in the Amazon basin or anywhere else in the world. But the tropical culture itself was remarkably uniform. There were regional differences like the blowgun, which is used only by tribes on the upper Rio Negro and in western Amazonia; but the pattern of life, determined by the same basic ecological conditions, was the same everywhere: because the soil was usually exhausted within five years, the villages had to be small and mobile. Because of the difficulty of procuring food, population control, either by contraceptive plant or by infant murder, was generally practiced. The Indians developed a complex animism, identifying with the spirits of the animals they hunted, and a material culture derived mainly from the riot of plants which enveloped them. The Amazon Indian is a vegetable Indian, unlike the Eskimos or plains Indians, whose material culture is mainly derived from skin and bones of animals. By trial and error, the Indians learned the properties of the plants: certain reeds were good for arrows; certain toxic vines, beaten on the water, stupefied fish; the seeds of *Bixa orellana* smeared over the skin gave it a bright red color; the resins or infused leaves of some trees had a hallucinogenic effect.

By 3000 B.C., manioc was being cultivated along the upper Orinoco River, and its use spread into Amazonia, where it is the main staple today. Corn arrived from Mexico by 1 B.C. Along the banks of the Amazon proper, from the mouth of the Napo River to Marajó Island, a civilization with marked differences in social status, flattened foreheads, and a polychromatic style of pottery, arose, tilling the rich soil of the *várzea* and harvesting the teeming fishes in the river. When Francisco de Orellana came down the Putumayo River and made the first European descent of the Amazon in 1541–2, he passed "many villages and large ones, which shone white." They belonged to the Omaguas, the most powerful and sophisticated tribe in Amazonia. "There was not from village to village a crossbow shot," Friar Gaspar de Carvajal, Orellana's chronicler, wrote, "and the one which was farthest [from the next] was not half a league away, and there was one settlement that stretched for five leagues without there intervening any space from house to house."

Estimates of the pre-Columbian Indian population in the Amazon run as high as six million. But war, disease, and the slave trade took their devastating toll and by the beginning of the eighteenth century many of the villages along the main rivers were deserted. Those who were able to escape fled into the forest and up the tributaries. Some were protected by the *cachoeiras,* or cataracts which most tributaries have as they break down from the highlands, from contact with white men until only a few years ago. Most tribes, like the Cayapo, who migrated from the savannahs near São Luis in the state of Maranhão into the deep jungle of southern Pará, underwent cultural devolution, regressing to the nomadic hunting and gathering life. The bitter memory of abuse made them hostile to all *civilizados.*

Typical is the story of the Xavantes, a northern Mato Grosso tribe and one of the proudest in Amazonia. In the beginning of the eighteenth century two thousand *bandeirantes,* or pioneers, led by a Captain de Moto, settled on the Rio das Mortes, in the heart of Xavante country. De Moto won the confidence of the Xavantes by giving them a lot of gifts. But one day a *bandeirante* killed a Xavante, and the next morning the Xavantes came and wiped out the entire settlement. In 1765 the governor of the state of Goiás sent a man named Tristao de Cunha to re-establish friendly relations with the Xavantes. He succeeded in getting a few thousand of the Indians to move near the city of Goiás. The Indians soon ate all the food in the city and the order was given to Portuguese soldiers to drive them away. Half of the Xavantes were killed. The rest retreated behind the Rio das Mortes and killed every white man on sight until 1942, when they allowed an anthropologist to come and study them.

Many of the Indians who remained along the main rivers degenerated into beggary and drunkenness. Henry Walter Bates, the British naturalist who also found unspoiled villages, describes a village which he entered in 1854: "On the afternoon of the 9th [we] arrived at Matari, a miserable little settlement of Mura Indians. Here we again anchored and went ashore. The place consisted of about twenty slightly built mud hovels and had a most forlorn appearance, notwithstanding the luxuriant forests in its rear.... The absence of the usual cultivated trees and plants gave the place a naked and poverty-stricken aspect. I entered one of the hovels, where several women were employed cooking a meal. Portions of a large fish were roasting over a fire made in the middle of the low chamber, and the entrails were scattered about the floor, on which the women with their children were squatted. ... They offered us no civilities; they did not even pass the ordinary salutes, which all the semi-civilized and many savage Indians offer on a first meeting. The men persecuted Penna for *cachaça,* which they seemed to consider the only good thing the white man brings with him."

Few of the eighteenth- and nineteenth-century travelers in the Amazon were impressed with the Indians they encountered. "How difficult to recognize in this infancy of society, this collection of dull, taciturn, and unimpassioned Indians," Alexander von Humboldt wrote in 1800, "the original character of our species. Human nature is not seen here arrayed in that gentle simplicity of which poets in every language have drawn such enchanting pictures ... these natives of the soil . . . their bodies covered with earth and grease, and their eyes stupidly fixed for whole hours on the drink which they are preparing, far from being the original type of our species, are a degenerate race, the feeble remains of nations which after being long scattered in the forests, have been again immersed in barbarism."

In such a dispirited condition, the Indians to whom white men had access were easily exploited. Some of the most sordid atrocities on record were committed in Julio Cesar Arana's rubber empire on the Putumayo River at the turn of this century. Men were shackled in chain gangs and if they failed to produce a certain quota of latex they were burned alive or strung up and quartered or had their testicles shot off for the amusement of Arana's captains. The women were herded to "breeding farms." When the law finally caught up with Arana in 1914, fifty thousand Indians had died along the Putumayo.

The only respite in the ruthless persecution of the Indians that began with the arrival of the Spanish and Portuguese and has continued almost into the present came in the eighteenth century when the Jesuits, who wanted their souls, made an honest effort to protect them from the slave traders and other entrepreneurs who wanted their bodies. The Indians were institutionalized in missions called Reductions, forced to wear clothes and to adapt to a spartan routine of work and worship. "The transition to the rigid discipline of the Reductions," Robin Fourneaux writes, "was made easier for the In-

dians by the fact that, long before the Jesuits' appearance, flagella-
tion had played an important part in their religious and erotic
lives." Under pressure from the business interests, the King of Portugal threw the Jesuits out of the Amazon in 1769.

Missionaries continue to be an important factor. The Salesians,
who are Roman Catholic, are still making converts throughout the
basin, and there are a number of other Catholic and Protestant
groups, but the most important one in recent years has been the
non-denominational Summer Institute of Linguistics. The SIL was
organized in the nineteen thirties by an American named Cameron
Townsend. He started in Mexico, where there are one hundred and
fifty native languages. The idea was to teach the indigenous populations how to read and write in their own tongue, with the ultimate
goal of having them translate the New Testament. Today the SIL is
operating in twenty-four countries. Until 1977 it had missions with
forty-three tribes in Brazil. In Peru and Colombia it is the only
agency that is doing anything for the Indians. In 1976 the SIL was
nearly thrown out of Peru. People had begun to suspect that the
organization, with all its airplanes and radios, was subversive, and
had linked it with the CIA. Some charged that the SIL was pacifying
the Indians to get at the oil on their land. Others resented the fact
that an American group, and a non-Catholic one at that, was working with the Indians. No one else offered to do the work, however,
and in 1976 the SIL's contract with the government of Peru was
renewed.

In 1977 FUNAI, without explaining why, did not renew the SIL's
contract. The Brazilian newspapers reported that one of the missionaries had been found with soil-testing equipment. The man
claimed he was only trying to help the Indians improve their crop
yield, but rumors about an American plot to usurp Brazilian natural
resources, and of the SIL being a CIA front, began to circulate. In
any case there had long been friction between FUNAI's anthropologists and the gospel spreaders.

I talked with Jim Wheatley, the organization's man in Brasília
when the SIL was still operating. After a decade in the Amazon, he
said, the first translations of the New Testament—one in Kayangung
and the other in Ishkariani—were almost finished. The Christian
message did not take with every tribe, he admitted, and in many
cases the health and agricultural assistance and the introduction of
the written word were the real contributions. For many Indians,
Christianity is only of interest because it has a certain status value: if
one can dress in western clothes and sing "Glory, Glory, Halleluia,"

one has a better chance of impressing the women in another
village.

Today, the Brazilian Indians' main champions are FUNAI and
the foreign anthropologists working among them. FUNAI is the successor of the Indian Protection Service, founded in 1910 by Colonel
Candido Mariano da Silva Rondon. Rondon, who was part Indian,
was one of the Amazon's great explorers; he accompanied Theodore Roosevelt in 1914 on a nearly fatal descent of the unknown
"River of Doubt," which turned out to be a tributary of the Madeira
River and eventually became known as Rio Roosevelt. The SPI's policy was based on the following principles:

1) respect for the Indian and for tribal institutions and communities;
2) guarantee of permanent ownership of the lands they live on
   and exclusive use of the natural resources and all the
   utilities to be found there;
3) preservation of the Indian's cultural and biological equilibrium, in their contact with the national society;
4) protection of the Indian against spontaneous acculturation,
   so that his socio-economic evolution can go ahead without
   sharp changes. Legally, the unintegrated Indian was clas-
   sified as an incompetent ward of the state, with the SPI as
   his responsible guardian.

The SPI mediated conflicts between the Indians and the local
civilizados—the rubber and Brazil-nut gatherers, the skin-hunters,
caboclos (peasants), *garimpeiros* (prospectors), and *fazendeiros*
(ranchers)—many of whom are of Indian descent themselves, but
still have a redneck prejudice against the aborigines and covet their
land. The organization also performed the perilous job of contact-
ing remote tribes, explaining that they were citizens of a country
called Brazil, and setting up posts from which medicine, tools,
clothing, fishing line, and other useful items could be distributed.
Today there are one hundred and seventy-two *postos indigenos* in
Brazil, with most of them in the Amazon.

Some of the SPI's employees were extraordinarily dedicated,
while others abused their powers shamelessly. In 1967 the organization was implicated in wholesale slaughter of Indians by dynamite,
machine guns, and sugar laced with arsenic. The SPI's head, Major
Luis Neves, was charged with forty-three crimes, including complic-
ity in murder, embezzlement, and theft of Indian lands. The organization was condemned by the Brazilian Congress as "a den of cor-

ruption and indiscriminate killings," and dissolved, to be replaced by FUNAI, the National Indian Foundation.

Things have gone better for the Indians under FUNAI. There are still frequent clashes with the *civilizados,* however. In the fall of 1976, for instance, a land war erupted in the territory of Rondônia between five thousand poor white settlers and the partially contacted Surui tribe. "It's just like a *bangy-bangy,"* a Brazilian who had been there told me. "You've got the good guys, the bad guys, and the Indians." *Bangy-bangys* are the American westerns frequently shown on Brazilian television and in theaters. FUNAI arbitrated a settlement: the *civilizados* could stay on the land they had usurped until their crops came in, but then they would have to leave.

FUNAI has its critics, chiefly the foreign anthropologists who complain of lack of support for their field projects, and claim that only four to thirty percent (depending on whom you talk to) of the organization's budget is actually spent at the posts and thus tangibly benefits the Indians. A few recent scandals in which money owed to Indians landed in personal bank accounts haven't helped. Another problem is that FUNAI is under the Ministry of the Interior, which decides its budget although it has no say in how the money is to be spent. Pressure is sometimes exerted by development-oriented superiors. Sometimes, too, critics say, FUNAI gets so involved in its formidable bureaucracy that it forgets whom it is supposed to be helping; but few would deny that the new organization as a whole is well-intentioned, or that Brazil should be credited with having such an organization, which is more than most Latin American countries have. At its headquarters in Brasília a group of bright young anthropologists supervises the field work and reviews applications to visit the Indians; no one is allowed on Indian land without authorization from FUNAI, which requires impressive credentials and can take months to get. It is not a good idea to try and sneak in, either, as many tribes are in the practice of instantly killing any strangers they run into.

"The personal contacts between anthropologists and Indians have been extremely important for the defense of Indian land against farmers and ranchers, for health assistance to the Indian population, and even for protection against threats of physical violence," George Zarur, head of the field research division, told me. "FUNAI until recently used to exploit Indian labor, pay them a pittance to gather nuts. Now a female anthropologist working with the Gaviões is teaching them the value of numbers, how to manipulate the market, bargain in a marketplace situation, and make contact with the big nut buyers in Belém." Outside his office a stone-faced lobby of three Gavião nut-gatherers was waiting for an appointment.

"We hope there will be the day when the Indians take over FUNAI," Zarur went on. "It's a very uncomfortable position because the Indians are not here yet."

The most delicate part of Indian work is making contact with a new tribe. The men who do this are called *sertanistas,* and their creed, set down by Colonel Rondon himself, is "die if necessary, but never kill." Theirs is a true diplomatic mission, in which months and often years may pass before any real success is achieved.

The first step is to enter the area of the uncontacted tribe and to make a large clearing for the *posto de atração,* or approach post. Then a well-protected house, a FUNAI pamphlet explains, is built, "preferably sheathed in corrugated iron and fenced around with barbed wire to ward off attacks and shield the team from the hail of arrows to which they are likely to be exposed. At the same time they till a stretch of land to grow food on for the group and to arouse the interest of the Indians. While this preparatory work is going on, the use of firearms is avoided, even when hunting, so as not to intimidate or antagonize the Indians.

"During the first few days after the Post has been organized, the man in charge of the approach, or his immediate assistants, explore the surrounding jungle accompanied by interpreters. Along the trails and at the watering-places most used by the Indians, they put up small huts called 'tapiris,' where they leave knives, machetes, billhooks, scissors, glass beads, and other gifts. When the Indians discover the Post, they begin to watch the approach team constantly, keeping well out of sight, but attacking any careless worker who gets separated from his companions.

"This period of intense surveillance is followed by a phase marked by open hostility on the part of the Indians who, in successive attacks, do their best to get rid of the invaders. This is an important phase because it affords an opportunity of showing the friendly intentions of the expeditionaries and their firm resolution not to engage in hostilities. It is, however, necessary to be firm as well as affable, and let the Indians know that the teamsmen have weapons and know how to use them (in hunting, for instance), are well defended, and do not attack because they have no desire to do so.

"As a rule, after the first fruitless attempts to scare off the new-comers, they move their village farther back and return periodically to assault the Post at dawn. It takes months of efforts for them to realize that these white men are quite different from those others, their enemies, who made war on them. Only then do some bolder Indians venture surreptitiously into the clearing made to attract them. They draw nearer and nearer and no longer destroy the huts to make the acceptance of presents look like plunder, but begin to leave gifts of their own in exchange. The expeditionaries also grow more daring and when they sense the presence of the Indians, they come out of cover and talk to them with the help of the interpreters, urging them to make friends. 'Flirting' is the name given to this phase of approach in which the Indians start to accept presents and even ask for more, leaving rough models of machetes or scissors to show just what they want. Any abuse of trust is extremely dangerous at this stage. A misunderstood gesture may trigger an outbreak of renewed hostilities, wipe out the efforts already made and even make it necessary for a time to abandon the enterprise."

On the next page there is a very interesting paragraph:

"In most cases the Indians think it is they who have tamed the white man. Many of the tribes approached were, in fact, anxious to come to terms with the whites, but they did not know how to set about it, and whenever they tried, they were received with bullets. It was often their own way of approach that led to misunderstandings. It was customary for the Umutina, for instance, when meeting a group of strangers on the Upper Sepotouba, to show their friendly intentions by staging as realistic an attack as possible, even drawing their bows and feigning to let go their arrows, only catching them back at the last moment. Naturally a group that does not share this strange form of politeness, is not likely to realize that so sudden and well-simulated an assault is by way of being a friendly greeting. When, however, it is accepted without retaliation, they consider they have pacified and tamed the white man."

There are eighty to two hundred and fifty thousand tribal Indians in Brazil today, the largest number in any Latin American country, with twenty to fifty thousand still isolated in the Amazon. Of the two hundred and sixty Amazonian tribal groups known to have existed in 1900 only one hundred and forty-three are left. Perhaps another forty groups remain to be contacted. Among them are the Yanomamo, scattered in the remote forests of northernmost Brazil and southern Venezuela; they number about fifteen thousand. Many of their *maloccas,* or communal round houses, have never been seen by white men. In western Amazonia several villages of Amahuaca, Machiguenga, and the head-hunting Jivaros, well back from the main rivers, have yet to be contacted. In Acre State, along the Peruvian frontier, are the Mayoluno, and some of the more remote Mayarunas; in Amazonas, the Macu and several other small groups with no names which people have flown over; in Rondônia, the Cabeça-Secas or "Dry-Heads," some of the Surui and some of the Cintas-Largas or "Wide-Belts," a collective name for three separate tribes who live in at least eighteen villages; in Pará, three Cayapo and one Kreen-akroare village; and even in Mato Grosso, where all the Indians were thought to have been contacted, a new tribe has recently been found.

One of the most persistently hostile groups is the five hundred or so Waimiri-Atroari, who live in nine villages only a hundred and fifty miles north of Manaus. In 1969 they massacred all but one of a party of fourteen led by a missionary named Father Jean Calero, who had come up the Alalau River to make friends with them. The survivor reported that the padre had mismanaged the encounter by firing into the air and frightening them. In 1974 they killed three laborers working on the construction of an international highway between Manaus and Venezuela.

FUNAI has two Waimiri approach posts for which few volunteer. "We are beginning to approach the time of year—the wet season, from September to January—when the Waimiri traditionally massacre their *sertanistas,"* General Ismarth Araujo de Oliveira, the head of FUNAI, told me in his office. "They have been massacring our men for more than thirty years. More than fifty *sertanistas* have been killed. We think there is some anthropological reason for it. Maybe it is part of some ritual of initiation. The last one was killed in 1974. He was living with them for more than seven years."

No white man was more loved and trusted by the Waimiri than the *sertanista* Gilberto Pinto. Late in December, 1974, a cheerful delegation of Waimiri came to his post to exchange presents. But by December 28 Pinto had run out of presents, and the Indians began to get irritated. At six a.m. on the morning of the twenty-ninth they killed him.

Two months earlier, on October 2, thirteen Waimiri came to the other FUNAI post in search of presents, although they had brought nothing to trade for them. Adão Vasconcelos, a laborer, gave them what he had and called Gilberto Pinto on the radio to tell him that he had some importunate Indians on his hands. Pinto advised him to be careful.

When he turned in that night Adão noticed that someone had removed the bullets from his rifle. In the morning he found the Indians standing at his door, but they were not armed. Adão went about his work as if nothing were out of the ordinary, sewing his pants and waiting to make his customary nine o'clock radio call to Gilberto Pinto. At 7:30 one of the Indians came up to him and began to stroke his hair. Looking back on it, Adão realized that this was a prearranged signal. The Indians jumped him, breaking his collarbone, but he managed to struggle free and jump into the river. Several Waimiri pursued in a canoe, firing arrows at him, while the others ran along the bank. When Adão got to the other bank he faced them and said, "Papa Gilberto." The Indians turned back. They killed Odoncil, another worker at the post.

At the moment, General Ismarth told me, the Waimiri seemed to be making peaceful overtures, but knowing that they do not hesitate to attack a small group, he had thirty armed men at each of the *postos*. "You have to carry your gun all the time," a FUNAI employee told me, "or they will get you. And it has to be a big caliber. The .22's don't intimidate them."

One evening in a bar in Brasília a retired *sertanista* told me the sad story of the Kreen-akroare, one of the most recently contacted tribes of Amazonia. A primitive semi-nomadic group, they occupied a territory of some five thousand square kilometers southwest of the Air Force base at Cachimbo in the state of Pará. "Five years ago they didn't know the canoe and were living in the Stone Age," the *sertanista* said. "They didn't know how to make pots or manioc bread like most of the other tribes. They were another humanity. Essential human ideas were missing from their minds."

The Kreen-akroare lived in three villages, going on hunting treks that could last for months at a time and cover hundreds of kilometers. There were perhaps three hundred of them. In 1957 their traditional enemies, the Menkranoti, armed with shotguns, attacked one of the villages. The Kreen-akroare had never seen guns and fled in terror. Fifteen were killed.

In 1961 the Kreen-akroare ambushed and killed Richard Mason, an English botanist working near the Air Force base at Cachimbo. The Menkranoti identified the arrows.

In 1962 two *caboclos,* Amazonian peasants, contacted them, and gifts were exchanged. But when the *caboclos* returned with guns, the Kreen-akroare deserted their village and fled into the woods.

In 1967 a two-engine Air Force plane flew over another village. Thinking it was a big bird, one of the Kreen-akroare took aim and, with a lucky shot, brought it down with an arrow. All twenty passengers were killed in the crash.

In 1968 the Menkranoti attacked again, killing thirty-five and carrying off five children. The Kreen-akroare took the corpses of their dead to the Air Force base at Cachimbo, hoping that the white men would help avenge their deaths. But when the commander saw them, he panicked and fired off a few shots into the air, and the Kreen-akroare ran off in terror. He sent out an SOS over the radio that the base was under massive Indian attack, but by the time reinforcements arrived there were no Kreen-akroare to be found.

By 1969 the Kreen-akroare had still not been effectively contacted, the ex-*sertanista* went on, and he drew a map to explain what was happening. It showed the Cachimbo Air Force base to the north, an army base to the south, and two highways under construction which would pass right through the middle of their country.

That year Brazil's most famous *sertanistas,* Claudio and Orlando Villas-Boas, made the first of two attempts to contact the Kreen-akroare. The Villas-Boas brothers had been nominated for the Nobel prize for setting up the Xingú National Park, an area of about 12,000 square miles in Mato Grosso where eighteen tribes live in their traditional way, protected by FUNAI. After several months the Villas-Boas brothers finally saw some Kreen-akroare staring at them from the other side of a river. They had Indians with them who knew fourteen languages, and they tried shouting in each tongue across the water. But the Kreen-akroare just looked at them with puzzlement, then disappeared into the forest. Adrian Cowell, a British anthropologist with the expedition, was able to film them and to use the footage in a superb documentary called "The Tribe That Hides From Man."

In 1970 Claudio Villas-Boas returned and waited for a year in one spot, leaving gifts in a clearing near where he thought their village might be, withdrawing, and coming back again. The gifts were taken, and sensing that he was on the verge of contact,

Claudio summoned his brother. Finally, in February of 1971 three Kreen-akroare appeared on the other side of the river. Claudio and Orlando and a few others threw down their guns, got into a canoe, and paddled over to them. Orlando got out and embraced them. One of the Kreen-akroare made a speech for an hour which no one understood.

A few days later two Kreen-akroare showed up at their camp. The Villas-Boas brothers knew that there were other Indians around and that if these two were harmed, they would attack. The two visitors were showered with presents. A few days later forty Kreen-akroare showed up with their women and had a dance. The Xavante and Xinguano Indians with the expedition did their dances, which the Kreen-akroare seemed to enjoy.

A contact is usually in three stages. First you exchange gifts, then you get the Indians to come to your camp, and finally you enter their village. The first two stages had been passed, but Claudio refused to finish the contact. He knew that if the road construction through their country continued, the Kreen-akroare would not survive. Many would die of disease. Others, thinking that all white men would treat them as well as the Villas-Boas brothers had, would be abused. Claudio could not stop the roads, and left in disgust. Another *sertanista* named Apuena Murelles finished the contact.

In 1972, forty Kreen-akroare died of pneumonia contracted from the road crews. The Cuiaba-Santarém highway was now two kilometers from one of their villages. The Indians abandoned it and its plantations, and crowded together in another village. Soon they were reduced to eating *urucu* seeds, from which a red body paint is derived, and earth. Finally a famous picture in *O Globo,* a Brazilian newspaper, showed several starving Kreen-akroare, begging on the highway.

By December, 1974, there were only seventy-nine Kreen-akroare left. Three-quarters of the tribe had been wiped out by pneumonia, flu, and malaria. With their homeland usurped, the Villas-Boas brothers arranged for them to be moved to Xingú National Park, where the Kyabi had agreed to give them their village of Prepuri and its plantations. There were many adjustments for the dislocated tribe. They had to adapt to living in two houses, when they had previously lived in four, one for each moiety or clan group. They had to learn to transport themselves by canoe and to fish with hook and line, when they had been used to bow and arrow fishing in clear, fast-running streams. When the Kyabi showed

them the manioc root, they wanted to eat it immediately, not knowing that the toxic prussic acid must first be extracted. To make matters worse the other Xinguano tribes would call on the Kreen-
akroare and stay for a week, so that within three months the tribe
was out of food and had to move in with the Txucurramai.

Life with the paternalistic Txucurramai, who tried to marry
their women and make them adopt their ways, was difficult. Finally,
the Kreen-akroare moved to a third village a kilometer from the
Suya, with whom they have become big friends. The Suya have
been very helpful, and Richard Heelas, the British anthropologist
now living with the Kreen-akroare, reports that they have started to
hold their traditional festivals for the first time since they were up-
rooted, and are beginning to open up about themselves.

While the Kreen-akroare are beginning to recover from their
traumatic contact with civilization, they are dangerously close to the
lowest population they can have and still survive. As of January,
1976, they were only sixty-four, and because of their system of marriage, only ten women can have socially acceptable children.

"The future for the Indians in Amazonia looks black," the *sertanista* told me, staring down at his beer. "The Indians don't con-
tribute to the economy so to the technocrats they are only a barrier."

As Claudio Villas-Boas has pointed out, to integrate the Indians
is the work of generations. It can't be done in two or three years.
General Ismarth agrees. "The ideal policy in Xingú and the other
primitive areas of Amazonia," he told me, "is to keep the Indians
isolated and slowly expose them to the contact that will inevitably
come."

But not everyone is as sensitive to the problem. "We are going
to create a policy of integrating the Indian population into Brazilian
national society as rapidly as possible," Rangell Reiss, Minister of the
Interior, said in 1974. "We think that the ideals of preserving the
Indian population within its own habitat are very beautiful ideas,
but unrealistic."

What happens to Indians who are thrust directly from the
Stone Age into the twentieth century is one of the great tragedies of
Amazonia. "Amazonia is full of them," Claudio Villas-Boas said, "wit-
less, detribalized remnants of a once vital people, passive morons of
civilization waiting for decisions to be made in their behalf."

I didn't meet any of these "passive morons," but in Iquitos,
Peru, I heard about jungle lodges to which tourists are taken to

meet some real, live Jivaro Indians. The tour director tacks a ten-*sole* note to a tree and the first Indian who hits it with a dart from his blowgun gets to keep it. Deeper in the jungle unacculturated Jivaros are still raiding each other's villages, carrying off the women, and shrinking the heads of their male victims.

FUNAI recently put a stop to an outfit called Green Hell Tours which had been taking boatloads of tourists from Leticia, Colombia, to a Tucano village in the Brazilian Amazon to see a ceremony called "the plucking of the virgin's hair." But not every tribe endures passively the destruction of its culture. On the Brazil-Peru border, the Mayarunas, whose numbers have dropped from two thousand to four hundred since their land was penetrated by an oil company in 1972, have reacted by killing their babies. Paulo Lucena, a Brazilian anthropologist living among them, reports that the tribe has killed female children in the past to ensure an even balance of the sexes, "but now, desperate, and feeling that they have no place to go, they have decided to die, and are summarily executing male children as well."

Even more serious than the loss of identity or even life from too abrupt acculturation are the diseases that the white man brings. The Indian has no resistance to flu, pneumonia, measles, or tuberculosis, and once he is smitten, he often decides that the evil is too strong to resist, and lies in his hammock waiting for death. When a whole village is seized with an epidemic, the food gathering system breaks down, and more actually die of starvation than of the disease itself. According to an estimate by Professor Paulo Duarte, Brazil's indigenous population dropped from 250,000 to 80,000 between 1963 and 1968, years when many of the last remote tribes were finally contacted.

But each culture has its own life expectancy and can't be kept alive or isolated artificially. Many of the Indians I met who had been slightly exposed to civilization wanted to know more: they wanted to see Manaus and ride in a plane and meet the women they'd been hearing about. I sensed they could take care of themselves; many Amazonian Indians have in fact become experts at manipulating *civilizados* (myself included) into getting what they want. There is a side to them that they never show to the white man. Far from being forgotten, their culture and the lessons they learned from the jungle act as powerful spiritual forces that enable them to keep things in perspective the deeper they get into our way of life.

"There is no such thing as an integrated Indian," General Ismarth remarked recently. "There are Indians who are in permanent contact with society, but that does not mean that they are integrated."

In the Villas-Boas brothers' book, *Xingú, the Indians, their Myths,* there is a passage about a Waura chief named Taxapuh, who was taken out of his village and flown to São Paulo for a hernia operation. "How could you return to this world after seeing how we live?" he asked when he had been in the city for a few days. "How can you breathe this foul air or sleep with these noises [the traffic]? How can you eat this food made to have tastes not its own? Why would you want to have intercourse with these women who seem afraid to be women and hide themselves and cover their eyes? Who are these men with guns who stand in the paths of the village?"

℘ 5 ℘

Menkranoti

It took two weeks for us to receive our permits and another two weeks for Gustaaf Verswijver, the young Belgian anthropologist who had been asked to take us into the village he was studying, to get his visa extended. If one is not an anthropologist, FUNAI requires that an anthropologist goes along. It also requires a complete physical check-up, including chest X-rays to show that one is free of tuberculosis.

We spent most of the second fortnight with Gustaaf, laying in a grubstake for the month we would be with the Indians and buying presents for them. Having lived with them on and off for the last two years he had picked up the quick, fluid Indian way of walking, and it had been hard to keep up with him on the sidewalks of Brasília. He had also begun to think like an Indian, always turning over what he was going to say before speaking, and never answering a direct question directly. Added to these qualities were the manners of a gentleman; he was descended from Flemish nobility on his mother's side. His father had died when Gustaaf was in his teens. The boy had enlisted in the Merchant Marines and there, on lonely midnight watches, he had formulated his ambition to live with and study the Indians of the Amazon. After two years of besieging FUNAI, Brazil's National Indian Foundation, with letters, his application was finally accepted. Now he was one of the most respected young anthropologists at FUNAI, with an intuitive understanding of the Indians to which few white men could lay claim. He spoke perfect Flemish, English, French, German, Portuguese, and passable Cayapo. He was only twenty-two, cadaverously thin, with intense blue eyes and a dirty blonde beard.

We had originally applied to visit the Xingú National Park. Created in 1961, it is the most ambitious attempt to cushion and protect the indigenous population of Amazonia. More different tribal groups live in its confines than in any area of comparable size. It seemed important, then, for us to go there. But at FUNAI we learned that the Park had not been entirely successful. The most effective way of saving scattered Indian groups was undoubtedly to move them all to a central location, but many of the groups were traditional enemies, and conflicts arose. For other groups the move from land they had occupied for centuries was traumatic. But the worst debacle was the highway that was built right through the Park in 1971, after the land had been supposedly set aside for the Indians in perpetuity. We heard that the Xinguano Indians had been visited by so many anthropologists that they were getting to be like the Navajos, drawing up their own kinship charts and selling them to the anthropologists. FUNAI had closed the Park to all but the scientists who were already working there. There had recently been an unfortunate incident in which a female American graduate student had had a child by an Indian man. She had refused to breast-feed it and when it was time for her to return to the States, she had wanted to leave it with the tribe, knowing well that as a motherless child it would be killed. Orlando Villas-Boas had brought it to her as she was waiting for the plane. She had "forgotten" it as the plane took off. Villas-Boas had radioed the plane to come back. It was said that as soon as the girl had landed in civilization she gave the baby to a beggar woman. "It's probably dead," the man at FUNAI who told me this had speculated.

So we had been assigned to a Cayapo village called Menkranoti, several hundred miles northwest of the park, with Gustaaf to look after us. The more we heard about Menkranoti, the happier we were to be going there. Of the nineteen Indian villages Gustaaf had visited, this one, where he had spent most of his time, was his favorite, and the purest and most remote of the contacted Cayapo settlements. The word "Cayapo" means "resembling a monkey," and the Menkranoti are "the people with black faces," because they paint themselves with the black juice of genipape fruit. Like many of the indigenous tongues of South-Central Amazonia, their language belongs to the Jê linguistic group. It is not inflected. There are no words for "love," "thank you," or "goodbye." When you meet someone on a forest path you don't say "hello," because there is no word for it. You say *"Moina ga teng?"* (Where are you going?)

At last our twenty-seven pieces of luggage were loaded on the bus and we climbed aboard. As the bus sped north from Brasília through the wide open vistas of Goiás, Gustaaf reminded us that we should never ask an Indian his name directly; the proper way to do it was to turn to the nearest person and ask, "What's his name?" Gustaaf dictated a list of useful Cayapo words:

nãnã —where is it?
moina —what's up?
kuben —stranger
krĩ—village
puru —plantation
prù —path
moi prù —which path?
djunwa —father
nirùa —mother
kanikwoi —sister
kamu —brother

i kra —my child
a kra —your child
na —rain
a mre tẽ —come here
ùrù tẽ —go
adjum —later
arùpket —it's finished
kati —no
ne —yes
tãn —that's right
punure —bad

Meikumrex —the *ei* is spoken in a drawn-out falsetto and punctuated with two or more emphatic slaps of the upper arm against the rib cage. Meaning: good.

Twelve hours later we had covered a third of the distance along the Belém-Brasília highway back to Belém, and the bus dropped us off at a place called Mira Norte, North Lookout. It was two in the morning and the town was asleep. We roused a boy who had slumped on the counter of a bar and asked where we could find a truck to hire. He took us to a *bombeiro,* a fireman, who had a new pickup and offered to drive us the one hundred and eighty kilometers to Araguaçema for sixty dollars. The price was steep, but we agreed to it. We had no choice, and the *bombeiro,* whose name was Ratinlo, Little Rat, needed the money; his wife had been burned by boiling water a few weeks before, he told us, and it had taken everything he had to save her life. "The women in Araguaçema are fire," he said, as we passed through an outpost called Dós Irmãos, Two Brothers. Four hours later, shortly after dawn, we pulled into a small landing field outside of Araguaçema on which there were two Cessna bush planes.

The planes belonged to the Unevangelized Fields Service, an American missionary group, and their pilot, a Californian named Skip Parrish, was one of the few people who knew the way to Menkranoti. Parrish, however, was not particularly hungry for our business. Hardly looking up from the bench on which he was stripping a piece of machinery, he said he would be busy for the next few days after which, if the weather was alright, he might be able to find the time to fly us in. There was nothing to do but head on into Araguaçema and wait.

Time flowed at a different pace, as they say, in Araguaçema. There was not much *movimento,* as our hotelkeeper told us apologetically. Several dogs and chickens were running around in the lobby. The cook came out and grabbed one of the chickens. Outside it was very hot, like walking into a wall. We went to the end of the main street and watched naked children, some with piranha scars on their thighs, swimming in the Araguaya River. "You missed school," a mother shouted down from the wall to one of them. "You're going to get it when you get home." The current was smooth and deceptive. I made for a pile of black basaltic rocks fifty yards out at a fast crawl and was carried in a sweeping arc far below them. There had been a drowning here the previous July. On a sandbar midway across the milky green water a fishing party had beached a long dugout and was roasting its catch on a driftwood fire.

That evening we sat with a friend of Gustaaf's in a bamboo-sided *barraca,* where there was a record player and watched young teen-age girls doing the folk-dances of Pará—the Carimbo, the Serimbo, and the Seria—shuffling along gaily with their hands on their hips. The older women were all married and working on outlying *fazendas,* ranches, Gustaaf's friend told us.

The next afternoon a shirtless man with his hair in a braid and sunglasses riding on the top of his head burst into our hotel, uncorked a bottle of *pinga** and started to pick his guitar. Rane, as the man was called, was a bush pilot—what every boy in Araguaçema dreamed to be, and, even more awesome, he had been to the United States, where he learned to fly helicopters. More than anything, he told us, he valued his freedom, and only those who knew the freedom of the skyways could understand what he was talking about.

Rane took us to his favorite bar, and we shot pool in front of most of the youth of Araguaçema. At the approaching drone of a plane everyone ran into the street and threw up a wild cheer as a green and white Cessna roared by only twenty feet overhead. The

---

*Pinga, cachaça and *aguardiente* are different names for the white rum distilled from sugar cane, which, after water, is perhaps the most important fluid in Amazonia.

pilot, who was Rane's partner, rolled back over the river and buzzed us two or three more times. Then a car passed in which Gustaaf's friend was urging everyone through a battery-powered bullhorn to vote for the challenger in the upcoming elections for the *prefeito,* or mayor, of Araguaçema. Rane borrowed the bullhorn and extemporized a speech about democracy and freedom and family life in Araguaçema which brought tears to the eyes of a handsome pregnant woman who sat in a doorway, painting flowers on a sheet.

We decided we would much rather fly with Rane than with Parrish. Rane said he had been to Menkranoti once eight years before, with the man who had taught him to fly (the man had died shortly afterwards in a crash which had left Rane with scars on his shoulders). He thought he could find it again with the help of Gustaaf, who had made the run a dozen times now. The next morning he put us and our gear on the scales and did some calculating. We could carry enough fuel, he announced, to stay in the air for six hours. The course which he drew carefully on the aeronautical map ran a few degrees north of true west for about four hundred kilometers. There would be enough gas left over to cruise for fifteen minutes once we got in the general vicinity of Menkranoti; and if we didn't find it by then we would have to turn back.

Once in the sky Rane became dead serious. He pushed the plane through a low cloud layer and leveled it off below a second layer of overcast, and we flew in the clear space between. Occasionally the way was blocked by an ugly thunderhead to which Rane would give as wide a berth as he dared without losing his bearings. The only way to verify the course was with the rivers below and the *serras,* the mountain ranges which occasionally wrinkled the otherwise smooth blanket of green. On the far side of the Araguaya the low cloud layer began to dissipate and we saw below us the perfect square of a newly-cleared *fazenda,* then a few palm-thatch huts of *caboclos,* or Amazonian frontiersmen, with small plantations of bananas and manioc, and then there were no more signs of culture. Below us the planet's vastest wooded wilderness stretched to every point of the horizon. It seemed like an ocean to which there was no limit, and this was only a small part of it: the same sight would be repeated whenever I took to the air in another part of the valley.

This section, a square some three hundred miles on a side, lying between the Araguaya River and the Serra do Cachimbo, is one of the most deserted and unknown parts of the Amazon basin. It is the exclusive domain of the Cayapo Indians. Gustaaf had visited most of the contacted villages: Menkranoti, population, 286; Kubenkrãnkegn, population, 504; Gorotire, population, 420; Kokraimoro, population, 120; Bau, population, 47; Kararáô, population, 28 (only two men and six or seven women of childbearing age are left, the rest were carried off by malaria, and the children are deformed by incest); two villages of Xikrin, further north, population, 190 and 110; and two villages of Txucurramai in the Xingú National Park, population, 120 each. Somewhere down in there were three more uncontacted villages, he said, with populations of between thirty and eighty each. They had been started by disaffected bands of Cayapo who had split from the main settlements in the nineteen thirties. Their inhabitants had no guns and wore nothing except for body paint, penis sheaths, and *botocs,* red wooden plates in their lower lips.

The territorial requirements of the Cayapo are staggering. Gustaaf estimated that the Menkranoti alone hunt and defend and are intimately familiar with an area of six thousand square kilometers. They have had guns since 1930, twenty-five years before their first friendly contact with white men, having taken them in raids on the *caboclos.* This has given them a huge advantage over the other Indians in the area, and enables them to defend their ample territory.

In 1972 they clubbed down seven white men after giving them a week's notice to get off their land. "Three years ago," Gustaaf told us, "they killed their last white man, an old *caboclo* they had always liked and allowed to live in their country. But they killed him for his new revolver."

The traditional Cayapo weapon is a meter-long bat made of a dense red wood called *kô.* Gustaaf had seen the clubs in action. Once he had been sitting with a group of men when one of them had said *"queixada"*—wild boars. Gustaaf heard nothing. Very slowly and silently the men had gotten their clubs and gone to the creek. Just as fifteen boars were crossing they were surrounded by the Indians who pulled them out of the water by their feet and dispatched them with the clubs. None of them had gotten away.

The plane passed the Serra do Gradaos to the north and the Serra do Matao to the south, sudden zigzag ridges in a flat land. A flock of large white birds with black flight feathers—wood storks—glided aimlessly far below. Here and there the golden crown of a *Vochysia* tree, flat and sometimes two hundred feet in diameter, emerged from its dull surroundings. Every once in a while the ancient black rock of the Brazilian Shield would crop up, and the oxbow of a sinuous river would gleam up through the trees. Danny pointed to a spectacular waterfall plunging into a deep gorge. Much of this wilderness had probably never been walked on by humans, not even Indians. It was unknown, a blank white space on the map except for the block letters RELIEF DATA UNRELIABLE.

But the rivers were on the map. They appeared on schedule every thirty minutes or so, winding their way north. First the Rio Fresco, a tributary of the Xingú, then the Xingú itself, full of sand bars and ruffled with *cachoeiras,* or cataracts, as it broke down from the crystalline highlands into the lower valley. We passed between two islands in the Xingú at 1:20 p.m., right on the nose of the plotted course; then over the Rio Petita, a short tributary of the Xingú, then the Iriri, a long tributary of the Xingú; and finally the Xixê, a tributary of the Iriri.

Now at the fifteen-minute deadline we had to find the Rasgado, a creek which came into the Xixê from the west. Menkranoti was forty kilometers up it. The creek was small and we could easily pass it hidden beneath the trees. But the Indians had planted a garden some years before at the Rasgado's mouth, and this was what we were looking for. Rane turned north up the Xixê, and everyone kept his eyes peeled on the left bank. "There it is," Gustaaf shouted, pointing down to a small, ragged clearing filled with the star-shaped bursts of banana plants.

What would they think, I wondered, of the tall, pale strangers who would soon be dropping out of the sky? The first time Gustaaf went in, the FUNAI *chefe de posto* was out of the village and so were the two missionary women. He found himself alone with two hundred and eighty Indians. "You sure you want to stay?" the pilot had asked. The Indians who had swarmed around the plane had wanted to know everything about him. "What's your name?" "What's your father's name?" "What's your mother's name?" Gustaaf was alone with them for several weeks.

Recognizing the hills ahead Gustaaf pointed to a thin swath in the forest beneath them. "The landing strip," he said. It and the village lay in a natural amphitheater with a semicircle of hills to the north and west, and flatter, more open ground running to the south and east. Now we were banking over two concentric rings of huts with a bare earth plaza in the middle and one hut—the men's house—in the middle of the plaza. Several clusters of dark naked people were standing in the plaza looking up at us, shielding their eyes with their hands. Others were running down to the strip. Rane brought down the plane and taxied up to a group of men and boys. Some of the men had hastily put on pants, shirts, hats, and sunglasses for the occasion. The purpose of this apparel was purely ornamental. Others wore only cones holding up their penises and, wedged in a hole beneath their lower lip, a red wooden disc the size of a hockey puck. The women sat in the grass on the edge of the strip smoking large, goblet-shaped pipes, and nursing their babies. Most were naked with intricate, black geometric designs painted all over their bodies and bright red dye on their faces and feet. A few had on torn calico dresses.

In the chaos that followed everyone was hugging each other and laughing. Several of the men filled bottles with gasoline from the wing-tank for their cigarette lighters. Others shouldered our gear and headed for the village. A little boy with blue and white beaded bracelets on his upper arms and strong rippling designs on his cheeks took my hand and led me up the path; a powerfully built man of about eighteen who could have passed for a Cherokee fell in on the other side of me. I stared at the vegetation which stood up in shocks and smothered the ridge. I had never seen such a tangled, frothing mass of plants. The older of my escorts stepped on a thorn and cried, "Ai. Paritoklu."

"What's he saying?" I asked Gustaaf.

"Ow. My foot hurts."

Standing on the path we met an emaciated, densely freckled white man of about fifty-five with sunken eyes shaded by a straw hat, large holes in his distended ears, grey stubble on his chin, and not much left of his teeth. Benmoti was his name, and he had been living with the Menkranoti since he was a child, when he was stolen from a *caboclo* family. Benmoti had forgotten Portuguese and had no memory of his former life. He had two sons and a daughter by a Cayapo woman who had died, and now he was the only old bachelor of the village. The men joked with him about getting married again, but he wasn't interested. He knew more of the old dances and myths than many of the Menkranoti themselves. A few years ago someone from FUNAI discovered that he had a sister living in the city of Altamira, five hundred miles to the north. Asked if he wanted to see her, Benmoti said no, but, in true Indian fashion, gave him a list of things he wanted her to send him.

The hut that the men had built for Gustaaf was in the second ring, and it was like the others except that it had an earthen hearth with several grills and a split-pole table with benches at which Gustaaf conducted his interviews. A large crowd followed us into the hut, and others too shy to enter — mostly teenage girls — stared at us between the palings, lashed together with bark, which formed the walls. Danny held up his pocket watch for some boys to listen to. One of the women filled Gustaaf in on what had happened in the past three months. "Nobody died," he translated, "and there were two births."

The crowd parted for Bebgogti, the chief. He was a tall, magnificently preserved man of about sixty-five, with hair streaming to his shoulders. His eyes shone merrily, and his mouth spread in a broad, childlike grin as he hugged Gustaaf and slapped us on the back. "Capitão," he said, pointing to himself. "I am the captain." In his day he had killed fifteen men, and that was why he was chief.

The Menkranoti had been isolated until twenty-five years ago. They numbered about six hundred and lived about 130 miles southeast of their present village. Their chief was Kretire, and Bebgogti was the second chief. In 1953 Claudio Villas-Boas contacted their first cousins, the Txucurramai, who lived near the Xingú River and had Kremoro for their chief. The two villages were not fighting, and a party of Txucurramai came to Menkranoti talking about Villas-Boas. The Menkranoti wanted to kill him to get his goods, as they were used to doing with *civilizados*. So a large expedition of Menkranoti under Kretire went to Txucurramai. Although Kremoro had told Claudio he'd better get out, he stayed, and when Kretire came Claudio threw his arms around him and began to recite Kant in Portuguese. Claudio had spent many hours in his hammock reading Kant, and although they didn't understand a word of the recital, they were impressed by his speaking voice — an attribute they associate with a leader. Because they liked him and his presents and promises, they moved nearer the Xingú and stayed two or three years. But then Kremoro and Bebgogti fought. Bebgogti moved with Kretire and about seven hundred and fifty Indians back to their old village. In 1958 another *sertanista* from FUNAI, Chico Mureles, approached the Menkranoti and promised to give them a post with an infirmary and to supply them with tools and ammunition if they moved north to the Iriri River. They agreed to his request and moved to the river to wait for him. But Mureles couldn't get the money and half of the Menkranoti died from malaria and other diseases during the two years they waited there for him to return. Many died in infancy and now there were only seven *menôrônùre* — bachelors in the fourteen- to twenty-year-old age group, as opposed to sixty adults; the normal ratio is about one to two. There should have been twenty-five to thirty *menôrônùre*.

In 1963 Kretire decided to move back to the Xingù. Bebgogti and two hundred of the Menkranoti stayed. Kretire came back three times, asking for Bebgogti to join him. The third time Bebgogti agreed, but on the way back to the Xingú, Kretire died of influenza, and so Bebgogti stayed where he was. Now there are two Txucurramai villages near the Xingú. Bebgogti won't go to the one run by Kremoro because he would have to fight with him. But Robni's village is Kretire's people—only a hundred and twenty left—and they are on good terms with the Menkranoti. Bebgogti was expecting Robni to visit next month. When Robni arrived, the two chiefs would weep ceremoniously because they had not seen each other in six years. There would be dancing and long speeches in Robni's honor.

Opening a suitcase, Gustaaf distributed a dozen pink rubber balls to the children and took out a soccer ball, which he inflated. Then he started walking down toward the river. The men and boys followed, and the women and girls returned to their huts. As we walked through the plaza, several emaciated and parasite-infested dogs ran up, barking. Dogs had entered the village in the 1950s. The Menkranoti had gotten them from the Txucurramai, who had gotten them from the *caboclos*. They were the typical medium-sized mongrel with a predominance of hound found throughout Latin America. Now there were about three hundred of them. The Menkranoti made no attempt to train or feed them. They lived their own lives, attaching themselves to the household they were born in and living off scraps. They served as watchdogs and scavengers, cleaning up whatever was edible, much as the *urubús,* or vultures, police an Amazonian marketplace. Whenever the men went into the forest they followed.

The huts were roofed with several layers of *babaçu (Orbygnia martiana),* palm fronds which shed water but let out smoke. The fronds had been laid horizontally across pole rafters, doubled over, and lashed in place with strips of bark, and enormous wishbone tree crotches straddled the roofs to hold them down. The crotches were favorite perches of the twenty-five or so *araras*—raucous red macaws. The Menkranoti had captured the birds in the jungle, waiting below a big *kadioti* tree until the birds came to feed on the dripping black fruit, then stunning them with blunt-tipped arrows. The huts were sided with mud and wattle. Their design had been copied from the *caboclos* and is known as the "neo-Brazilian" hut style. Until fifteen years ago, the Menkranoti had lived in lean-tos of a much simpler construction. The women sitting in the doorways of the huts, grating manioc and grooming their children, looked up and smiled now as we passed them. They were healthy women, with wide hips, heavy shanks, and breasts pulled down by their numerous offspring.

The Menkranoti are deeply aware of their own passage through time. Their society is organized by this awareness, and the most important moments in their lives occur when they pass from one time of life to another. When a boy becomes eight years old he leaves his mother's house and goes to live in the men's house. With other boys of his age he becomes part of an inseparable group of peers that hunts and takes part in ceremonies together. Later, when he becomes a father himself, thus consummating his trial marriage, he moves into his mother-in-law's house and joins his first moiety. Gustaaf had discovered that there were two moieties divided into three men's societies and one of *menônônùre*. And the soccer game that now materialized on the makeshift field was split into moieties. I had the twenty- to thirty-year-olds on my side. Those who were over thirty played with Gustaaf and Danny, and the ones under twenty went on both sides. The men were bowlegged with small hips, tight buttocks, and broad muscular shoulders, the opposite of the women who bulged at the hips like guitars and after their first child lost the definition of their waists. It was a free-for-all. One man would get the ball and try to take it as far as he could. The field was filled with flailing legs and arms, whoops and yells, and the thunder of bare feet on the earth, much as it must have been when the Indians of North America got together for a game of lacrosse. It was a tough, hard-fought game in which each man fought for the honor of his moiety. Whenever someone was knocked to the ground everybody would laugh, but not maliciously, and he would get up and play twice as hard, hiding his pain. Whenever a goal was made the shrill, good-humored cries of "GOL," would come from the victors, and the game would begin with fresh zest.

After several hours of exhausting play we headed for the creek. The men shouted down the path to let the women know that they were coming. Each sex had its own time at the swimming hole, which was part of a larger dualistic pattern. Unless they were working together in the plantations, the men and women led separate lives during the day, coming together only after the sun had gone down. The women gathered up their clothes, filled their pots and gourds with water, and headed back to the village. The men who had acquired shorts in trade took them off, and if they had nothing on underneath they cupped their hands modestly over their pubic areas until they got into the water. The others wore one of two types of penis coverings which they never removed in public.*

---

*One is a cone of woven palm leaves that holds the penis shaft upright; the other is a string around the waist, under which the foreskin is tucked. Every boy receives a penis covering, or *muoyê*, at puberty in a ceremony which asserts social control over his sexuality. The word means "original clothing."

Like most Indians, the Menkranoti are very fastidious and bathe in the Rasgado several times a day. With the boys cannonballing from a high branch that leaned out over the water, it seemed little different from the scene at a peaceful swimming hole somewhere in rural America. A swarm of several hundred butterflies of the species *Phoebis philea* was drinking in the moist sand at the water's edge, and when three women returning from the plantations laden with bananas and puffing on their pipes crossed the creek on a fallen tree-trunk, the butterflies rose, enveloping them in a shower of orange and yellow flakes. There were dangerous things in the water—piranha, stingrays, anacondas, jacares (the black alligator), but one seldom encountered them. A few months before we arrived, an American anthropologist climbing out of the water had put his hand on a log and been stung by a scorpion. He had felt nothing for thirty minutes, then been seized with such violent convulsions that he had to be flown out to a hospital.

That night we were beseiged with requests for salt, needles, fish hooks, and line (the ones who wanted a fishhook put a finger in their mouth and yanked it to one side, as if they had just been hooked). All medical problems were referred to Danny, who soon found himself with several dozen patients, mostly children. Some had bloated bellies and were treated for worms. Others got pills to stop their diarrhea. One had a dead eye about which nothing could be done. The chief himself came in complaining of pain in his testicles and emissions of pus. "It sounds like gonorrhea," Gustaaf said. "Several months ago there was a big epidemic. Half the village had it." We started Bebgogti on a week-long treatment of tetracycline.

The chief left and shortly afterwards, as we swung in our hammocks, we could hear him walking around the plaza and explaining that *menibiok,* a festival in which girls between the ages of two and eight received ceremonial names, would take place in three weeks, that the women must bring in many bananas from the gardens and Brazil nuts from the forest, that the men must hunt a lot of good meat and gather a lot of tortoises, that everyone must look out for the newly arrived *kuben* —strangers. His speech was punctuated with violent rhetorical grunts as if someone was slamming a fist in his stomach.

I lay in my hammock and listened to the village sleeping, the heavy breathing and snoring that came from the nearby huts, the occasional cough or startled cry of a baby finding itself awake, the sound of a fire being poked back to life. Fire is a symbol of civilization for the Menkranoti, and they sleep close to burning flames to keep warm, preferring to inhale smoke than to be preyed on by mosquitoes and vampire bats in their sleep.

A dense field of rhythmic sounds surrounded the sleeping village. Katydids of the family *Tettigonidae* were producing a loud, steady hum, while giant cockroaches hissed, tree frogs rattled, and other insects tirelessly repeated chk-chk-chk in alternating octaves. Bats, in an effort to echolocate prey, emitted soft pings at regular intervals, but each bat had begun transmitting at a different time, and the whole effect was that of a random staccato patchwork of sound, like rain falling on a tin roof. I was reminded of the heavy rhythm sections in the *samba* bands I had heard in Brasília. I wouldn't be surprised if *samba* and other kinds of tropical music, most of which emphasize percussion rather than melody, were originally inspired by the nocturnal sounds of the jungle.

Somewhere around midnight I was awakened by an unearthly sound coming from deep within the jungle. It was the cascading roars of the howler monkeys. Maybe two clans had come near each other where their home ranges overlapped, and they were engaging in a loud vocal battle until one of them backed off; or maybe the monkeys were roaring at the approach of a big cat or a solitary bachelor howler. It sounded as if there were hundreds of them, but they were probably much fewer. The roars were of long duration and blended into each other in a harrowing continuum. I had never heard anything so wild and terrifying. It was like wind rushing out of the portals of Hades. "The whole larynx is much enlarged," Marston Bates, the tropical biologist, wrote, "with the hyoid bone of the throat forming a sort of boxlike resonator, larger in the male than in the female, but present in both sexes. A howling chorus can be heard from at least a mile away." The roars are produced, he explained, when the howlers contract their stomach and chest muscles, forcing air under pressure across an opening at the top of their sound boxes.

The perpetrators of these monstrous sounds were in fact quite small and meek, vegetarians who spend four to six hours a day eating leaves and fruit directly from the stem, pulling the food toward them rather than picking it and eating it in their hands. According to C.R. Carpenter, who made the classic study of howlers forty years ago on an island in Panama, they don't come to the ground to drink, but lick water from leaves and drink rain as it streams down the trees.

Marston Bates called them "democratic" monkeys, as opposed to the "totalitarian" monkeys of the Old World, because their clans seem to have no leader. He conjectured that they had developed the habit of roaring because "vocal battles are less damaging." I heard them in many parts of the valley and grew to relish the roars of the howler monkeys, and the fact that I never once saw the animals

67

only increased the disembodied, otherwordly quality of their howl-ing. It was like the music of the spheres, on the same order of terrible inhuman beauty as the singing of humpback whales.

Towards dawn a chorus of raw female chanting started in the men's house. The usual ban against women being there, on pain of rape or even death, was lifted during the weeks before *menibiok*. Each morning now the women would sit on the floor of the men's house among sooty palm wisps and shavings from whittled spears, and, pumping their arms up and down, they would join in a slow, *acapella* chant that connected with a part of my being I had never been aware of. A phrase introduced by one or two women would be picked up by all of them, and other phrases with terminal or internal rhymes would follow until after five to ten minutes the possibilities had been exhausted, and a new chant with a new set of rhymes would begin. Gustaaf couldn't understand what they were saying. "The language is being ceremonially deformed," he said. "I won't be able to understand it until I transcribe it." Every so often one of the women would let out a scream like someone overcome at a gospel meeting. The singing went on for about an hour and reached a crescendo as the light came. At the critical moment the women gave a great shout, broke up, and went about their business.

On the third morning of listening from my hammock I slipped into the men's house with my tape recorder and turned it on, very surreptitiously I thought. But after about fifteen minutes of taping, one of the women pointed to my machine. Everyone stopped chanting. They were more interested in hearing what they sounded like. I felt as if I had ruined their service. Our voyeuristic presence was making the Menkranoti self-conscious. Not long before this in-cident Gustaaf had heard a teenage girl in one of the huts singing a beautiful song as she swept the floor, and he had rushed for his tape recorder. But as he approached the hut again he heard the girl's mother order her to stop singing.

In the morning we went to the men's house with presents for Bebgogti and the second chief, a taciturn man in his forties who was sitting on a palm mat and weaving a beautiful headdress of red, blue, and green *arara* feathers. The second chief had seven scars on his chest, self-inflicted with piranha teeth, which corresponded to the number of men he had killed. All his family had died from white man's diseases in Bau, a more acculturated Cayapo village a hundred and fifty miles to the north. He had met one of Bebgogti's daughters there, married her, and come here.

We turned half of our goods over immediately — two hammocks, an assortment of machetes, hunting and paring knives, fish hooks and line, salt, red twine for women's sashes, cooking pots, mirrors, lighters, flashlights and batteries for night hunting, twisted coils of strong black tobacco called *fumo de corda,* balls of red string for the sashes young girls wore when they reached sexual maturity. The rest we kept to pay people who brought food and did us other favors.

Gustaaf had found two hundred and two items in the Menkranoti's own material culture. To qualify for his list an item had to have a name and a use and to have been worked on; a simple leaf or a stick, for which there were countless uses, did not count. In addition, the Menkranoti had accepted the following things from the outside:

lighters
matches
watches
beads
cloth
dresses, shirts, shoes, socks, hats, shorts
salt
paper (ten could write)
the *caboclo* hut design
guns (called onomatopoetically *katonk*)
flashlights (called *robno,* the eye of the jaguar)
dogs
nails, needles
shower slippers
dolls, rubber balls
steel axes
machetes
soap, razor blades
wheelbarrows
hoes, shovels
medicine
hammocks
nylon fishing line and hooks
pots, bottles, kerosene lamps
ammunition bags
suitcases
combs
hammers, saws
files (to sharpen fishhooks and nails into spear points)

rope
locks
guitars
radios (three)
a tape recorder (owned by Bepkum)
airplanes (called *màdu-kà* — they were used to seeing them
overhead)

As a final step to easing us into the Menkranoti culture Gustaaf
arranged to have us painted. The three body-painting specialists
also happened to be the most beautiful women in the village. Or at
least they came closest to embodying the curvaceous, thin-waisted
type of beauty that is admired in our society. Most of the Menkranoti
mentioned these three when asked who their most beautiful
women were, but when asked what was most desirable in a woman,
they said a strong, fat body for bearing children and hauling
firewood, and an easy and compliant disposition. These women
were beautiful, but they knew it and were among the most difficult
wives to live with.

Nhàk-ba, the one who had agreed to stain my body, came with
a palm mat and a bowl made out of the scooped-out husk of a fruit
called *cuilha* in Portuguese. In it was a black paste from the pul-
verized, olive-green berries of the genipape tree which she periodically lubricated with spit. The pulp had been masticated and mixed
with charcoal, and it had oxidized to produce a black paint that
would last for a few weeks. After placing me carefully on the mat
she smeared the fingers of her left hand with the paste and wiped
them on a flexible stylus only one eighth of an inch wide made
from the midrib of a leaf which she held in her right hand. Then
she placed the stylus on my left cheek, pressed down, and pulled it
off, leaving a line several inches long running parallel to my lower
jaw. She repeated this process, occasionally running the stylus
through her lips to moisten it, until she had impressed a bold design consisting of several rectangles inside each other, with an outer
fringe of teeth, first on one cheek, then on the other. Then she went
to work on my chest, laying down bars which flowed over my rib-
cage like contour lines. Then she painted rings around the thin
parts of my upper arms and calves and blackened my thighs with
her hands. The whole job took the better part of the afternoon, with
Nhàk-ba alternately giggling at the results and shouting at me to
keep still. Danny, who had been in the hands of another woman,
turned out a little differently than I did; the painting had followed

the same basic pattern, but there were personal touches in each artist's work which Gustaaf had been able to recognize. The women finished us at about the same time, and we took a stroll through the plaza, feeling conspicuous, which brought everyone to the entrance of his hut with rousing shouts of approval.

In our new plumage we were more acceptable to the Menkranoti, and within a few days the initial fuss over us began to die down. Gustaaf thought up some Cayapo names for us: I was Kubentire — the big stranger, and Danny, Kubenaka — the white stranger. They caught on immediately, and that was how we were known from then on. Tewet, Nhàk-ba's father, carved a beautiful pipe, stained it red with *urucu* juice, and presented it to me. It was shaped like a wineglass, like the chillums of North Africa, and called a *warikoko*. Tewet eventually adopted me as his brother, and we did many things together. He was very quiet and a fine craftsman.

The Cayapo women are probably the most skilled body painters in the Amazon valley. Most of their attention is lavished on their children. A decorated child may have leg and armbands of crocheted cotton, stained red with *urucu* juice, and adorned with tiers of blue and white beads; cigar-shaped plugs of reddened wood in his earlobes; a string of beads dripping from a starter hole for a lip disc below his lower lip; several dozen strands of blue beads around his neck and waist; the hair long on the side and shaven back from the scalp; and swirling black lines all over his body, making it look like an anatomical diagram.

The men seldom get spruced up except for a festival or a raid, and their paint jobs are smeared on rudely with the fingers. The red dye, derived from the seeds of the *urucu* bush, *Bixa orellana,* is associated with health, vitality, and quickness of mind and body, and also with belligerence and bellicosity. The women apply it to each other's faces, feet, and hands. The ornamentation of the ears and mouth may be related to the symbolic meaning of the organs: the Cayapo words for hearing and knowing are the same, and speech is associated with masculine self-assertiveness, with the thundering oratory the men make in the plaza at dusk. Lip discs are fading out of the culture. They serve to make the wearer look threatening to his enemies, and since this is probably the last generation of warriors, lip discs no longer have a function. Besides, the Menkranoti feel self-conscious wearing them under the stares of white men. Only a few of the men in the twenty to thirty age group have them, none in the fourteen to twenty age group, and the young boys will get no further than starter holes. All the older men's lower lips have been stretched, but they usually go around without the discs in them, and when they smoke, they drool through the hole.

After walking around with the camera around his neck for two days so people would get used to it, Danny started taking pictures, and I began the work I had applied to FUNAI to do: to make a study of the plants the Menkranoti use, especially their medicinal plants, which they call *pidio.* I started with Pukatire* because he knew a little Portuguese. He had lived for a while in Bau and was the most urbane and sophisticated of the Menkranoti, the self-appointed cultural attache for white visitors. He usually wore a black dinner jacket, a wristwatch, red shorts, and a brimless red military-type cap he had made himself on the *chefe de posto's* sewing machine. He had been to Belém four times and had learned to do such exotic things as ride a bicycle. On the first trip, two men in a bar had offered him a beer. Pukatire had said he didn't drink, but the men had insisted, placing the bottle in front of him. He had picked it up, smashed it on the counter, and walked out.

On the last trip he had had to wait two months for FUNAI to fly him back to the village. Finally he had gone to one of the officials and said, "I want a plane. Today." The official had said, "I'm sorry, but that's not possible." Pukatire had taken out a gun and fired it into the wall several inches from the official's head. Rather than cause an incident the man had gotten right on the radio, and Pukatire had been back in the village that afternoon.

Pukatire began by showing me the wild edible fruit trees. The Menkranoti harvest some sixty jungle trees, but their fruits, while often delicious, are in little danger of being exploited commercially because they have big pits and too little pulp to make it worthwhile. An exception is *kubenkräkti,* the cacao tree, from which chocolate is made and whose white pulp is tasty eaten raw. Pukatire found one of the trees and "swarmed" it, putting his hands around it, pulling his feet up to his hands, and repeating the process until he had reached the fruits, which were some twenty-five feet overhead. After we had gorged ourselves, he cut a yard-long section from a

---

*In Cayapo -i is a frequent ending, as in Pukati, Menkranoti, and Kubenti. A longer form, -ire, as in Pukatire, Menkranotire, and Kubentire, is used just as often.

thick vine in the genus *Davilla* and held it over his mouth. In a few seconds cool water began to drip from it. The water wouldn't come out unless you cut the vine on both ends. *Davilla* vines and the prop-roots of *Pourouma* trees are ready sources of water for those who can recognize them. Vines that look like *Davilla* but flow red or yellow when you cut them open are apt to be poisonous.

"The heads these guys must have," Danny said as we followed Pukatire. "The thoughts that must run through their minds from living in the jungle."

Pukatire pointed to an elaborate scaffold which the Menkranoti had built to a bee's nest in the crown of a tree a hundred and twenty feet up. "Is that to get the honey?" I asked.

"No," Pukatire said. "The young men go up there to get stung. It makes them strong." On the way back he showed us a plant called *mekraketdja* which his wife had taken as a contraceptive two years ago after one of the shamans had told her she would not survive another childbirth. There had been no children since.

Pukatire was only thirty, and there were many plants known only to the elders. Almost every old person was a *wayanga* or medicine man. Most had a specialty. Bebgogti, for example, was the *wayanga* for fish sickness, Bote the one for freshwater clam sickness, Koti for turtle sickness, Pakux for scorpion bite, Karekra for dog bite, and Krakiêro for snake bite. Tewet and Eketi were general practitioners. Eketi was, at five-eleven, the tallest man in the village, a powerfully built and handsome man with hair streaming down to his shoulders who seemed in the prime of manhood though he was about fifty. The only sign of physical deterioration was that he was losing his sight in one eye. His feet were huge, and their soles were like leather, and as he walked through the forest he planted them so solidly that the ground seemed to shake in his wake, yet he moved with such fluid strides that I had to rush to keep up with him.

Eight years earlier Bebgogti had sent Eketi to spy on the Kreen-akroare village; he had scouted out the situation for six months, and then the Menkranoti had struck at dawn. It had been a devastating raid; Menkranoti's finest hour. Thirty-five people were killed, and five children taken captive. Two of the children had died and the oldest, Remrare, was about twelve now. She had the joyful, self-absorbed innocence of a child, but her breasts were beginning to swell, and the men were beginning to look at her in a different way, making her feel confused and self-conscious. At night she would come to our hut and listen to the singing, but she was always too shy to join in. Eketi seemed to have adopted her, as she spent most of the time over at his hut, doing chores with his wife and daughters and playing with their children. Soon she would have her first menstruation, upon which she would go into solitary retreat for a few days. After the first man had taken her to the *kikra-bua,* the zone between the jungle and the edge of the village where lovers met at night, she could let her hair grow and wear a red sash, meaning "her virginity has been taken," at ceremonies with the other women. But because she was a captive, she could never marry. Remrare seemed to be perfectly happy with her fate.

Eketi would show up early in the morning at our hut and take me walking in the woods for a few hours, stopping whenever he came across a medicinal or edible plant. He would tell me its name, and I would write it down and make a sketch of it, to his amused fascination. Most of the *pidio* were for stomach disorders: *podpidio* was for sickness from eating anteater, *kapranpidio* for sickness from eating tortoise, *kukoi* for sickness of monkey, *kukrùtpidio* for sickness of tapir, *pêiàti* for sickness of a gregarious oriole called the *joãocongo* or yellow-rumped cacique. Most of the thirty-one plants I collected and took to Manaus for identification turned out to be in the chemically active *Menispiermaceae, Bignoniaceae,* and *Apocynaceae* families. The four contraceptive plants and the one abortifacient all probably had some physiological foundation. Others seemed to have been chosen because of their resemblance to the animal for which they were meant to be an antidote. The sharp leaves of the *piperaceae,* for example, looked like the sting of a scorpion; the speckled juvenile leaves of the araceous vine* resembled a snake; the broad, jagged foliage of the *passiflora* seemed visually appropriate as a remedy for someone who had been attacked by a jaguar. This sort of association was to be expected of a society which had to find in its own environment plausible, if not totally effective, solutions to the afflictions that beset it. Medieval herbals are full of cases of plants whose use was suggested by their appearance. This practice was called the Doctrine of Signatures. The Menkranoti believe in their plants and in the power of the shamans who administer them, but they are turning increasingly toward the white strangers whose *pidio* miraculously stops diarrhea, reduces

---

*Curiously, this plant bears a close resemblance to rattlesnake plantain, an orchid used by the Eastern Woodlands Indians of North America as a remedy for rattlesnake bite.

fevers, and expels worms. Two years before we arrived a woman had tried to club her father to death because he had been badly gored by wild pigs, and she didn't think he would recover. A well-placed blow with a club, resulting in quick death, is usually used for infanticide, murder, and mercy killing. But now the Menkranoti have the help of western medicine, and this kind of killing doesn't take place any more. Bebgogti remembered well that it was a FUNAI *enfermeiro* who had brought him back from near death several years ago. He believed in the old ways, but also realized that the white men had things his people needed. He continued to treat the rheumatism in his right arm by wrapping it in a medicinal vine, but he also knew that it was largely through the good works of FUNAI that the village's growth rate was now up to ten percent. The Menkranoti need to keep alive their old ways to ensure their spiritual well-being, and they need to cooperate with the white strangers to ensure their physical survival. Bebgogti's ambivalence toward western culture was reflected in his dress. One minute he would be wearing a shirt and pants, the next only a penis sheath.

Mine was the first ethnobotanical study of Menkranoti. Of particular interest were the plants used for birth control. Nearly every tribe has a contraceptive plant, and many have several. Some enterprising graduate student might analyze them and discover the safe contraceptive our society still lacks. Pukatire's plant, taken once, lasted two years.

The entire pharmacological potential of the Amazonian flora has hardly been explored. A German chemist whose job it was to develop new drugs told me before my trip that, as far as he was concerned, there were no useful chemical compounds left to be discovered in the Amazon. Fifty percent of the flora, he said, all of the genera, and all chemical possibilities, were known; the botanical work that remained, describing new species, was only of taxonomic interest. The man's attitude typified the reluctance of drug companies to become involved in the Amazon. There are several reasons for this reluctance: 1) the risk: it takes a great investment to collect and analyze a plant that may or may not prove to be commercially exploitable; 2) a contraceptive product that must be taken only once every two years is obviously less desirable, from the point of view of making money, than one that must be taken daily; and 3) a drug company may in fact be involved in the analysis of a certain plant, but because of the intense competition for new products, isn't saying anything about it. Dr. Ghillean Prance of the New York Botanical Garden is now analyzing *Curarea tecunarum,* a contraceptive vine in use among the Dení Indians of the Rio Cunhuá. It is the only study of this kind that I know of.

The dean of Amazonian ethnobotany is Dr. Richard Evans Schultes of Harvard, who has spent more than thirty years among Indian tribes collecting their medicinal, toxic, and narcotic plants. I wrote him of my conversation with the German druggist, and he replied:

> "All I can say about your pharmacologist adviser is that he is woefully ignorant of both botany and the Amazon—and you may quote me, if you wish. This ignorance is far from uncommon.

> "There are 62,000 known species from the Amazon valley—and experts estimate there may be 20-25% still to be discovered.* Only a mere fraction have even *superficially* been looked at chemically. . . .

> "One has only to remember the whole procession of 'wonder drugs' discovered from plants in the 30's, 40's, and 50's, several of them from a flora as well known as New England, to realize the potentialities."

Perhaps ten percent of the Amazonian flora has been analyzed chemically. The antibiotic compounds in the fungi are not at all studied, nor are the bacteria-inhibiting compounds and chemovars in the lichens or the sesquiterpenoid lactones, ecdysones, alkaloids, and cyanogenic glycosides in the ferns and their allies. The angiosperms are better known, but they, too, abound with genera that have never been subjected to phytochemical scrutiny. The need for well-trained ethnobotanists right now is particularly critical, as Schultes explains:

> "While there is certainly no reason to presume that people in primitive cultures possess any particular insight into the discovery of biodynamic plants, it is true that they do live in a much more intimate relationship with their ambient vegetation than do those of urbanized, advanced civilizations. Trial and error and the experience of centuries have built up a rich store of folklore. It is, therefore, a shortcut, as it were, for us today to use to our advantage. . . .

---

*These figures differ significantly from those of Dr. Murça Pires.

"Civilization is closing in on many, if not most, parts of the world still sacred to aboriginal peoples. Our great concern lies in the progressive divorcement of man in the less advanced societies from the dependence on his immediate environment. A prime example is the Amazon Valley—an area with an indigenous flora of at least 60,000 species, still only partially known, and with peoples characterized by exceedingly penetrating perspicacity concerning the uses of unusual biodynamic properties of their plants. Yet, one after another aboriginal cultures in this vast area are rapidly being lost. We must, for both academic and practical purposes, salvage some of the medicobotanical lore of this part of the world, before it shall have been forever entombed with the culture that gave it birth."

In the evening, as I was pressing the day's collection, people were always coming in and banging on my guitar for a while, then handing it to me and saying *"Nre,* play." They had already learned "Glory, Glory, Halleluia," from the two missionary women, who had left the village a month before. I taught them two more American songs, "Irene Good Night" and "Jimmy Crack Corn." The boys would watch my lips and reproduce a split second later the sounds that were coming out of my mouth; they were such good mimics that I thought they must have understood what they were saying, but when I stopped and indicated for them to go on by themselves, they became shy and tongue-tied. We made up a Cayapo version of Jimmy Crack Corn that went like this:

Moina ga tē, me bengokre
Moina ga tē, me bengokre
Moina ga tē, me bengokre
Boka nega te.

Where are we going, people of the watery places?
Where are we going, people of the watery places?
Where are we going, people of the watery places?
We're going into the woods.

Then we would go around the room, substituting someone's name for "people of the watery places." The person being sung about would blush with mortification, and the chorus would dissolve into laughter at the end of each verse. Even the shyest of the girls, who would normally only peer in through the palings, could not resist this song, and they would come inside and shriek each other's names as the next one to be sung about. After we had gone through the entire contents of the hut, everyone would usually want to start all over again, or to sing another round of "Irene Good Night," so whenever I picked up the guitar I could figure on having to play it for several hours.

After supper and the sing-along we would usually go over to José Roberto's, the *chefe de posto,* and play canasta with him and Guillermo, the male nurse.

Menkranoti became a *posto* in 1966. A year afterward the family Schneider of the Missão Cristão Evangelico came in. They were known to be gung-ho proselytizers, but in three years "they didn't evangelize one Indian," Gustaaf told us. Realizing it was too soon to evangelize, they concentrated on making an airstrip and treating the Indians with medicine. They had to leave in 1970 after a malaria epidemic in which 40 Indians were killed, both Schneider and his wife became comatose, the radio broke down, and their eight-year-old daughter took care of the village.

In 1970 a two-woman team from the Summer Institute of Linguistics, now on leave from the village, came in. In their absence, a dozen or so Indians, led by Pukatire, would hold services every Sunday afternoon, wearing the odd bit of western clothing they had acquired in trade—the loafers, necktie, or argyle socks.

Once on our way to José Roberto's we saw a bright yellow ball bobbing low in the northeastern sky. Its distance was hard to gauge, but it was clearly too near to be a star, and too far away and up in the sky to be a bioluminous insect. I thought it was a planet, but no planet I had ever seen had such an erratic wobble. Maybe our perception of it was being distorted by atmospheric disturbance. Two hours later, during a recess in the canasta game, the ball was still wobbling, but less dramatically, and sitting noticeably higher in the sky. Was it a balloon? But what would a balloon be doing all lit up, sailing over the Amazon rain forest in the dead of night? The ball remained a UFO for several months until I got a letter from my friend Tim Ferris, an authority in celestial matters. "The bright thing you saw climb slowly in the sky," he wrote, "was the planet Jupiter. Thermal currents can make bright stars and planets appear to waver and move in the sky when they are near the horizon, and the extreme brightness of Jupiter tends to make it seem nearby; the rate of climb you described, one-sixth of the way across the sky in two hours, is exactly the sidereal rate produced by the earth's spin on its axis.

"Incidentally, there are scattered reports that early Africans of some tribes had good enough eyesight to see Jupiter's four bright moons, or at least a couple of them. (For us, the task requires at least a pair of binoculars.) If you run into a sharp-eyed native, perhaps you could ask about this." We did ask a few Menkranoti about the strange yellow ball, but none of them ventured a theory or seemed to have the least interest in it. The Amazon Indian does not seem to be sky-oriented. Perhaps the vegetation takes up too much of his attention. At Menkranoti the blazing constellations of the southern sky—Taurus, the Pleiades, the Southern Cross—and the nightly meteor showers went almost unnoticed.

One morning Eketi came to me and said, "Do you want to see some bananas?" I said sure and followed him back to his hut. At the entrance his wife Pinkra and his pretty daughters Niokro and Raibote, and Remrare the captive Kreen-akroare girl, stood waiting with empty wicker pack baskets slung from their heads and machetes in their hands. "Eite, eite. Come here, come here," he called to his three dogs, and stooping over one of them squeezed three inchlong maggots out of its back, larvae of botflies that had been injected into the dogs by a *mutuca,* an insect on whose half-inch proboscis botflies lay their eggs.

The forest to the west of the village was hilly and dark. East of the village, I discovered, it was flatter, wetter, and more open. At one point in the space of fifty yards we had to ford the same creek three times. My inexperienced eyes could hardly make out the path, and I fell behind Eketi's family. Sticktights fastened themselves to my legs and I was stung by nettles. The *mutucas,* which are twice as painful as deerflies, were out in force, and clothing offered no protection against them. About five miles out I caught up with my companions. Eketi had hacked down a *Pourouma* tree, and he passed me a cluster of its fuzzy, purple berries, which looked like grapes and tasted of wintergreen. I noticed a small, leafless plant sticking up through the damp leaf mould. With its six-inch brown shaft and its white head covered with fine pink hairs, it looked very much like a penis. It was in fact a saprophyte in the *Balanophoraceae* family, I later learned.

I asked Eketi if the plant had any use. The women giggled. It was called *metuyarodjà,* he told me. A woman eats its head when she wants to have a baby. In fact, the Menkranoti believe that pregnancy is caused by the ingestion of this plant and the incantations of a shaman, who bathes the woman in a special leaf brew, cleanses her in the river, and sings over her until midnight. He repeats the process the following morning. Intercourse has nothing to do with it. There had never been a baby born in Menkranoti, Eketi claimed, without this due process. At the onset of labor the women go into the woods to have their babies, he went on; no man may witness the event. Unlike some tribes, the Menkranoti do not observe *couvade,* in which the expectant father confines himself to his hammock while the woman is in labor; here, he stays in his hut and does nothing. After the child is born he goes hunting and cannot come back until he has found good meat.

Early in the afternoon we arrived at Eketi's new garden. Since the arrival of FUNAI and the missionaries, the Menkranoti have become more sedentary and have adapted themselves to farming. Now there are big plantations in every direction from the village. The Indians grow twelve kinds of banana, twenty-two kinds of sweet potato, four kinds of corn, six kinds of manioc, and two kinds of cotton, along with sugar cane, tobacco, papaya, pineapple, *urucu,* and *genipape.* Each family, with the sons-in-law it has acquired, tends its own patch. Eketi's garden had six of the more common varieties of banana found in Brazil at large: *banana comprida* or plantain, which is long and pink inside and eaten raw or roasted; *banana roxa,* fat little claret bananas which are sweet and delicious; *banana d'agua, curta,* or *maçã,* the common short banana; *banana costela,* three-sided and fat-skinned; *banana prata,* like *maçã* but with a green skin, used medicinally for dysentery and vomiting, especially by children; and *banana noa,* same size as *roxa,* but with a yellow center. The great mystery is where the Menkranoti, and other Indians like the Kreen-akroare who have supposedly never had contact with the Brazilian national society, got their bananas. Edible bananas are not native to South America. According to T. W. Purseglove, whose three-volume *Tropical Crops* is the best book on the subject, the banana originated in the Burma-Thailand area, was taken to West Africa and from there to the Canary Islands by the Portuguese, who introduced the first clone to the New World on Hispaniola in 1516. How it managed to make its way to almost every tropical-forest tribe in South America has yet to be explained.

Several women were sitting before huge bunches of green bananas, and a man was rapidly weaving a palm basket. The women passed around a warm, seedy papaya and Eketi shucked a few stalks of cane for us. His little grandson *Kokonù* brought two bird eggs and ate them raw. There was much laughter.

After this pleasant break one of the women loaded two bunches of about a hundred fingers each—at least eighty pounds

—on her back. She slipped the bark tumpline, or sling, which would bear most of the weight, over the top of her head and picked up two burning sticks from the fire to keep her pipe going as she set out on the ten-mile trek back to the village. Eketi indicated that I should go with her. A small load of about forty fingers was prepared for me, and I followed the woman and two others laden with a similar burden of bananas. They placed their hands at their temples under the tumpline and walked along, breasts jiggling, pipes smoking. My neck felt as if it was going to break; I had never used these muscles. We made frequent rest stops, and the women would sit on a wild banana leaf and pick lice from each other's hair, or take a dip in the creek. There was a lot of joking around; the joking, I am sure, was a way of distracting themselves from the boring, back-breaking work, just as singing is an outlet for the women in certain African tribes. Trying to imitate the way they walked across a log, pigeon-toed, I slipped and fell into the creek. My tumpline broke. One of the women cut a gash with her machete in the side of a tree, in the family *Annonaceae,* put her fingers under the bark, and ripped up until she had torn off a thin, twenty-foot strip. Then she stepped on either end of the machete, ran the strip under the flat edge of the blade, and pulled up, separating the inner bark—soon to become my new strap—from the outer bark. She was the chief's roly-poly fourth daughter, whose husband had left her several months before. Because none of the men in Menkranoti had wanted her, she had taken one of her two children and walked for sixteen days through the jungle, living off fruits and nuts, to the village of Bau, where she married within a week. Since she was the chief's daughter, a delegation of Menkranoti men had come and brought her back. Now she was pregnant with a baby that she didn't want, and she said she was going to kill it. Leaving the women I hurried on alone, to reach the village by nightfall, scaring up a flock of curassows, plump black relatives of the turkey with scarlet legs and bills, who fluttered up awkwardly into the lianas.

That night I went to the creek for water, and as I approached the bank something very big flopped into the water and drifted downstream with the current. I kept it in the weak beam of my flashlight until it disappeared under a fallen tree, but all I could make out was a black and tan form slithering in a way that would suggest anaconda and swimming with its head up in a way that would suggest alligator. The year before a sixteen-foot anaconda— an adult of medium size—was killed near the village.

Our cook, the son of Benmoti, the white captive, had borrowed our strongest flashlight earlier in the evening to go hunting, and as he returned to the village he stepped on a scorpion. We found him in the morning lying in his parent's hut. His sister was rubbing tobacco leaves all over him and applying a vine tourniquet to retard the spread of the poison. His father was fanning him with a palm leaf. He was shuddering spasmodically and had lost control of his speech. The family was gravely concerned, but to the rest of the village the accident seemed to be a source of amusement. Within a week, he had recovered fully.

I spent the next few days in the village. Most of the men had gone to the woods for several weeks to hunt and catch tortoises for the *menibiok* festival. It was quiet in the village, and as I walked from hut to hut the women would beckon to me and offer me a banana or a sweet potato, or show me a pair of earrings, a flute, or an arrow that they wanted to trade. A typical hut had three doors, three fires, three families, two raised platform beds, one woven palm sleeping mat, three stools, and eight faded hammocks, some with tassels. Eight-foot arrows with assorted points were stuck in the thatch. Hanging from poles and on the walls were bows, baskets, guns, clubs, spears, spindles, gourds containing feathers, ammunition bags, slings for carrying children, axes, hoes, straw hats, a necklace of tapir hoofs, cooking pots, machetes, clusters of nuts, and glass bottles with cocoanut oil for the hair. The light poured into the dark interior through chinks in the wattle walls, and smoke from dying fires curled in the light. Perhaps the extended families of the Menkranoti, as in many societies that are close to nature, are matrilocal, because in nature, among animals, the mother is the figure of continuity; often the father is not even known.

Djonare and Mruprire had stayed behind to make *farinha* for the approaching festival. A heap of manioc roots had been brought in from the plantations and soaked for a day or so, then crushed in a wooden press to remove the prussic acid in them and left to dry overnight. Two women were grating the processed roots into a trough made from a hollowed-out log, and the moist pulp was then roasted in a huge metal frying-pan donated by FUNAI. Djonare and Mruprire kept stirring it with round wooden paddles and feeding the flames until the hard, golden nuggets were ready to be transferred into a second hollowed-out log.

While I was at the manioc shed, an outcry went up in the village. Djonare and Mruprire grabbed their guns and ran to the plaza where everyone was watching a jabiru stork circling overhead. Finally the bird made the mistake of landing in front of Eketi's house. Mruprire crept up on it and shot it in the head. Then, followed by the women and children, he carried it triumphantly through the plaza and held it out to the chief, who pulled off a few black primary feathers. I realized that even half-deserted, the village was in a state of combat readiness.

That afternoon three boys stoned a dog to death. Two held it down, and the third kept on coshing it over the head with a rock. It struggled free and they ran after it, beating it with sticks. It was nobody's dog, so nobody stopped them. Bothered by this gratuitous cruelty I walked to the edge of the village and sat alone on a log. "Why is he sad?" the boys asked Gustaaf. At Menkranoti, no one is ever by himself by choice. Being alone at night in the jungle, where you might be attacked by a jaguar or possessed by a spirit, is especially to be avoided. Time spent alone is dead time, as far as they are concerned, and they depend on each other for company, love, structure, and safety. Only rarely does someone break from the tight communal bonds and go berserk or *aybānh*. But this too is accepted behavior; perhaps a necessary outlet in one of the few Amazon tribes that has no alcoholic beverages or hallucinogens. There was a man who had gone *aybānh* a few years before. He had shot his brother in the head and run screaming into the woods. A week later he returned, calm again. The rest of the village treated him as if nothing was out of the ordinary, according to Gustaaf, and now the incident was forgotten.

The next day I had diarrhea and just lay in my hammock, stewing. When an attack came I had to rush behind the hut and squat over a hole in which a large *Mygales* spider, the type that eats finches and is known in Portuguese as the *caranguejeira,* lived. After half a dozen trips I became profoundly apathetic and drifted into a nightmare of complete deterioration, of wandering around South America no longer caring where I was or what was happening. The jungle was beginning to get on my nerves. The steady hum of billions of tiny *pium* flies who lived in the village, feeding on excrement and banana peels, swarming around our ankles as we walked through the plaza and forming a palpable cloud six inches from the ground, was beginning to prey on my sanity. There were other painful and irritating insects: chiggers, ticks, scabietic mites, and *bichos de pe,* who lay their eggs in the soles of your feet, buttocks, or any other part of the body in contact with the ground, and whose egg-sacks have to be dug out with a needle. Certain things about the Indians were also wearing on me. The women were always pestering us for salt and needles, and some of the men had become complete beggars. If you said *arùpket,* meaning that you didn't have any more of what they were asking for, they would just ask for something else. Gustaaf said that after you had run out of everything they stopped bothering you, but this did not alter the fact that many of the Menkranoti were highly materialistic people whose main interest in relating to you was to get the goods you had brought. Another thing that took a little getting used to was their habit of spitting wherever and whenever they wanted to. You would be sitting next to a nice old lady who was puffing away abstractedly on her *warikoko* when suddenly she would conjure up a juicy quid and deposit it several inches from your feet. I found that the best way of dealing with this situation was to conjure up an even bigger quid and to deposit it as close as possible to where the original had landed.

The jungle either accepts you or it doesn't, as someone once wrote. I was beginning to think that I was not one of the chosen. The countless *pium* bites on my legs, scratched by dirty fingernails, had begun to infect and swell; in another few days walking would become excruciatingly painful and long treks in the jungle impossible. I was getting stir-crazy. I was beginning to feel "the stupefying boredom that drives men to the brink of madness," as one explorer described the effect of being confined by the humid, claustrophobic rain forest. My feelings vacillated between thinking I had the privilege to be a witness of the life of some of the last humans to be living in a natural state, and listless, enervated withdrawal. The two environments, village and jungle, offered escape from one another. But within a short time both became unbearable.

As I lay in my hammock, a day-flying *Uranea* moth, jet-black with swallowtails and opal bars, flew in and fluttered under the latticework of the ceiling. I pulled myself together. With such an exquisite sight in range of my hammock, think of what there would be to see if I got outside. I joined a crowd of women and children who were running to the other side of the village. Bepkum had come back from the forest with four tortoises—too small for the festival—and some tapir and peccary meat. His mother put her hand on her forehead and sobbed uncontrollably for all the days that he'd been gone. Several women comforted her. Everyone else crowded around Bepkum with outstretched hands as he distributed the meat.

That night the thunder boomed and lightning lit up the edges of the thunderheads that hung over the hills around the village. We could hear the chief telling stories to his family in the next hut. The Cayapo have some eighty myths. They call themselves "the people who came from a hole in the sky." Originally, according to them, the earth was uninhabited. Everyone lived in the sky. One day an old man was digging out an armadillo burrow when he broke through the undersurface of the sky and saw the earth far below. He summoned his fellow villagers, who made a long rope out of vines. Half of them, led by a daring youth called "the son of the people," climbed down the rope, and we are all descended from them.

In the morning we went out with Bepkum and twelve others between the ages of ten and twenty-four. We walked for several hours, crossing creeks on logs, the young men cutting loose with full-throated yodels as they loped along with hundred-pound baskets of *farinha*. They were happy to become animal again, open to every sight and smell, away from the domesticating influence of the village.

Reaching a flat place near water, the young men set down their loads and without talking, set up camp. The youngest boys cleared the ground with machetes. Others ripped fresh long strips of bark from nearby trees, cut four poles with a fork at one end and a sharpened point at the other. They planted the sharpened point into the ground. Then they cut two long horizontal poles and lashed them to the crotches with the bark strips. Others returned with saplings about fifteen feet long, which they planted into the ground, bending them over the first horizontal pole, and lashing them to the second. A fourth party came back with trains of palm fronds which they tied to the wall of vertical saplings and threw in twos over the arching roof. The final product, a palm hut, was ready in fifteen minutes. It was six by thirty feet, fully waterproof, and could sleep twenty comfortably. The rest of the day was left for hunting.

Half a mile from the camp Kadiure suddenly stopped, rubbed a sapling several inches from its base, and smelled his hand. It had a strong, musky odor. *Kukrùt,* he said—tapir. We broke up into groups of two and three, keeping in contact with high, dove-like hoots, snapping twigs to retrace our way. I went with Bepkum and Wakontire. They led me to a huge tree with flaring buttresses, in the sheltered nook between two of which the tapir had last slept. We trailed the animal to a stream and saw his fresh, ungulate prints in the sand, then lost them in the water. Bepkum examined some holes in the riverbank which he said were inhabited by snakes. The dogs took off in a yelping frenzy after a deer. Looking up, Bepkum motioned for us to freeze. *Macaco.* A troop of monkeys was swinging through the trees, but the foliage was thick, and they were too high for him to pick off with his .22 rifle. We came upon some women who had cut down a Brazil-nut tree and were roasting the nuts. It must have taken them a day to fell the monarch, which was about eight feet in diameter; and it would take several more to gather all the nuts, roast them, and carry them back to the village. The fruit of the *Bertholetia excelsa* (Brazil-nut tree) is a woody ball or pixidium the size of a grapefruit, containing eighteen to twenty-five nuts. A good-sized tree may produce hundreds of balls. People have been killed by the falling fruit. After roasting the whole pixidium in an open fire, the women open it with their axes and pour the nuts into their baskets. The Menkranoti shell Brazil nuts with a single, well-placed bite. We sampled a handful. The nut has moist white meat, richer than coconut.

With Wakontire in the lead, we entered a *mata de cipó,* a wood consisting mostly of vines. I had the feeling that if I had not been there he wouldn't have been slashing down everything in our path, which I was sure was alerting every animal within earshot to our presence. But the Menkranoti are very protective of the *kuben,* the strangers who are living with them. They call them *no ket,* no eyes; like children, the *kuben* cannot see, and they must be carefully supervised so they don't get into trouble.

We came across a bee's nest in a dead tree, and Bepkum pried it off with a pole, wrapped the honey capsules in a leaf and passed it around. We took turns squeezing the bittersweet nectar into our waiting mouths. Just as Eskimos recognize over sixty kinds of snow, the Cayapo have names for twenty-eight species of bees. Most of them, like these bees, do not sting, so you can raid their hives with impunity.

Suddenly a shotgun popped twice in the distance. Bepkum and Wakontire dropped the stake with which they had been reaming out a hole and ran toward the sound. Twenty minutes later we joined the rest of the party. Kadiure had shot the tapir. The others were butchering the animal — which weighed at least three hundred pounds — and carrying it back to the camp. You could see how well it was adapted to a close, sticky environment: its hair was short, sparse, and spiny; its ears, neck, legs and tail elongated — the better to pass off body heat.

A fire was made, and stones piled on it, and strips of the flesh laid to roast on the stones. The liver, heart, and other organs were boiled in a pot; two fish, an ibis, and a guan were suspended over the flames on a spit. Several plantains were deposited in the ashes. For the rest of the afternoon we lazed in camp, chewing on the tapir meat, smoking, and naming the birds that sang: the watery

Overleaf *Cayapo boy bringing wild banana leaves for the roof of a lean-to. By Danny Delaney.*

Left *The Author and Tewet, the plant doctor, Menkranoti. By Danny Delaney.*

Right *The chief's son, Menkranoti. By Danny Delaney.*

Ruby, the Aika hunter, shooting a fish on the Rio Catrimani. By Alex Shoumatoff.

Facing Page *The vegetation at 11,000 feet in the upper Apurimac Valley.*
By Alex Shoumatoff.

Left *Maria building a fire, on the Rio Catrimani. By Alex Shoumatoff.*

Right *Maria, on the Rio Catrimani. By Alex Shoumatoff.*

Cayapo men in the plaza, Menkranoti. By Danny Delaney.

Cayapo women in the plaza, Menkranoti. By Danny Delaney.

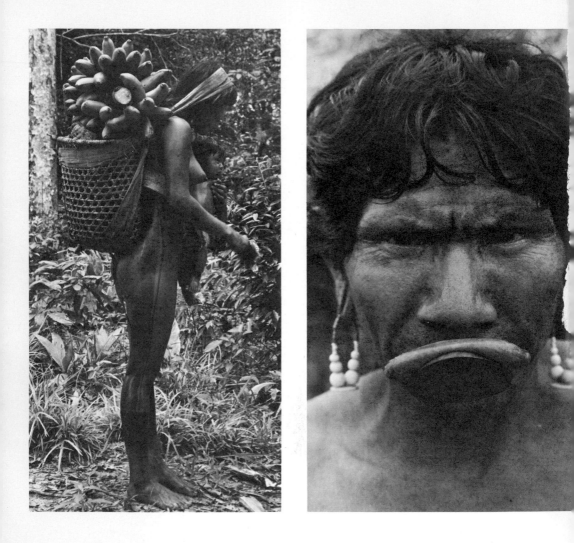

Left *Cayapo woman carrying bananas back to the village, Menkranoti. By Danny Delaney.*

Right *Cayapo man with lip disc, Menkranoti. By Danny Delaney.*

gurgles were a *wanamariket,* the piercing whistles a *tanokororina.* With vivid eyes and excited gestures, Kadiure told how he had shot the tapir. Kopran, fifteen, the youngest husband in the village, showed me how to make a *warikoko:* finding a certain tree, you carve out the goblet shape, hold it between your knees, and bore out the pith by rolling the stem of a tough grass back and forth quickly in your palms. Danny introduced the group to Wrigley's spearmint gum, clutching his throat with his hands to show that it was not to be swallowed. Hundreds of sweat bees swarmed over us, and to escape them we would periodically go and sit in the creek. Monekabo taught me how to count to ten:

1) *pudi*
2) *amaikrut*
3) *amaikrutikeke*
4) *amaikrutamaikrut*
5) *amaikrutamaikrutikeke*
6) *amaikrutamaikrutamaikrut*
7) *amaikrutamaikrutamaikrutikeke*
8) *amaikrutamaikrutamaikrutamaikrut*
9) *amaikrutamaikrutamaikrutamaikrutikeke*
10) *amaikrutamaikrutamaikrutamaikrutamaikrut*

Clearly, the Cayapo have little use for numbers.

That night Danny and I slept in our hammocks, and the men and boys lay on the floor of the hut, sleeping against each other in a great curled-up ball of snoring bodies. Whenever one of them turned over, the others would all turn by chain reaction. At their feet smouldering faggots of deadwood kept the animals away. Fire, which the Cayapo believe they got from the jaguar, is their protector at night in the woods. Cooking itself is regarded as a civilizing process, representing the transformation of raw, bloody meat into something palatable to humans. Their word for community, *tchet,* also means "baked" or "roasted." They are at a loss to explain why the word should have these two meanings.

In the middle of the night the rainy season began in earnest. We could hear the water pounding the leaves, but so dense was the canopy that for minutes we felt nothing. Then the rain broke through the saturated treetops and we scrambled into the lean-to, spending the rest of the night huddled among warm bodies. Bepiakoti, twenty-four, my right-hand neighbor, was fascinated with the hairs on my chest, and he pulled them and played with them while

I struggled with my inhibitions at being touched so freely by a member of the same sex.

In the morning as I took down my soggy hammock it ripped down the middle. After two weeks in the jungle, the cloth was already rotten. The Indians broke camp, walked for three hours, and set up a new one exactly as they had done the previous morning. Krâtùk and Kàprõt left for the village with slabs of tapir meat and we went with them.

That night, at about two-thirty in the morning, a chorus of heart-rending shrieks and wails went up in the village. An infant child had died of diarrhea. At dawn Karekra, the closest male relative, fired off two shots. Three shots would have meant a birth. The child who died was a twin. Her sister had been "allowed" to die some months before, probably clubbed to death by her mother, who was unmarried and in no position to bring up children. Karekra, the head male of her household and thus the person in charge of curing the child, had refused to go to FUNAI; Guillerme would have given him lomotil tablets, which quickly stop diarrhea. Karekra also refused to let the child have water, in the belief that it would only be excreted—so that she probably died of dehydration. Her death was not seen as a great tragedy because there were already ten extra females in the adult population and an even greater surplus in her own generation. The mother went about work as usual that day, except that her eyes seemed sad, and she spoke slowly, as if stunned, and in a low voice. In the afternoon, the child was buried at the edge of the village with her beaded armbands and necklaces, and a cone of sand was piled up on the spot. Afterwards the old women came to the mother and took all of her possessions from her. We debated why the woman should be subjected to further bereavement. Gustaaf's explanation seemed the most reasonable: if you lost a child, you lost everything, and had to start all over again.

We stayed away from the funeral and from Karekra's house; it was no time for *kuben* to be poking around. Tewet took me to his hut and played five songs for me on his bamboo flute, which only had four holes. The songs had a purity and a simplicity which western music could not command; I felt as if I were listening to a beautiful bird. Afterwards, Tewet tied a bark strap to his old Winchester repeater and set off to climb Kraenprekti, the high hill that overlooks the village. The vegetation was frothing over the summit cone, and we slashed for an hour through vines and saplings armed with thorns, until suddenly the land fell away on all sides, and I realized we were at the top. A cool breeze blew up the leaves, and between them we could see the morning mist rising over hundreds of miles of jungle. Tewet fired up his pipe and smoked. His lashless almond eyes were shining, and as he looked my way his thick lips spread into an engaging smile that revealed his upper gum.

On the way down he spotted a *buriti* palm tree, built a makeshift ladder, stood it up to the trunk, climbed up, and hacked down the fruit cluster. Within minutes he had woven two baskets of palm fronds for us to take the nuts, which tasted like soapy apricots, back to the village. At the base of the mountain he carefully cleared a place among the dead leaves, and as he was planting one of the nuts in the earth he heard the faint drone of an engine. *Màdu-kà,"* he said, looking up. Our plane had come.

6

On the River

The Indians showed no emotion as we loaded our gear into the plane, climbed in, and were spirited away. I looked at the group around the plane and realized that I still hadn't a clue about their inner thoughts. My attempts to come to terms with the Menkranoti had been hopelessly subjective and culture-bound. I had duly recorded that the lip disc was about the size of a hockey puck, knowing that the observation was without bearing for the people who wore them. At first I had been overwhelmed by the gulf between us. Then I had started to think that maybe we weren't so different; why, this man is *just* like so-and-so back home. Now I didn't know what I thought. We had been there too short a time, I decided, for the Indians to let down their guard. I met understanding in the eyes of Gustaaf, who stood beside the chief and would be staying in the village until after *menibiok*. Then we became airborne and the brave little circle of huts was soon swallowed up in the ocean of trees.

For me, at least, the leaving was emotional: I had learned that people who live in harmony with nature still exist, and after this brief exposure to their existence, my life could never be the same. At the same time I had been freed of whatever romantic illusions I had entertained about living in the jungle. I knew now why the Indian of the tropical forest has stayed where he is for ten thousand years while civilization has gotten to the moon. I had thought before I got there that it was because the environment was so easy that there was no incentive. All you had to do was reach out and pick a banana. Now I realized that it is because the environment is so hard. Food and game are not abundant. It is a full-time struggle to survive. The temperate regions, which force one to plan ahead, are hard in a different way. The semi-nomadic hunter-gatherer is induced to become a sedentary farmer. Once there is agriculture, there is civilization, and then the trouble begins: nature stops being a medium and becomes an obstacle.

We were heading northwest to Itaituba, a city on the Tapajós River. After forty minutes of featureless jungle we came to the Jamanxim River and followed its north-running path, ruffled with *cachoeiras,* to its meeting with the Tapajós. Just east of it, a thin reddish line, the new highway from Cuiabá to Santarém, sliced through the forest. Only the week before, our pilot told us, the President of Brazil had opened the road at a ceremony in Santarém, but there were no buses on it yet. Under good conditions, the journey from city to city took two days. West of the Jamanxim, he said, was rich mining country; the rivers all had gold in them, and far upstream were diamonds. The area was filled with *garimpeiros,* prospectors, who occasionally fought with the Mundurucu Indians.

For the first time in a month I set and wound my pocket-watch. We were already back in the world of clock time. In fact, it was costing us $150 an hour to be in this plane. What day was it? November 1. An important day on the next continent; the American people were deciding their next President. An important day in Brazil, too—*All Souls' Day.* As we flew in low over Itaituba we saw a gaily dressed crowd in the cemetery placing wreaths and lighted candles on the graves of their departed relatives.

Itaituba had all the excitement of a boom town. Parts of its new prosperity reflected the mineral wealth of the Tapajós. The streets were lined with establishments that stated in bold lettering COMRA-SE-OURO—we buy gold—at forty cruzeiros a gram; and there were numerous *pensoes de garimpeiros,* prospectors' inns. Part of the boom was due to the road: Itaituba is on the Transamazonica, the road that is opening up the Amazon much as the Alcan Highway united the remote fastnesses of Alaska and the Yukon with the rest of North America. Furthermore, on the opposite bank is the crossroads of the Transamazonica and the new Cuiabá-Santarém highway, a factor that will make Itaituba even more important. Already shiny new pickup trucks and sedans were rolling down the dirt streets, scattering pigs and chickens; elegant houses with flowered tiles were spreading block by block; and men with sunglasses and safari jackets were sitting in lush gardens, clinking glasses of *cachaça* at the closing of a deal.

We checked into a hotel overlooking the river, sat under the arbor of an outdoor restaurant, and drank our first cold beer in a long while. I got a haircut, and Danny made friends with a Swiss soldier of fortune in his early thirties named Uri. Having entered the Amazon system from Ecuador by taking a dugout canoe down the Putumayo River, Uri planned to spend a few more months exploring before returning to Zurich. He had been in Itaituba for several weeks; it was the most agreeable Amazon town he had found. He had a dugout canoe and a high-powered rifle; a few days before he had paddled downstream at dusk and said he had seen a black panther (actually a melanistic variety of the jaguar, *Panthera onça palustris*) on the beach. He planned to set out in a few days for the *garimpeiro* country, filling his boat with bottles of *cachaça* and fifty-litre cans of kerosene for which the prospectors would pay in pure gold. He figured to sell his canoe and its contents, catch the next bush plane to Itaituba, cash in the gold, and make enough of a profit to earn his way home. By taking periodic leaves of absence from the family shoe business, he had visited every country in the world but three.

While in Itaituba we inquired about the success of the Transamazonica. Five years before our arrival, a directive for "national integration" had been issued in Brasília, and a system of highways, running up, down, and around the Amazon basin, linking places hitherto accessible only by river or by air—17,855 kilometers in total length—was begun. The Transamazonica was to run parallel to the Amazon, crossing the southern tributaries below where they encountered the Brazilian shield and navigation by large barges was no longer possible. It was now open from Tocantinopolis on the Transbrasiliana to Humaita, where construction was halted because the road crew had hit emeralds. The date of its arrival at its final destination, Pucallpa, Peru, was indefinite; because of the rampant inflation Brazil was experiencing it had been set aside until "next year," as I was told in Brasília. Besides its primary objective, "to open up vast areas of the world's last frontier," the road was being built for national security—to protect the Brazilian part of the basin from its covetous neighbors. The government also hoped that by connecting the Amazon with the Northeast, there would be a salubrious redistribution of the population: thirty million *nordestinos* live in arid poverty, growing by one million a year, while there are only eight million people in the Amazon, which takes up fifty-nine percent of Brazil. INCRA, the National Institute for Colonization of Agrarian Reform, subdivided a twenty-kilometer-wide strip along the stretch from Maraba to Itaituba and launched a massive advertising campaign: hundred-hectare lots were available for $700, payable over twenty years, and two-room houses were available for $100, payable over the same time period. Every ten kilometers there was to be an *agrovila* — a government-built community of forty-four to sixty-six houses with a medical post, primary school, a government-run general store, and an office of the agricultural extension service; every 100 kilometers there was to be an *agropolis* with a secondary school, a hospital, light industry and warehouses; every 200 kilometers there would be a *ruropolis,* with 20,000 inhabitants, a trade school, banks, hotels, and an airport.

By December 1976, only 5,717 *nordestino* families, whose average size was six, had shown up; the projected migration had fallen short by a factor of more than ten. There was also a significant population of migrant workers, squatters, and government employees. The homesteads were more popular with the independent-minded *nordestinos* than the *agrovilas.* Practical considerations also favored the homestead: to make a go of it in the Amazon, a farmer must always be there on his land, protecting his rice and corn from pests, and his pigs and chickens from the depredation of Virginia opossums and forest cats. Some people received good land; most didn't. There were messy disputes over the ownership of jungle land that until recently was considered worthless. In July, 1976, John Davis, a rancher from Alabama, and his two sons were gunned down by squatters on their particularly fertile spread near Maraba. An American who knew the man said that he should have compromised with the squatters, allowing the established ones to remain in return for keeping out new arrivals. "Davis was a tough character. But he thought he was back in the United States, where the law says that a man owns every inch of his land, and the authorities back him up. There, you got to negotiate with the police, the authorities, the squatters, with everybody. And if you end up with less land than you expected, you still have enough land to make it worth your while." Davis and his sons were bushwhacked by a group of about thirty of the squatters on his land. Brazilian law says a property owner can evict squatters but must reimburse them for the improvements they have made. When you have two thousand squatters, as Davis did, it gets to be a problem.

Other problems on the Transamazonica are malaria and gastroenteritis, a major cause of infant mortality brought about by drinking water contaminated with feces. "Children defecate promiscuously in backyards," reported Nigel Smith, a British geographer who has studied the settlement along the Transamazonica, "while adults generally prefer the discretion of a banana or maize patch."

With all these setbacks, the government was beginning to move away from the colonization project, and to sell more and more of the land along the highway to large companies — an ecological tragedy, as this would mean more large-scale clearing, leading to rapid depletion of the soil and less shifting, slash-and-burn agriculture by individuals, which seems the best human adaptation to the Amazonian rain forest. The impact of the Transamazonica, the major occurrence in the Amazon today, was profound on the areas contiguous to the road, but still quite negligible on the basin as a whole. The impression I had received in the United States was exaggerated. "The programme of massive development and settlement on the forest margins along the new Transamazon highway has run into difficulties," Smith concluded, "and forest destruction has so far been much less than was expected." But his study was made as the large corporations were just moving in, and it may be time for a new assessment.

While the Transamazonica has run into problems, some people — merchants, hotelkeepers, and restaurateurs mostly — are getting rich because of the road, and it has siphoned freight from the rivers. "Because of the high cost of inefficient operation and rampant pilferage," wrote a Brazilian geographer named Hilgard O'Reilly Sternburg, "shippers were ready to forsake the waterways in favor of the quicker, safer, and, all things considered, cheaper transportation of the truck, as soon as this alternative became available," and the impact of the road on Itaituba, which a few years before must have been a sluggish installation like Araguaçema, has been dramatic. The outlook is bright for Itaituba, I thought that night as I stood under a pipe from which gushed the soothing waters of a natural hotspring. But for the time being, we could not get a hot meal. The town was out of cooking gas.

In the morning we shipped out on a *motor,* a sleek, two-story affair crammed with passengers, pigs, river turtles, and baskets of *farinha.* The upper deck was open with a white railing and a flat tin roof under which the 20 or so passengers were swinging in the colorful hammocks they had brought with them. The Tapajós was clean and beautiful and without mosquitoes, and the next few days of serene gliding fulfilled the dreams I had of Amazon river travel. The *motor* would put in beneath a row of colorful storefronts to pick up a shipment of chickens, or dock at a *sitio,* a little farm on the riverbank, to discharge a passenger. People were constantly paddling up in dugout canoes and offering us melons; once in the middle of the night, a regal-looking mulatto woman with a white parasol came aboard but debarked before I awoke again. During the heat of the afternoon we lay suspended in our hammocks or played cards with the crew. At night we watched the benign fins of freshwater dolphins cutting the lambent, ghostly sheet of moonlit water, and waved to pretty barefooted women who came running out of their palm-thatched huts and stood on the bank with babies in their arms. On the second evening we stopped at Fordlandia, Henry Ford's attempt to resurrect the rubber boom. Ford had put in the immense plantation in 1928, but he soon found out that by planting the rubber trees all in a row, he was only setting them up for their natural enemies, three kinds of leaf blight fungus from which rubber trees are protected in their natural state, scattered in the forest. Ford recruited the local people and paid well, but many were not used to working regular hours, and it was impossible to maintain the steady reservoir of labor that such a large operation required. Discouraged, he sold Fordlândia to the Brazilian government in 1943, and it has been going downhill ever since. The situation was especially bad at the moment because of the low price of rubber.

The next day was my birthday, and I commemorated the occasion with the following entry in my notebook: "the Tapajós is widening—three miles now, perhaps—at its mouth it is wider than the Amazon. Two men are gambling over the motor, everyone else is hanging like a cocoon in his hammock. It is 12 o'clock. I have the shits and have just turned 30."

That afternoon, at another rubber plantation called Bela Terra, forty kilometers from Santarém, we took on a crew-cut Catholic priest whose name was Brother Norbert. A native of Kentucky, he was responsible for administering to the religious needs of the people up and down the Tapajós, whom he reached by *lancha,* a long dugout canoe with a motor and a makeshift palm-thatch roof, being gone sometimes for weeks at a time. He told us about the Vaughans and the Reicherts—Confederate families who fled to the Amazon after the Civil War and whose descendants are still in Santarém—and the abundance of artifacts that the bishop of Santarém had found under his plough on his farm outside of the city, relics of the pre-Columbian culture that flourished at the mouth of the Tapajós. Soon we passed the big modern hotel that Varig, the Brazilian airline, had built in Santarém to encourage tourism, and the hill whose top had been clipped off because it was a hazard to aircraft; then crossed the *encontra das aguas,* the meeting of the crystal blue Tapajós with the café-au-lait Amazon. Along the line of contact fish lay stunned by the sudden change in temperature and turbidity.

The *motor* pulled in beside dozens of other riverboats of similar construction. A plank was extended to the sandy beach, where several hundred people were milling around. We forged through the crowd and checked into the nearest hotel, the Macarongo, a dilapidated fortress on the waterfront with a Mansard roof, fifteen-foot ceilings, and rats in the walls — "the House of Dracula," as the owner called it. The scene in the dining room, with the Amazon gliding by the windows, a breeze ruffling pin-ups of nude women, and a dozen or so solitary old men eating in silence at separate tables, was out of a Fellini film. Santarém, the largest city we'd been in since Brasília, was dead in a pleasant, relentless sort of way. Perhaps it was overwhelmed psychologically by the immensity of the river. Out of our window we watched men piling stones in chicken-wire cages along the bank against the coming wet season. The year before the river had risen into the main street. We took in a *bangy-bangy* in the gagging heat of a movie theater whose fans were not working, bought some lovely hammocks to send home, and went down to the beach to ask about the next boat to Manaus.

At seven p.m., Saturday, November 6, in the light of the full moon, we shipped out on the *Cidade do Parintins,* a larger *motor* than the one that took us down the Tapajós. About forty passengers hung their hammocks on the upper deck; Danny and I took one of the boat's two cabins. I rode for a while with the man behind the wheel. The biggest dangers, he said, were sandbars and sunken trees. He was constantly playing his headbeam over the water and reading the swirling muddy surface for submerged danger. All sorts of debris floated by: entire trees from banks that had slumped in the river; *matudas,* floating islands of the grass, *canarana,* from far upstream. The pilot stood at the wheel, impassively threading his way through them, occasionally crossing to a deeper channel on the other side, through the night and until 3:30 on the afternoon of the next day — a twenty-hour shift. Most of the passengers stayed in their hammocks, talking and reading. The most popular reading matter, I noticed, was the Bible. I spent most of the day playing dominoes with the crew.

At lunch time the table was cleared and we ate *tambaquí* — a large fish with the taste of swordfish that locates the fruits it eats by the sound of their dropping into the water. Along the bluffs we passed slabs of *pirarucú,* the most important commercial fish of the Amazon, about the size and shape of a muskelunge, drying in the sun; and many flourishing *sitios,* planted with corn, tomatoes, pepper, cane, jute, and manioc. The fertile soil of the *várzea* can only be farmed during the dry season, and when the water rises, the *sitios* are abandoned. We could see the water-line of last year's wet season half-way up the trees. The lower eight feet or so of the vegetation were still completely muddied and festooned with grass and other flotsam that had caught in its branches. The most common species was the *sumaumeira,* or silk-cotton tree; a century ago it was still being used by the Indians to make beautiful fabrics. We passed an anhinga in a tree, drying its wings, and a floating brothel making its way downstream to the next military installation, the women laughing and lounging in their hammocks.

I met a woman called Lucia Maria who was returning to Manaus from Santarém, where she had been visiting relatives with her four-year-old child, having left the seven- and ten-year olds with her grandparents. Her husband had been killed by the bite of a *jararacussu,* a fer-de-lance, a few years before while gathering rubber on the Rio Negro. Now she worked on an assembly line in a television factory, earning eighty dollars a month, and lived with an aunt in the suburb of Alvorado. She was twenty-eight, but looked older, despite a strong face and a fine white-toothed smile. Lucia Maria hated the jungle. She would stay in Manaus, and whenever she went up the Rio Negro to be with her husband she would return pregnant. "I'd probably be pregnant now if he were still alive," she said.

On the fourth morning the right-hand wall of rain forest gave way to an immense body of water that flowed the color of dark Darjeeling tea. This was the Rio Negro — the Amazon's most important tributary. Its discharge alone, 67,000 cubic meters per second, is four times as much water as the Mississippi dumps into the Gulf of Mexico, and forty percent of the total volume the Amazon pours a thousand miles later into the Atlantic (160,000 cubic meters per second, which is fifteen percent of all the fresh water passed into all the oceans on earth.) Several miles up the Negro, on its east bank, there suddenly appeared an enormous city — tall needles of steel gleaming in the sun, and beneath them ocean-going freighters being unloaded by gigantic cranes. It was as improbable an apparition in the middle of the rain forest as Brasília had been in the great central plain.

7

The Capital of the Jungle

Manaus began in 1660 as a fortress built by the Portuguese from which sloops called *montarias,* laden with cacao, cotton, and turtle oil for house and street lamps, would make the thousand-mile journey to Belém. Deep in the jungle and far from any constraining social influence, it was a dangerous, anarchic place. "Morals in Barra [as Manaus was then called] are perhaps at the lowest ebb in any civilized community," Alfred Russell Wallace, who formulated the theory of evolution at the same time as Darwin, reported in 1849. By the turn of the century, Manaus was the only source of rubber in the world. There was so much money in Manaus that the rubber barons, the Amazonian equivalent of our robber barons, would send their laundry to Paris. At the end of the rubber boom in 1912, 43,000 tons were exported from Manaus. By 1913, Malaya and Ceylon were even with Amazonia in rubber production. The seeds that Henry Wickham had shipped out of the Amazon in 1876 and planted in Kew Gardens were now trees in the Far East. The trees, far from their natural enemies, could be planted in rows; and there was a reservoir of cheap labor to tap them. The rubber barons who had recently impressed visitors by lighting cigars with bills of large denomination watched helplessly as the bottom fell out of their business. But the city survived.

In the last few years, because of its status as a free port and the most important city in western Amazonia, Manaus's sudden growth has disrupted public services and the gracious living pattern that survives in Belém and Santarém. Brazilians flock to Manaus to buy tax-free cameras, televisions, and the like, and there is a thriving black market in precious and colored stones, in spotted cat skins, river turtles, and other contraband produce of the valley. The city is full of young women who are escaping the boredom of the hinterland. Many become unwed mothers and turn to prostitution. Parts of Manaus are instantly familiar: commercial strips with neon lights, new subdivisions with barbecue grills in each yard, a welcome station at the beginning of a real estate development with a map showing how the land is going to be carved up, a few model homes to walk through. At the modern airport, suited businessmen with briefcases step off the plane, transact their business, and fly home the same day, as in any other city. The western world has arrived and begun to spread its tentacles—dead-straight roads with charred, clearcut borders—around the valley. Unlike the earlier civilizations which the jungle has swallowed up without a trace, this one seems here to stay. No place, however wild and forbidding, seems strong enough to withstand it—not even the Amazon. The day will undoubtedly come when every Amazonian owns a television and an air-conditioner, when humanity succeeds in insulating and isolating itself from its environment as it has in the temperate zone. In most of the valley it is still the palm-thatch hut with a dirt floor and insects into everything that prevails. Many of the kinks in the conquering technology have still to be ironed out: elevators in Manaus have a disturbing tendency to go up when you push down, weekly power failures plunge the city into darkness for hours at a time, local telephone calls can take an hour to go through, roads are torn up for repair and forgotten, and planes are often hours behind schedule.

Manaus is an anarchic patchwork of skyscrapers and shack cities, stucco *conjuntos,* or subdivisions, and relict stands of stately French and Victorian architecture left from the rubber boom. Many of the barons' dreamhouses—their minarets, chalets, and chateaux—were imported brick by brick. But the most fabulous structure is the Teatro do Amazonas, built with the twenty percent tax which the state of Amazonas levied on exported rubber. "To visit the famous opera house in Manaus," a visitor wrote, "is to be reminded of the bizarre and grandiose opulence which, like some Amazonian orchid, grew out of rottenness." Approximately 66,000 blue and gold tiles from Alsace-Lorraine gild its gawdy dome, which, illuminated at night, can be seen from many parts of the city. The dome sits on an elegant gray base with white trim and winding balustraded stairs leading to a columned portico. The base was recently painted gray, the color of all federal buildings, which caused an uproar as it had been pink for many years. In the reception foyer rich golden drapes and tall vases of Sevres porcelain are offset by soaring cream and coral pillars of Carrara marble flanked by carved jacaranda wood chairs. With four tiers of boxes adorned with angels and cherubs, the opera house seats an audience of 1,600.

The night we reached Manaus Danny flew home. Brazil had been more expensive than he had expected. His month with the Cayapo, which he had documented with splendid photographs, would have to stand as his experience of the Amazon. He flew to America, but America, he would soon write, would never be the same.

I went back to my hotel, a one-flight walkup just downhill from the hot merchandise district of the free port. By accident I opened my neighbor's door and found a man with a large moustache and a degenerate grin sitting on a bed that was strewn with several hundred cut stones—diamonds, emeralds, amethysts, and topazes of both the orange and smoky variety. With him was a young Canadian dressed as a hippie, who was holding the stones up to a penlight and examining them for flaws. My neighbor invited me in and explained that he was a diamond smuggler. He unwrapped five fifty-two faceted, clearwater diamonds from brown paper and placed them in a metal rule with graded holes for measuring the size of standard-cut stones. They weighed from one to one-tenth of a karat. He had bought the stones *brute,* or uncut, and had them cut by his own lapidary. Every so often he would take a bush plane into the wilds of Porto Velho or Roraima and buy a load of *brute* stones directly from the *garimpeiros.* "When you go in there," he said, "you take a gun, and you'd better know how to use it. Two to four *garimpeiros* work a claim together. They're a mean lot. Some have fake Bolivian or Paraguayan passports. Some don't have any passports. They go in there for two months, and if they're lucky they come out rich and if they're not they lose everything they have.

"I once sat for a week on a fist-sized *brute,"* the smuggler went on, "which had been responsible for the deaths of three people. And I know a farmer in Porto Velho who has a wooden suitcase filled with amethyst crystals, each of which is the size of a small drinking glass. The man is sixty-five, and it took half his life to collect the gems. He says he will begin to sell them when his last daughter is married." The smuggler then picked up his metal ruler and pointed to two of the holes. "From 1.98 karats—here—to 2 karats—here—there is a big jump in value," he said, "from three to 18,000 dollars."

My plan was to stay a month in Manaus and to learn what I could about INPA, the National Research Institute of Amazonia. On the outskirts of the city, INPA is a well-equipped, modern scientific facility whose buildings are nestled in luxuriant vegetation. The forest on the property is so well preserved that there are even thirty or so resident sloths. After Danny left I bought some clothes, got a haircut, and presented myself to Warwick Kerr, the director, a respected scientist who has made his mark in the study of social insects. It was from his laboratory in São Paulo, due to the carelessness of a visiting beekeeper, that the notorious "killer bees" absconded a few years before. They have been moving north at the rate of two hundred miles a year, hybridizing with native species along the way. They were now in Surinam, and much of their aggressiveness and the potency of their sting, which was exaggerated by the press in the first place, had been bred out.

Dr. Kerr welcomed me warmly and explained the goals of INPA and some of the ground-breaking scientific work being done there. He arranged for me to share a comfortable apartment on campus with a Czechoslovak specialist in water plants who also collected beetles. My roommate deserted me almost immediately to return two weeks later sun-beaten and exultant from an expedition to some distant, cast-off loop of the main river where the water was clear and the wildlife prolific. There he had discovered three new plants in the family of his specialty and two new beetles. The beetles, unwrapped lovingly from tissues and laid on his night-table, were brilliantly arrayed, impressively armed with harmless horns, and, in typical Amazonian fashion, many times the size of most beetles in the rest of the world. They had names appropriate to their grandeur like *Megasoma, Acteon, Dynastis,* and *Titanus.*

"Beetles eat almost nothing," my roommate explained. "Their life is very short: two days, eight days, fourteen days. There are few carnivores. Most, like the *scarabs,* are coprophagous. The enormous hissing cockroach of the Amazon, which grows to a length of two inches, is omnipresent and omnivorous, and is not a beetle, which is a *Coleoptera,* but an *Orthoptera,* related to the grasshoppers and the crickets. For a taxonomist INPA was probably one of the most exciting places to be in the world. Every day scientists were returning from the field with new species to describe. A medical entomologist expressed the collective sense of discovery when he burst in on our group at the cantina, exclaiming, "Seven new species of dobsonfly! What a world I have around me!"

While at INPA I underwent a thorough physical examination to ascertain the effects on my system of my month-long sojourn in the jungle. First my stool was checked for amoebas and worms. A piece of my feces was dissolved in a beaker of water. "One out of every two Amazonians has worms," the doctor who conducted the examination told me, holding the beaker to the light, "so it is very probable that you have them too." Filtering the solution with cheesecloth, the doctor poured it into two test tubes. "Ameobas," he said, "are mainly transmitted in cyst form by people handling food with dirty fingernails. The cysts flourish in the humid microenvironment of the fingernail." "Once in the digestive tract," he continued, "the cyst metamorphoses into its trophozoite form and begins to multiply in the large intestine, by binary division." The doctor put the tube in a centrifuge and gave it a two-minute whirl. "Then the trophozoites metamorphose back into cysts, which come out in the feces.

"Sometimes the amoebas cause small ulcerations, mycosis, and gradual disintegration of the intestinal wall. After many years they can cause abscess of the liver. The symptoms of amoebiasis are colic and blood and mucus in the feces." He placed a few drops of the solution under a microscope and took a look. "Nothing but normal bacteria swimming around," he pronounced. "I can tell you with ninety percent certainty that you are parasite-free. There are still a few worms which wouldn't show up for a month, but you definitely don't have amoeba or giardia, another unicellular parasite."

While I had been given a clean bill of health internally, the external surfaces of my body were under devastating attack. We were approaching the 149-day winter, from January to June, during which heavy rains fall daily on central Amazonia. The eighty-five percent relative humidity and the mean temperature of 82.4°F are psychologically depressing. Several quarts of water must be consumed daily to replace the loss from perspiration. Every pore becomes involved in the heat-regulating process. The back sweats. The thighs sweat. The body acquires the sweet, stale stench of an organism constantly exuding fluid. Pockets of fat melt away. On top of constant thirst, one feels a gnawing hunger for which the ingestion of food offers only temporary relief. Part of the explanation for the constant craving for food is that significant amounts of zinc, a micronutrient essential to the human diet, are lost while sweating, and zinc is absorbed most readily in meat and other sources of protein.

We were approaching the humid season when fungal infections are rampant. Both of my inner thighs became raw and inflamed with the disorder known as "crotch rot," and a red patch burned in the crook of my left elbow for several weeks; it took twice-daily applications of cortisone and antihistamine ointments to get rid of the lesion. My cellular immune mechanism had broken down; there were six purulent excrescences the size of apricots on my legs, and my body could not manufacture enough antibodies to keep out the toxic parasites that had invaded it. Every morning I had to grip the muscle of my left thigh and inject a penicillin derivative called benzotol into it. The infections raged and crested; I could not get up without going white and nearly fainting from the pain, and walking was agony. One morning the heads of two white maggots broke the surface of the largest of the pussy lumps. I pulled them out with the tweezers of my Swiss Army knife. They were an inch long and left two holes whose bottom I could not see. My right calf looked as if it had been punctured by two .22-caliber bullets. The maggots were larvae of the human botfly, *Dermatobia hominis,* which had been fattening themselves inside me for forty days.

At the medical research division of INPA I found out the progress being made to understand and bring under control the more virulent Amazonian diseases. A young Panamanian, Dr. Jorge Arias, was working on leishmaniasis, whose victims often suffer the hideous lesions associated with leprosy. I asked if leishmaniasis was serious in Amazonia, and Dr. Arias said, "Serious? During the mid-rainy season, the peak of transmission time, military groups going into the jungle suffer up to eighty percent leishmaniasis. Of the five people working here on the disease we've had six cases of leishmaniasis; I've had it twice. Is that serious?"

"Leishmaniasis," he explained, "is a parasite transmitted by sandflies. It invades the lymphatic system and can eventually cause extensive muco-cutaneous damage, attacking the nose and palate and eating them away in from two to twenty years."

Dr. Jorge showed me the picture of a patient with nothing left of the central part of his face, his eyes and mouth widened in a silent scream reminiscent of a painting by Francis Bacon. "Depending on the species of parasite, the first symptom appears in from one to nine months. It is an open sore on the arm or leg surrounded by a red crest like a little volcano. It will either close spontaneously or become nasty. When someone comes in with one of these sores a skin biopsy is run or a direct print is made of his tissue section. The leishmaniasis will usually show up. The disease is treated with thirty intravenous injections of pentavalent antimony over fifty to 140 days. The trouble with the antimony is its side effects — cardiac involvement and artificial swelling of the joints. So sometimes a five-month treatment of an antibiotic called Rifampicin is administered instead. There is a great deal still to be learned about the epidemiology of the disease. There are different vectors in different areas. In Manaus there are six species of sandflies, two of which are vectors. We need to know more about their life history, and whether the sandfly is the only vector, and about the course of the disease in man. And of course there's the left-field research like trying to develop a prophylactic vaccine. That's not going to happen but it sure would be nice."

Several doctors at INPA were doing new work on malaria. One group was trying to develop a "biological insecticide" in the laboratory by breeding a strain of *Anopheles* mosquito with nine "Y" chromosomes which, when released into the forest, would produce only male offspring and gradually reduce the female population; only females transmit malaria. Others were trying to develop a vaccine similar to one in use against Chagas disease, perhaps by injecting a non-infective strain of the malaria plasmodium that would help build up antibodies. I was told by one of the doctors that it was useless to take my weekly prophylactic pill of cloroquine since cloroquine was only good for *Vivax* malaria and the chances that the malaria I came down with would be *Vivax* did not justify the damage the drug would do to my liver. The best thing was to keep an emergency killing dose of cloroquine for *Vivax* of ten tablets, four to be taken on the first day of fever, and three each on the following two; and three tablets of *Fansidar,* a sulfa-based drug for *Falciperum* malaria, to be taken at once; and to pray that the malaria was not one of the resistant strains. A few months later, one of the entomologists at INPA came down with a resistant strain and died.

"Every study done here," Dr. Kerr told me one afternoon, "is geared to have a return for Amazonia. For example, we are involved in planning cattle pastures for Manaus, but instead of burning the cleared wood, we suggest that it be used — for making paper. We also recommend that strips of trees be left at certain intervals to reseed the pastures. That way you maintain the genetic variability of the forest.

"We are involved in the development of better rural housing and are integrating agronomy and chemistry to improve the diet of the average Amazonian. We avoid the distribution of high oxalate foods, which make kidney stones, like *taioba* [*taro,* in the *Araceae* family], and substitute cabbage, our own variety of green pepper developed here, *cubiu* [a vegetable in the tomato family], several species of green bean, Asian and African spinach, and a variety of manioc selected for its high Vitamin A content.

"Our ichthyology department is studying the biology of fish and the technology of fish culture." Dr. Kerr handed me a handsome wallet made of *pirarucú* hide. "We are especially concerned with protecting and increasing the drastically diminishing populations of such endangered species as the *pirarucú* and the manatee. The *pirarucú* population around Manaus is about one percent that of 1969. There are now 700 fishing boats, whereas in 1969 there were only sixty. The *pirarucú* is a typical k-adapted species,* laying only 200 eggs and caring for its brood; it is incapable of withstanding the fishing pressure currently exerted on it.

"Another of our goals, to set up a system of forest preserves, is coming along well. We have three outside of Manaus, one near Belém, one at Rio Aripuana, a tributary of the Rio Roosevelt, and three to come at Cuiabá in the state of Mato Grosso."

The challenge for INPA was the one that faces any academic institution: how to get the fruits of one's research into the "real world." In Amazonia, the gulf between theoretical knowledge and practical application is particularly wide. "Any program," as Charles Wagley has pointed out in his classic anthropological study, *Amazon Town,* "which would introduce modern technology and industry among a 'backward' people must realize the far-reaching cultural changes implied." To get people to eat well, to accept medicine and develop habits that will reduce their susceptibility to disease and to conserve dwindling resources like the manatee, the otter, and the

---

*K-adapted animals produce less young less often than r-adapted ones, whose strategy is to produce many more than will survive and are thus better able to withstand predation.

river turtle, one must first understand their needs and attitudes. One must adapt the information to the Amazonian mentality and present it as a feasible and practical alternative.

There is no public transportation to the leprosarium outside of Manaus, and I started down the fifteen-kilometer road on foot, the wind kicking up sand in my face, the *urubús* wheeling in the up-drafts like charred scraps of paper. I rode in a succession of trucks. The last one left me three kilometers from the colony. The patients had few visitors, the driver told me, and there was no telephone to the hospital.

I knew something about the disease, having visited the United States national leprosarium in Carville, Louisiana. Leprosy, or Hansen's disease, as it is now generally called, is grossly exaggerated in the public mind. Only in cases that have been allowed to go untreated for many years do the hideous disfigurations associated with the word leprosy result. In the United States only about 3,500 people have it, and these have a history of the disease in the family and have come into prolonged and intimate contact with it, so it is not considered a threat to the public health; but in Amazonia the number of patients is a good deal higher, and the theory that you must first be genetically susceptible in order to contract it is not taken seriously. There are four kinds of leprosy in the valley: lepromatous, tuberculoid, and two intermediate varieties. Tuberculoid leprosy can usually be eliminated after a few years of treatment with sulfone drugs, but the lepromatous kind can only be *arrested;* the symptoms may disappear, only to return without warning years later. *Mycobacterium leprae* is a microbe that thrives in the colder extremities of the body: fingers, toes, nose, ears, cheekbones. It deadens nerve endings and makes the area it infests anesthetic, or insensitive to heat or cold. Reddish hyperpigmented or pale hypopigmented patches in the skin are usually the first visible signs of its presence. But patches of this kind can be many other things.

I came to a bar that had been lowered across the road and beside it a gatekeeper's booth, which was empty. Down in a gulch to the right, in the shade of several expansive trees, was a stucco cottage with neither whitewash nor windowpanes. I followed the well-worn path from the booth to the door of the hut and gave a halloo. Presently an old man appeared. He served me a cool glass of water from a clay jug, and we sat together in the dooryard on some crates under one of the trees. The old man looked up to the hill where I could make out the outlines of several large buildings among the trees.

"When I got here, on November 3, 1959," he said, "the place was in ruins. People were dying of starvation. There was only one meal—lunch—and if you didn't have money you couldn't get it. Now there's a clinic, with physiotherapy and serology." One of the therapists, white-suited and wearing goggles, skirted the lowered bar on a motor scooter. "He's Japanese," the gatekeeper went on. "He knows all about machines and electricity, and he's a really good photographer."

"It's a cooperative," he said. "Some work in a brick factory, some in the lumbermill, others go out in boats on the river and fish for *pirarucú, tambaqui, tucunare, jaraci.* We grow fish in the lake, raise chickens, and run a *lavoura,* a plantation of manioc and *macaxeira* (sweet manioc). "Some work, some don't. You have people of all kinds, from all over Amazonas. It is a city. Some don't have the spirit of camaraderie and hide in self-pity. Some won't take their pills, others won't leave even though they've been cured. The more open they are, the easier it is to be cured."

The old man seemed philosophical about the blight that had set him apart from the rest of mankind. He'd been taking a sulfone tablet every day for fifteen years. I remarked that the disease had left few marks on his exterior. "Only this," he said, holding up his right hand, whose five fingers were all missing the first knuckle. "Because of the sulfone I lost my teeth, but there is no question that it helped me overcome leprosy. I suppose I could have left long ago, but I didn't know where to go so I stayed. And I think I was a little scared. Now my brother has written from Parantins. He's got a beautiful farm and wants me to join him. I'll be going in April."

I walked up the hill. In the heat of noon no one was about. On top of the hill was a pavilion with several semi-detached clinics and a cement courtyard in the middle. A few patients were sitting in the shade of the tin roofs. A nurse in the brown habit of the Franciscan order asked me who I was and learning I had made no appointment to visit the colony led me to the staff's quarters and fed me fruit juice and sandwiches. The *esprit de corps* at the hospital, she said, was very high. One man was an artist who painted still-lifes of flowers, holding the brush between his teeth. She attributed the high rate of leprosy among Amazonians to the heat and lack of hygiene. The staff stressed hygiene. "Where you have water, soap, and hygiene," she said, "leprosy diminishes." None of the sisters had come down with the disease, though some had been working at the hospital for years.

Wandering in the fish market in Manaus one afternoon I stumbled on a stall full of magical potions, bundles of herbs, hooves of animals, dried fish, and plaster statues of the spirits whom believers in *macumba* and *espiritisme* hold in awe. Antonio Matos, the proprietor, a small, vigorous man, explained the uses of some of the items to which I pointed; there were literally hundreds of folk remedies for every conceivable ailment. A decoction of a shrub called *pedra unica* was for diabetes, the bark of *xixuasha* for rheumatism, the twigs of *arbuto* for fever, the bark of *carapanauba* for ulcers, the ground seeds of *paxuri* for indigestion and diarrhea, the herb *quebra pedra* for gallstones, the leaves of *casca de sacaca* for inflammation of the intestines, the tapir hooves for hernia, the spiny seed capsules of *buxina* for sinusitis; "They're good," Senhor Matos said, "drunk with a little *cachaça.*" Then he showed me various aromatic baths and incenses used to protect against evil spirits, propitiatory candles, a crystal ball, a dried fish called *abota* used as a talisman, the statue of a North American Indian with drawn bow called Yara, and of the other spirits — Maria Lunga, Pai Joachim Angola, Pai Jacobi. "They are all white spirits," he said, "but can be used for bad purposes." A man and a woman came up and the woman asked for some *catuaba,* and Senhor Matos handed the couple a bundle of bark. "What's that for?" I asked. The proprietor and the little crowd that had gathered around me laughed. "That's for man."

8

The Economy of
Light

While still in the United States I had met Dr. Ghillean Prance, the curator of Amazonian botany at the New York Botanical Garden. A full-bearded Englishman, he recalled Richard Spruce, the intrepid Scottish plant explorer who a century before spent fourteen years in the Amazon. Dr. Prance was giving a course at INPA on the systematic botany of Amazonia, which he invited me to audit. Having a fairly good grasp of the flora of our Northeast, I thought that I would be able to come to grips with the Amazonian flora at least in a superficial way. But a month was not enough. No one knows how many species of plants there are in the Amazon. At least 25,000 have been identified; Dr. Murça Pires at Belém had guessed that at least as many remain to be discovered. On a typical acre of woods in the American Northeast there may be a dozen kinds of trees; recently, on an acre of *terra firme* forest outside of Manaus, a botanist had identified 290 species. The oaks and maples of my woods broadcast their identity, but Amazonian trees seem all the same, running up straight as telephone poles, branching and bearing broad, glossy leaves with minute flowers only at their crowns. Of the 160 families of angiosperms found in the Amazon valley, many have no representatives in the temperate zone, and can be distinguished only by dissecting their flowers under a microscope.

Angiosperms, the class of plants to which hardwood trees and wildflowers belong, are thought to have originated in the tropics during the Cretaceous Period, when the continents of North and South America, Africa, and Asia were fused in a single land mass called Gondwanaland. The earliest known angiosperm, whose pollen was discovered in Africa is 125 million years old. By that time Africa and South America had already begun to separate. Fifteen million years later fossils and pollen of the most primitive extant sub-class of angiosperms — the *Magnolidae* — were preserved on all three continents. Eighty to ninety million years ago the separation between Africa and South America was complete, and the direct exchange of plants between the continents was no longer possible. But the continents were still less than 600 kilometers apart, and there was an archipelago between them. Birds could still ingest the fruit of a plant on one continent and defecate its seeds on another, and many seeds, especially in the *Monimiaceae, Lauraceae,* and *Annonaceae* families were buoyant and had water-resistant cases that enabled them to ride the currents and germinate on distant shores. Paleobotanists are still trying to decide which species now found on both continents evolved before the split, and which drifted over later. The presence of the same species on two continents is *prima facie* evidence that the populations must have at one time shared the same gene pool; it is by definition impossible for a single species to come into being in two separate places.

Beginning about sixty-five million years ago, new species began to pullulate in the Amazon basin, while Africa underwent widespread dessication and lost much of its flora. The flora of Amazonia is much closer to that of tropical Asia and of Madagascar, which were spared the dessication, than to that of Africa; as I pored over descriptions of the flora of the Amazon I would occasionally come across an obscure genus with the following range: "Found only on the upper Rio Negro and in Madagascar."

Five to ten million years ago Central America emerged from the sea, and the South American creosote bush spread north up the land bridge, reaching North America several million years ago, while the North American firs, alders, sweetgums, beeches, walnuts, and elms headed south. They were in southern Mexico sixteen million years ago; walnut had reached South America by eight million years ago, alders by 700,000 years ago, and several species of oak by 150,000. Today one of North America's fifty species of willow grows in the Amazon; while one member of the typically Amazonian family, *Melastomaceae,* occurs naturally as far north as Rhode Island.

Of course, the animals were more mobile. Nineteen North American mammals recolonized South America, while twenty-four South American mammals, including the porcupine and the armadillo, headed north. By the late Pleistocene epoch, the opossum had recolonized North America, while many of the larger grazing mammals, like horses, glyptodonts, ground sloths, and camels, were extinct on both continents.

The Guyana and Brazilian shields, the crystalline massifs which form the northern and southern borders of the valley, are Archean—some of the oldest rock on earth, dating to 4600 million years ago. But the lower basin is Tertiary—only sixty-five million years old. It became a mediterranean sea in the Miocene Epoch, when the Andes were heaved up, then gradually filled in with sediments. During the Ice Age, with much of the earth's water frozen at the poles, sea level was much lower, and the Amazon River bit into its sediments and deepened its channel, becoming the deepest river on earth—250 feet deep in places. During the warm, dry spells between glaciers, the climate in the valley was more favorable to savannah, and the forest receded to a few isolated patches, high spots and other places that attracted rain, called refugia. In the refugia there was increased opportunity for speciation. Unlike the primitive angiosperms that went to the Indo-Malayan peninsula after the split-up of Gondwanaland, the ones in Amazonia were subjected to fluctuating stress, and being less genetically plastic than the modern taxa did not survive. Compared to Asia, the Amazon is poor in the first three sub-classes—*Magnoliidae, Hamamelidae,* and *Caryophillidae*—except on the shields and in the refugia, where there was less disturbance.

Dr. Prance's dozen students greeted with cheers his announcement that the class would be taking a four-day field trip at kilometer 400 on the new highway from Manaus to Caracaraí. The road had just been completed but was not officially open; to travel beyond kilometer 400 one needed permission from the military engineers. Beyond kilometer 400 the road entered the country of the Waimiri-Atroaris, who of all the tribes in the Amazon have most fiercely resisted assimilation. One did not want to have a breakdown between kilometers 400 and 550.

"Where you are going tomorrow there is resistant malaria," Dr. Prance told us, and he warned us to bring insect repellent and *mosquiteiros,* outer casings of mosquito netting to slip around our hammocks, to reduce our chances of being bitten by an infected *Anopheles.* The road to Caracaraí headed due north from Manaus. After a hundred miles or so even the occasional palm-thatch hut of a brave homesteader gave way to pure jungle. The road was dead straight. The land was hilly. Some of the hills had been clearcut and logjams of charred poles were scattered over hillsides whose rape was complete and senseless, since whatever agricultural or grazing potential they had would be washed away after the first season of rain.

At kilometer 400 we came to a western-style stockade inhabited by the Brazilian Sixth Battalion of Construction Engineers, who had built the road. The captain, a man in his thirties with a meticulous moustache and superb bearing—in every way the impeccable commanding officer—greeted us with an effusion of warmth and friendliness that was extraordinary even for Brazil. I complimented him on the stockade, which he said was *"tirado do bangy-bangy,"* inspired by our cowboy movies. After a sumptuous meal in the officer's mess, the captain invited me for a game of ping-pong. He was a fine player, but, having been stuck myself once in a remote military installation, I was able to hold my own. The captain was very proud of the road, which had taken six years to build and would be the last link of an international highway system joining the Brazilian Amazon and Venezuela. Conditions in Bôa Vista, the capital of Roraima Territory, hitherto accessible only by river and air, would be improved, he predicted, and the road would be rapidly colonized. "We are all working," he said, "for the same thing. To make Amazonia a place to live in. To make it work."

What about the Waimiri-Atroaris, through whose country the road had run? Just outside the door was a fifteen-foot dugout canoe, left by the Indians in 1974 after the massacre of *sertanista* Gilberto Pinto. "The Waimiri," he said, "are six miles up the road. In their language *marebom* is a friend, and *murupau* an enemy. You go up to them saying *marebom, marebom* many times and embrace them and give them something. They are *curiosissimos,* touching you all over, pulling the hairs on your chest, but they have no interest in getting to know our civilization. They wear vine belts and short hair. They have arrows with metal points but no guns. No one knows their language."

For 120 kilometers on both sides of the road an area had been left for the Waimiri as a *reserva indigena,* although they had not yet been notified that they were living in boundaries. Nine of their villages had been sighted from the air. They were *maloccas,* communal round houses, surrounded by banana and manioc gardens. No white man had ever entered them. One of the villages had lain three miles from the highway, and in 1974, as the construction was growing near, some Waimiri ambushed three of the roadworkers. Our botany class would pose for a photograph, the following day, at the cross that marked the place where their bodies, riddled with arrows, were found. After this incident, the captain told me, the Waimiri abandoned that village, and they had never troubled anyone on the road since; perhaps, he theorized, "because they have seen a greater force than their own. But sometimes they come out and stare and touch the workers." The nearest village was now twenty miles from the road.

In Brasília I had heard a disturbing rumor that the Waimiri problem had been taken care of by dropping napalm from planes on their villages; but if such a thing had happened it was hard to believe that the Sixth Corps of Engineers, and especially the captain, whose admiration for the Waimiri was obvious, could have been involved. "They come to the FUNAI posts to trade arrows and artifacts for shirts, shorts, and fishing line. You will see them one day and then the next you won't see them for two months." The captain took us to his office and showed us some of the artifacts and the slides he had taken of them during their last trading session, three months before. The bow was eight feet long. Dr. Prance identified the wood as *macacauba,* in the legume family. It was the first bow he had seen of that wood. The arrows, tipped with steel acquired in trade, were unusually short—three and a half feet in length. The cord for the bowstring and the hammock were made of fibers in the pineapple family. The Waimiri had also woven a beautifully designed basket with rippling designs made from *Marantaceae* stems, dyed black. The captain's slides showed Indians with superb musculature in their torsos and great dignity in their faces, climbing curiously over a yellow caterpillar tractor. Some of them had put on western clothing to trade in, but as they headed back to the forest you could see them taking it off.

That night we lay shrouded in *mosquiteiros* while the cascading roars of two rival bands of howler monkeys filled our minds with fear and wonder, and in the morning we walked down the road in the opposite direction from the Waimiri-Atroaris for several hundred yards and then turned into the forest. The rest of the day we would spend in a meticulous examination of the plant life, collecting everything that was in flower.

The flowers in the understory were already familiar to me from Menkranoti: the staggered blades of *Heliconia,* the wild banana, which the Indians had ground into a powder to make their cultivated bananas grow better; the pine-cone-like spike of a *Costus,* in the *Zingiberaceae* family. They were conspicuous because they were few and red; the lowland rain forest is remarkably lacking in color, because of the lack of showy flowers. The main flowering was going on a hundred feet above us. Some of the flowers, like the red pompons of a tree in the *Caryocaraceae,* had fallen to the foot of the trees; others Dr. Prance discovered by combing the canopy with fieldglasses. When a tree in flower was found, the INPA *mateiro* would cut it down; because of a hurt foot he was unable to climb the tree for its specimens, as he usually did. A dozen cuttings of the foliage, flowers, and fruit (if any) were placed between newspapers, stacked in a press, and dried overnight by kerosene burners, to be distributed to specialists around the world. The forest reacted to the sacrifice to science of one of its members with silence. The occasional low hum of a *jacamin,* a trumpeter, like a sword being swung through the air, or piercing whistles of a screaming pia, or warning hiss of a giant beetle on the path only accentuated the deceptively intense silence. The pia's screams, heard from the edge of the Atlantic to the base of the Andes, are the theme-song of the rain forest. I had heard the bird often only thirty feet above me for several months, but that day was the first chance I had to see it. I happened to look up and there was a small khaki-gray bird whose posture on its branch was that of an opera singer. It started out softly whistling the notes do—mi, do—mi, as if preparing for a more important announcement; then throwing its head back, opening its wings, and swelling its body, it let out, an octave higher, an earsplitting series of do—ti—do's. Amazonians call the bird *daí-à-pior,* "worse to come."

That a bird with such an incredible voice should be so visually unexciting is a function of its niche in the high understory. Alfred Russell Wallace was one of the first to observe, a hundred years ago, the difference of coloration among the birds of Amazonia. "The wrens, ovenbirds, antbirds, wood rail and tinamou," he wrote, "are brown flecked with lighter spots and blend into the pattern of light and shadow in the forest. These birds also have the habit of remaining motionless when an enemy comes near—an adaptive behavioral trait. The roof of the forest, where less danger exists from predators, is inhabited by many gorgeously colored birds such as toucans, tanagers, manikins, flycatchers, woodpeckers, trogons, and motmots, which have neither dull protective colors nor quiet habits." Between pia screams the overpowering silence of billions of leaves soliciting the sunlight fell again.

The physiognomy, or vertical structure, of the rain forest, is best understood in terms of the universal quest for light. Different plants have different light requirements, and therefore some are emergent species, others are content to produce their crowns below the canopy, while vines writhe to the treetops, then spread laterally in every direction to get the maximum exposure to the light. The leaf surface of many species is staggering, and so is the aerial vegetation which uses the trees only for scaffolding. No tree of any size stands alone, but must be encrusted with epiphytes, plastered with lichens, and cabled with vines. The older trees are usually hollow, their dark shafts inhabited by birds, bats, and other animals who pay rent for their quarters by enriching the soil beneath their tree with droppings rich in nitrogen and other minerals. It is not as if the trees decided to stop growing after reaching a certain height; the physiognomy of the forest is not neatly stratified, but rather a burst of growth will take place wherever space is available. The guiding principle is *horror vacui.*

The physiognomy of the forest is remarkably uniform throughout the Amazon valley, without significant variation from *terra firme* to *várzea* or *igapó.* Nor is it different-looking from the two other blocks of rain forest — the Indo-Malaysian and the African. Humboldt named the Amazonian jungle *hylaea* after the Greek word for forest. In 1898 A. F. W. Schimper introduced the term *tropische regenweld,* or tropical rain forest, defining it as "evergreen, hygrophilous in character, at least thiry meters high, rich in thick-stemmed lianas, and in woody as well as herbaceous epiphytes." The largest rain forest, about one billion acres, comprising one sixth of the total broadleaf forest of the world, is in the Amazon.

In every group of organism the number of species increases sharply toward the equator, achieving in the Amazon valley the most astonishing diversity. The profusion of life has been explained in several ways. One theory holds that the tropics, older and more stable, have not experienced drastic climatic changes like those in the temperate and arctic zones, and therefore their communities have had more time to develop. The longer an environment remains undisturbed, the greater the opportunity for evolution. Alfred Russell Wallace sensed this in 1878 as he was working out his theory on the origin of species. "The equatorial zone, in short," he wrote, "exhibits to us the result of comparatively continuous and unchecked organic forms . . . evolution has had a fair chance . . . an ancient world . . . in which the laws which have governed the progressive development of life . . . have resulted in those wonderful eccentricities of structure, of function, and of instinct — rich variety of colour, and that nicely balanced harmony of relations which delight and astonish us in the animal productions of all countries." The same hypothesis would hold for the plant kingdom. "The immense floristic riches of the Tropical Rain Forest," wrote P. W. Richards in 1966, "is no doubt largely due to its great antiquity; it has been the focus of plant evolution for an extremely long time."

But time is not the only factor. Tropical populations are generally more sedentary, facilitating the geographical isolation that is a prerequisite of speciation. A wide river or a small mountain range will act as a barrier for the dispersal of a species; so will a sudden gradient in temperature or rainfall. The high jungles of Colombia, Ecuador, and Peru boast more species than the flat basin because their topography is more diverse. For the same reason, in part, there are more species on the Brazilian and Guyana shields than in the lowlands. But the highlands are richer, too, because they did not undergo the traumatic cycles of flooding and dessication that the basin has experienced in the last two million years. Only one species in the genera *Magnolia* and *Talauma,* for example, grows in the lowlands, while there are many in the uplands, because these primitive trees are less capable of dealing with stress.

Another factor is the constant warm climate, which allows for the continual growth and proliferation of plant life and the production of more generations of animals per year. In general life in the tropics proceeds at a faster pace. There is greater productivity and more competition between organisms, a greater turnover of populations, and thus more selection for traits that will enable individual species to survive. Many of the plants have developed elaborate chemical and mechanical defenses against herbivory. The palms bear thorns, the figs and the dogbanes exude a toxic milk, the vines, hacked with a machete, flow purple, orange, or white with the strychnine, rotenone, and other poisons running in their veins. "Truly," as Richard Evans Schultes, Harvard's eminent ethnobotanist, writes, "plants live by their chemical wits." Still other plants, like the genus *Tachigalia* of the *Leguminosae* family, have established a symbiosis with fire ants, whom they allow to nest in their hollow petioles. In return the ants clean up all the other plants around them and within seconds, as I found out that afternoon, will attack anything that comes in contact with their host. The forearm that had brushed against one of the myrmicophilous shrubs burned through the night; I would give the plant a wide berth from now on.

In the case of the *Heliconius* butterflies and the passionflower vines, two of the most common groups of organism in Amazonia, dynamic co-adaptive evolution is still actively taking place. When *Heliconius ethilla* enters the large magenta flowers of *Passiflora kermesina,* the visit is of mutual benefit. As the butterfly drinks of the nectar its wings flutter, fertilizing the pistils of the flower with pollen carried from the stamens of other *kermesina* plants. But the larvae of *ethilla* also happen to feed on *kermesina* and can do extensive damage to the vines, so the plant had to find ways to defend itself. First it acquired chemical defenses — alkaloids and saponins — to discourage the herbivorous caterpillars. But the strategy failed because the insects learned to absorb the toxins, and so the vines developed a devious assortment of mechanical defenses. To encourage the larvae to eat their own eggs, the plant developed an egg mimic — a supernumerary yellow flower bud on its meri- stem tendril. It also developed modified hooked leaf hairs called trichomes, which are capable of puncturing the larvae's abdom- inal cuticle, causing death. As another ploy, it acquired decidu- ous stipules resembling small tendrils so the butterfly would lay its eggs on them, and the eggs, before hatching, would fall from the plant. Near the places where the heliconids are likely to oviposit, the passionflowers also have extrafloral nectaries that secrete sugar attractive to ants and other egg predators. The coiling tendrils also fasten to other plants, providing access. Other tendrils may crush the eggs or larvae as they are hatching.

The butterflies reacted with a number of counterstrategies. Their well-developed vision makes it difficult for even the most inconspicuous vine to escape detection, and they distinguish real from false eggs by probing with their antennae and proboscis and tapping with their forelegs. They also use their organs to determine plants unsuitable for oviposition because the plant isn't big enough to feed a brood of larvae, is diseased, or infested with egg predators like ants, spiders, and other *Heliconius* larvae. When they do lay, they choose the tendril tips, out of reach of ants. To avoid being slit open by the trichomes, the larvae walk gingerly on specially evolved silken pads, and finally the heliconids find the passion- flowers' toxins, evolved in self-defense, useful against *their own* predators. Birds find the butterflies unpalatable and avoid them for this reason.

I watched a colorful brown and orange *Heliconius* butterfly flapping lazily by. It can afford to be lazy and colorful, I thought, because of the alkaloids it has absorbed. Or was it one of the ithomid butterflies which can be told from heliconids only by the disposition of their veins and genitalia? Ithomids eat *Solanaceae,* another family with many poisonous members, and are also avoid- ed by birds. But maybe it was a pierid butterfly, which eats legumes and, because it is palatable, has adopted the coloration of the heliconids and ithomids to protect itself. Whatever the butterfly was, it was part of a dynamic contest between one group of insects, the plants they eat, the spiders which eat them, and the other butterflies which mimic them. And all of these organisms were still evolving strategies and counterstrategies for survival. It had begun when the heliconids had chosen passionflowers as their food plant. The niche had been available.

Of all the kinds of evolutionary adaptation the most fascinating is mimicry, and there are probably more mimetic complexes in Amazonia than anywhere. All around you are vines (the monkey-ladder vine, Bauhinia sp.) that look like snakes, plus a few snakes (the slender blue-grey *cobra de sipo,* non-venomous, eater of lizards, birds, and frogs) taking advantage of the situation by imitating the vines; hawk moths posing as hummingbirds, orchids mimicking the scent and sex organs of female bees, butterflies looking like leaves, other butterflies, or other parts of themselves. It is like a big game, with an infinite number of players employing an infinite number of strategies to be able to keep playing it. There are many kinds of mimicry. Batesian mimicry, first identified by Henry Walter Bates, occurs when an unprotected species like a pierid butterfly mimics a protected one like an ithomid. Mullerian mimics are two protected species like the heliconids and the ithomids, converging on the same color pattern—warning coloration, in other words. In Mertensian mimicry, a harmless or palatable species and a highly toxic one both take after a moderately toxic model. Coral snakes have Mertensian mimics. Some are more venomous than others, and the important thing is that the bite of the most abundant model is not always effective: the prey often survive. Cryptic mimicry is the resemblance to some common, inanimate and inedible object, like a leaf or a bird dropping. Twig caterpillars and bitterns, who straighten their necks so as to look like dead stumps, fall into this category. As well as several species of butterfly, there is a fish, *Monocirrhus polycanthus,* that is a leaf mimic, achieving the effect with mottled coloration and a flat, leaflike form. In the water it lies near the bottom, blending with the water-logged foliage, and even when scooped up in a net it is almost impossible to discern from the rest of the debris. In this ruse, immobility is as important as shape and coloration. A sub-type of cryptic mimicry is aggressive mimicry—the resemblance of a predator to something harmless, enabling it to get within striking range of prey. Certain female lampyrid (firefly) beetles are aggressive mimics, giving the light signals of other species; thinking they have been invited to copulate, the males are actually eaten. Certain butterflies, with a mock-head on their wings, are eye mimics. The orchid-bee complex is a case of reproductive mimicry. Bee-mimics buzz like bees, while scent-mimicking flowers smell of putrefaction. Cormorants and egrets are social mimics — their black and white coloration makes them stand out against their background and helps maintain the cohesion of the flock. In the high jungle of Ecuador, some species of birds flock with other species that look like them. But the overriding mimetic theme, and the most effective strategy for survival in the rain forest, is to keep a low profile, to remain indistinguishable from the green welter of life. Wallace knew that the drab uniformity of the jungle, with which he had chosen to surround himself for many years, had a reason. "The fact that first strikes us in our close examination of animals as a whole," he wrote in *Darwinism: An Exposition of the Theory of Natural Selection,* "is the close relation that exists between their colours and the general environment. Thus, white prevails among arctic animals, yellow or brown in desert species, while green is only a common color in tropical evergreen forests."

In one day we collected over forty plant families. The subtlety of the flowers, the multitude of species, and strategies for pollination were humbling, and I could see how a dedicated person like Dr. Prance could spend a lifetime in their study. An extraordinarily energetic man, Dr. Prance had already deposited some 25,000 specimens in the herbarium at INPA. I followed, taking notes. "That tree," he pointed, "with the fruit like Christmas tree balls is *Parkia pendula.* The Brazilians call it *visqueiro.* The top row of flowers are nectar-producing and sterile. Bats come to drink the nectar and, brushing against the pollen of the lower flowers, fertilize them. The fruits hang on long strings called peduncles to facilitate echolocation. Cecropias are bat-dispersed.

"Each flower on this *Crysobalanaceae* tree has three to nine hundred stamens," he said a little farther on. He slapped the braided, fluted bole of a tree called *Minguartia guyanensis,* the chosen wood for house studs in Amazonia because it is both decorative and as unbendable as structural steel. He found an unfamiliar shrub in *Erythroxylaceae,* the family to which the cocaine-yielding coca shrub belongs. It would go to Harvard for analysis by the specialist in *Erythroxylaceae* there. "You'd have to chew the leaves in an alkaline environment to find out if they were psychoactive." He held up the creeping inflorescent branch of an *Anonaceae* tree and exclaimed, "Isn't this fantastic? Why has it evolved this way? What animal pollinates it?"

The find of the day came crashing to the ground late in the afternoon. It was in the *Lecythidaceae* — the family to which the Brazil-nut tree belongs and in which Dr. Prance specializes. "The hidden stamens and raspberry flowers would put it in the genus *Corythophora,*" he mused. "But the leaves, the trunk, and the inflorescence are different from the three other species in the genus. The leaves are more coriaceous [leathery] than other *Corythophora* with red flowers. They resemble those on *Corythophora* with completely different flowers. And the trunk is deeply fissured." After an emotionally charged silence he declared, "I think this is a new species."

As the species multiplied in the rain forest they became highly specialized; sixty-eight species of plants and animals, for instance, restrict themselves to the pools of water trapped in bromeliads. There were eventually more species than niches, and the phenomenon known as niche-partitioning took place. Scientists are still puzzled by the great number of species in the Amazon that have no apparent ecological difference from one another. "The geological antiquity of the tropical zone, untouched by the ice ages that depauperated the temperate floras," Verne Grant writes in his *Origins of Adaptations,* "can only in part account for the relative floristic richness of the rain forest. The historical factor seems best fitted to explain why large numbers of ecologically diverse species are preserved extant. It does not tell us why mixtures of ecologically similar species of trees have been preserved; indeed the long time available for interspecific competition might have been expected to have reduced the number of competitor species to a few. The question remains, then, why many species of trees with no apparent ecological differentiation grow in mixed stands in the tropical forests."

Part of the answer, of course, is that the species are not as uniform as they seem. There are subtle differences in flowering time, genetic structure, anatomy, pollen fertility, resin components, and other secondary substances. The individuals of one species may all burst into flower the same day, in response to some light or temperature stimulus, while those of a closely related species will not bloom until two days later. In fact only a minute percentage of the total number of trees we saw that day were in flower, and many were visited by a particular insect species and devoured by its own species of predators. As the plant species multiplied, so did the insects associated with them; most of the pollinators and predators in Amazonia, in fact, are host-specific. In response to insect pressure the tree populations scattered; we never found two adult individuals of the same species within a hundred yards of one another. They avoid each other's company to reduce the possibility of having their entire population wiped out. The differences in the species may not be discernible to humans, but such discretion poses no problem for the insects.

Another explanation for the profusion of closely similar species is that they developed in isolation from each other, in separate island refugia when the rain forest receded and the valley was taken over by savannah. Later, as the rain forest re-coalesced, the species met for the first time. There were some extinctions due to competition, but the more common outcome in the new communities that were forming was that the species learned to coexist in the same niche. Dr. Prance had found on his collecting trips through Amazonia as many as ten species of *Lecythidaceae* without significant ecological variation in the same place; the sites, he felt, were probably some of these "secondary contact zones."

In terms of understanding the evolution and distribution of the flora and fauna of Amazonia and of protecting the unparalleled genetic potential of the region, the location and preservation of the refugia is the most important work that is being done today. The refugia are centers of endemism containing the greatest concentrations of species to be found in the basin, and the evidence for their existence, coming from many unrelated fields and coinciding surprisingly, is impressive. The refugia concept was proposed in 1969 by an ornithologist named J. Haffer. He identified twenty-three places in which the number of birds species seemed remarkably high. In 1970, a herpetologist named Paolo Vanzolini reported four places that had an extraordinary variety of lizards. In 1973, Dr. Prance proposed sixteen refugia covering a much larger area than those of the zoologists, and in 1976, a lepidopterist named Keith Brown conjectured from the striking diversification in colors and patterns of *Heliconius* butterflies throughout the valley that there were probably twenty-three refugia. Later that year Betty J. Meggers, an anthropologist with the Smithsonian Institution, announced that certain puzzling aspects in the linguistic and cultural distribution of the Amazon Indians seemed to corroborate the refugia theory. She pointed to the disjunct distribution of pole snares and simple nooses for trapping game and conjectured that between five and ten thousand years ago the Indians' formerly continuous range must have been disrupted because of the many linguistic subfamilies that developed at that time. She did not attempt, however, to define any refugia.

All told there are twenty-three areas in the Amazon which more than one scientist has proposed as refugia. The immediate task is to determine the minimum size at which the refugia ecosystems can survive, and to get the land set aside. In Brasília, Gary Wetterburg, an American specialist in forest management, is trying to persuade the Brazilian government to incorporate twenty-four reserves of 5,000 square kilometers each, based on the refugia proposed by the four scientists, into the existing national park system. "In world terms, compared with other countries," he told me, "this is a big area. But in Amazon terms it is small." At the moment there is only one national park in the Brazilian Amazon—Amazon Park, a hundred million hectares on the west bank of the Tapajós River. But it is a paper park, without guards or enforcement. The World Wildlife Fund is helping develop a management plan. "I don't think the park system by itself is going to assure the ecological survival of the Amazon. If the legislation is not going to be enforced this whole exercise is a waste of time." As of this writing, 93% of all land in Brazil is still privately owned or otherwise not safe.

Much remains to be learned about the structural dynamics of the refugia. Different organisms have different range requirements, and many of their interrelationships are still not fully understood, so the most intelligent approach is to aim for the preservation of the entire habitat. "We would be foolish," as Tom Lovejoy of the World Wildlife Fund told me in Washington, "to freeze our conservation plans to the current state of our knowledge. And if all we do is conserve the refugia, then our effect won't be much different from that of the Pleistocene glaciations that created them in the first place."

9

Fish Stories

A great riverine web with a multitude of colored strands, the Amazon spreads over an area nearly as large as the continental United States. The Amazon system is the richest freshwater medium on earth. The rivers are invariably *peixosos,* full of fish, and, as in the rain forest, what is in them is still at best only half known. The first serious collection of the fish was made by Louis Agassiz, the Swiss-American geologist, in 1865, when not over a hundred species were known. He estimated that he had collected 1,800 to 2,000 species. His colleagues, however, snickered, since this was more than the number known at that time to exist in the entire Atlantic Ocean. More than a century later, his collection of 80,000 specimens has yet to be fully studied, but it looks as if Agassiz may have been right.

Amazonian fish ecology is still in a primitive state. Little is known about the *piraçemas,* the big fish migrations that many species undertake to spawn, or to seek better feeding grounds after a seasonal fluctuation in the water level.

Amazonian fish taxonomy is in a state of confusion. There is no agreement over the total number of species yet discovered, or even over the morphological characteristics that should determine species. "You want names?" a numerical taxonomist said at INPA. "Well, I'll throw a few at you, as long as you realize that in a few years, when things get settled, they may all be different." The cautious say there are only 1,300 species in the valley, but others go up to 4,000. "From Belém to Leticia and in the major tributaries at least two thousand species have been described, with ten percent not yet described," Dr. Jacques Gery, a prominent phylogenetic, or evolutionary taxonomist, told me. "But when those ten percent have been described, there will still be ten percent. I have 100 species in France which I have not had time to describe. In every collection you have two to four percent new species."

The marine past—remember that between sixty and fifty million years ago much of the basin was an inland sea—and the vastness of the present system are reflected by many of the species. Great pelagic sawfish, twenty feet or more in length, enter the Amazon River and have been reported as far upstream as Obidos; they are probably the largest fish in the system. Freshwater bullsharks have been found as far upstream as Iquitos, Peru. I saw at INPA the skull of one with five nasty rows of replacement teeth waiting behind the active row. The shark had measured over three meters. Three species of stingray, shark relatives, lurk in shallows, hidden in the sand. A flick from their serrated stinging spine can inflict a serious wound and excruciating pain for twenty-four hours. One species of sole and three of sardines have also adapted to the sweet water of the Amazon system.

Another constant reminder of the sea is the freshwater porpoise (often called a dolphin). The pink *bôto* and the grey *tucuxi* are protected by the numerous superstitions that surround them, and by the toughness and oily blandness of their flesh. *Caboclos* believe the animals are almost human and that they lure women into the water to have intercourse with them. Their dried skin 'is used as a fumigant for snakebite or ray sting. Children wear porpoise teeth around their necks to cure diarrhea; a *bôto*'s ear, worn around the wrist, will guarantee a large and lasting erection, and the grated left eye is an aphrodisiac powder. Travelers on the Amazon system up to the cataracts are never far from the snort and the arching back of the friendly mammals. Besides by color, the two species can be told apart by their manner of surfacing. The *bôto* rises head first, then exposes its whole dorsal ridge. The *tucuxi,* as Bates explains, "rises horizontally, showing first its back fin; draws an inspiration, and then dives gently down, head foremost."

The king of the river and the largest freshwater fish in the world is the *pirarucú, Arapaima gigas.* Pea-green with large, gritty red-edged scales that make excellent fingernail files, the *pirarucú* grows to ten feet and 250 pounds. For a fish it is remarkably mammalian, caring for its young until they reach four months. Up to 160 fingerlings have been seen following around the mother, who secretes from pores in her head a milky fluid to which they home. The *pirarucú* has gills, but it also has one lung, and comes up for air every three minutes. The natives hunt it with a harpoon, calculating where it will come up next. *Pirarucús* belong to a primitive family that has few living members. Its closest relative, the *aruana,* hatches its young in its mouth, in which the fry thereafter take refuge.

The silurids, or catfish,* of the Amazon belong to nine families and number over 500 species—twenty-five times more than the species of the Mississippi. The largest is the *piraiba,* the giant catfish, which gets over six feet and 300 pounds and has been known to drag swimming children to the bottom and swallow them whole. Armored cats like the *pirarara* have bony plates in their heads and can pin your hand if you grab them behind the fin. The *piracatinga* has a foul smell, while the primitive and rather grotesque-looking *cuiu-cuiu* has side spines and can walk on its fins from one lagoon to another. When the rivers go down, the holes of *cuiu-cuius,* riddling the banks, are exposed. Most of the cats are fine eating, particularly the leopard-spotted *surubim* and the *jandia,* which tastes like steak.

The *candirus,* about thirty species, are small, parasitical catfish who suck the blood of *piraibas* and other large fish. The larger *candirus,* reaching eight inches, chew a hole directly into the flank of their host and are especially feared by the *caboclos,* since a particularly motivated school can skeletonize a human being in even less time than *piranha.* The smaller *candirus,* about the size of toothpicks, not only parasitize the gills of giant catfish but penetrate mammalian orifices like vaginas, anuses, nostrils, and urethras. Once inside they throw out an excruciatingly painful set of retrorse spines on their operculum, or gill cover, and can only be removed surgically; as Dr. Gery put it, "the *candiru* will give quite a sensation." *Candirus* are attracted to the smell of urine, and legend has it that they will even ascend the stream of a man who is urinating in the river. I was unable to find anyone who would either confirm or deny this. To the Yurimagua Indians, who live on the Solimoes, as the Amazon is called between Manaus and Iquitos, the *candiru* is one of the seven deadly plagues of the river, the others being the electric eel, the stingray, the alligator, the anaconda, the *piranha,* and the *piraiba.* To be penetrated by a *candiru* was the most ghastly fate I could imagine, and I took care never to bathe nude wherever there was the slightest possibility of the fish being around.

Besides the *pirarucú* and some of the catfish, the best-eating fish are the *tucunaré* (a cyclid), of which there are five species or races, depending on which taxonomist you talk to, and the *tam-*

---

*According to Tyson R. Roberts, forty-three percent of the fishes in the Amazon are characoids, thirty-nine percent silurids, and three percent gymnotids.

báqui. Tucunarés have three spots on their side, and the fruit-eating *tambaquis* get to be seventy pounds. A number of fish are being considered at INPA for the possibility of aquaculture. The most promising is the *matrincha,* a fast-water omnivore. It has a two to one conversion factor; in other words, two kilos of food will produce one of fish. At Manaus there is a ten-meter fluctuation in the level of the river. During low water the fish are concentrated, and the fishermen often load their boats with more fish than they can sell at the market. What can't be sold can't be stored, and sometimes thirty percent of their catch is wasted. During the high water, which peaks in March, the fish are scarce and expensive, and many of the region's poor come close to starvation. It is the period of stress for humans and other fish predators. If inexpensive and high-yielding methods of aquaculture can be developed, and there is no reason why they can't, one of the last barriers to the colonization of Amazonia — the protein shortage, especially during the wet season — will have been removed.

The *saporo,* or knifefish, is active at night and sends out an electric field with radar in its tail much as the bat echolocates its prey. *Saporos* can move backward, and their tails, bitten off when they backed into an already occupied hole, are often missing. But their emissions are much less jolting than those of the electric eels, of which there are some forty species, which can discharge up to 800 volts. The *traira* is the carnivorous flying fish of the Amazon. It flies so fast you don't see it, only its splash as it is returning to the water. It takes to the air to elude predators, but also flies when there are no predators around; perhaps (a shocking hypothesis) for the sheer fun of it. The *tralhoto* (Anableps), a top-minnow, has four large eyes, one set for aerial vision, the other for examining the water below. Frightened, the fish scatter; they can't dive because they are too buoyant. Other fish are adapted to living at the bottom. Some live in cataracts or torrents, stuck to the undersides of rocks. Small, blind, poorly pigmented, with fusiform bodies, flattened breasts, large pectoral fins, sucking mouths beneath and eyes turned up, they eat mud. The *curimata,* or lungfish, an ancient species, aestivates, burying itself in mud during the dry season. Its metabolism stops almost completely, and the fish lives off reserves of fat built up when the water was high.

The most famous fish in Amazonia, of course, is the *piranha.* Wickedly equipped with razor-sharp teeth, the *piranha* was brought to the world's attention by Theodore Roosevelt, who had a subgenus, *Taddyella,* named after him. "The piranha," he wrote, "is a short, deep-bodied fish with a blunt face and a heavily undershot or projecting jaw which gapes widely. The razor-sharp teeth are wedge-shaped like a shark's, and the jaw muscles possess great power." There are about twenty species. Not all are true *piranhas,* but *pirambebas,* which aren't as bad. The largest and meanest species, the *piranha preta,* can take a chunk out of your leg the size of a silver dollar. The fish are most dangerous when trapped in slow water in the dry season. The rest of the year you can swim in most of the Amazon without much fear of being molested; their reputation, like that of sharks, is exaggerated. The fish, however, are nervous and unpredictable, have no fear of man, and are attracted, rather than frightened, by any commotion in the water. A *piranha* could, out of sheer perversity, take a piece out of your thigh, and when that happened, every other fish in the neighborhood would come running. Menstruating women are advised to stay out of the water; but the fish don't only home to the smell of blood. I heard of a woman who was attacked when she stepped into the water with red-painted toenails. *Piranhas* are found in almost all neotropical waters, not only in the Amazon system. In northeastern Brazil children swimming in the São Francisco River drown sometimes in its whirlpools. Several days later their bodies, mutilated beyond recognition, float ashore.

The largest creature in Amazonia, on land or sea, is the *peixe-boi,* or manatee. An aquatic relative of the elephant, it grows to be several tons and propels itself along with graceful flicks of its tail fin. There are only a few other Syrenians—the family of herbivorous subungulates to which the *peixe-boi* belongs: the dugong of New Guinea, the Florida manatee, an African species about which little is known, and the Stellar's sea cow, a cold-water species of the Pacific Northwest that has been extinct for 200 years. The Amazonian manatee is distinguished by a white or pink chest patch. Fascinated by this bizarre mammal, Wallace described it with loving detail: "One day the fisherman brought in a fine *peixe-boi,* or cowfish . . . the body is perfectly smooth and without any projections or inequalities, gradually changing into a horizontal semicircular flat tail, with no appearance whatever of hind limbs. There is no distinct neck; the head is not very large, and is terminated by a large mouth and fleshy lips, somewhat resembling those of a cow. There are stiff bristles on the lips, and a few distantly scattered hairs over the body. Behind the head are two powerful oval fins, and just beneath them are the breasts, from which, on pressure being applied, flows a stream of beautiful white milk. The ears are minute holes, and the eyes are very small. The dung resembles that of a horse. The color is a dusky lead, with some large pinkish-white marbled blotches on the belly. The skin is about an inch thick on the back, and a quarter of an inch on the belly...."

Its blimplike shape and its lungs, which act like ballast tanks along the length of its dorsal section, make it perfectly adapted to floating horizontally and placidly munching grasses, hyacinths, and other aquatic plants like *maracarana* and *cabomba* in the lakes, shallows, and quiet backwaters of the Amazon system. *Peixe-bois* are traditionally hunted by *mariscadores,* the subsistence Amazonian fishermen who live along the tributaries of the tributaries. The *mariscador* harpoons the animals at night. The point of the harpoon detaches from the shaft and is connected by a cord to a wooden buoy which the *mariscador* clutches to his belly as the terrified creature pulls him and his canoe along in the attempt to struggle free. The *peixe-boi* must come up for air within ten minutes, and usually after the third dive it floats exhausted to the surface, and the *mariscador* administers the coup de grace by stuffing its nostrils with wooden plugs. The *peixe-boi* is towed home, quartered, and fried in its own fat. Its flesh tastes like ham and, stored in twenty-liter kerosene cans, keeps for years.

But the *mariscadors* complain that, while they used to bring in five *peixe-bois* in a night, they are lucky to find one in a week. No one knows how many of the animals are left. A scientist at INPA working on the *peixe-boi* offered "a ballpark estimate" of 10,000, but I think there must be more; every family I asked along the Rio Branco and along the Solimoes admitted to taking two or three a year. The *peixe-boi* is probably managing to keep just ahead of the rate at which it is being harvested. It is officially endangered, but rural Amazonians kill it on sight; it is a catch they can't afford to pass up.

The *mariscador* himself is a vanishing breed; displaced by the gill-net, which came into Amazonia about ten years ago. While it takes a certain skill to throw a harpoon, anybody can now stretch out a gill-net and catch five times as many *pirarucú, tambaqui,* and catfish as a *mariscador* can. The trouble is that fifty to sixty percent of the gill-net catch is usually lost. The fisherman usually works twenty nets. A fish caught in the net dies in fifteen minutes and, because of the high water temperature, begins to grow soft and to stink in half an hour. The fish that aren't spoiled are often devoured by *piranha.*

Another prized and therefore seriously depleted source of animal protein is the Amazon river turtle. There are three commercially important species in the genus *Podocnemis,* which belongs to the same sub-order, *Chalidae,* as the great marine turtles: *P. expansa,* the *tartaruga; P. expansa,* the *tracajá;* and *P. sextuburculata,* the *iaçá.* The only other *Podocnemis* in the world is found in Madagascar — further evidence of the connection of that mysterious island with the Amazon.

The *tartaruga* is the largest freshwater turtle in the world, living up to thirty years and reaching 150 pounds. Its carapace is greenish brown and round, it has two barbels, or cartilaginous projections, on its chin, and its eggs are round and white and could easily be mistaken for ping-pong balls. The *tracajá*'s carapace is grayer and more elliptical, and it has only one barbel, while the *iaçá* has only one barbel and a carapace that is much smaller, greenish, and narrows at the front. *Tracajá* and *iaçá* eggs are pink and oval, hardening and becoming white with age.

From August to the beginning of October, when the water is down and long, narrow sandbars called *taboleiros* are exposed on the lower reaches of the rivers, the turtles return, as they have for millions of years, to lay their eggs. The rivers that attract the most turtles are the Purus, Jurua, Branco, Trombetas, and Pará. No one knows their movements during the rest of the year, but it is quite certain that, like the green sea turtles, the same turtles return to the same beaches. Too few of the animals have been tagged, but there are *caboclos* who say they have seen the same albino *tartaruga* crawl out on the same beach, at exactly the same place, year after year.

The females congregate in the *pocos,* the pools of calm, shallow water between the sandbars and the riverbanks. At nightfall the *caboclos* say that one male and one female will climb out on the bar and walk in a circle to verify if the conditions are good. If there are any people on the beach they will return to the water. If the coast is clear there is a mass exodus. "The emergence of the gravid females," writes Paolo Vanzolini, who observed the phenomenon from a well-concealed post on the Rio Trombetas, "is impressively quiet, as is the ensuing phase. Under the full moon the beasts look like nothing but a procession of the ghosts of huge phosphorescent beetles, the carapace presenting a distinct bluish phosphorescence. . . . Once on the general laying grounds, the turtles get to walking in all directions, colliding, veering away, or climbing over each other, and from time to time scooping some sand with the front feet and throwing it over the back. This phase is still strangely silent." If the turtle doesn't find a place she likes, after walking all around, she will return to the water; if she does, she will excavate with her rear *patas* a chamber about twenty-five inches deep and an arm-length in circumference. Then, keeping her body at a forty-five-degree angle, almost vertical, she extrudes one by one ninety to a hundred eggs. The whole process takes a few hours. After it is done she lies still for a while, sighing deeply; then fills in the rest of the hole with sand. On the way back to the river some of the turtles stop to urinate, some drag their tails, others hold them high. Some leave a broad track in the sand, like a toboggan trail on a snowy hillside. They enter the water noisily, with much splashing.

The eggs lie for two months in the warm sand. Some are dug up and eaten by people, dogs, or small reptiles called *lagartas*. Breaking the shell with a special egg tooth, the turtle hatchlings, about the size of a pocket watch, start flailing toward the surface, passing the dirt behind them down to the next turtle. Their emergence takes two weeks, during which they live on yolk sacs attached to what would correspond with our navel. By the time they surface they have straightened out fully from the curved foetal position. Five to ten percent of the eggs are addled, *ovos de banho,* large, infertile, with more oil. The race to the water is fraught with peril, as many birds—hawks, *urubús,* caracaras, wood ibises, maguari and jabiru storks—like nothing better than a tasty morsel of newborn turtle. Once in the water the *filhotes,* as the hatchlings are called, encounter another set of predators—caymans, *piranhas, pirararas, piraibás, surubims.* Fewer than one hatchling in 500 survive the seven years to maturity. Twenty-five percent of all hatchlings are trapped in the sand and drown in unexpected rises of the river; eighty percent in a highwater year.

The destruction of the *tartaruga* has been going on unabated for centuries, and the fact that there are any left at all is testimony to how many there once were. Turtles figure prominently in the mythology of twenty-nine riverine Indian tribes, some of whom corraled them to keep a supply on hand during the wet season, others of whom (the Tapajós) made clay pots in the shape of turtles in which they burned oil expressed from the turtles' eggs. Although men of the Paumari tribe are said to have been able to swim to depths of thirty feet and catch the turtles by hand, the more common methods of catching them, still in use today, are to harpoon them with a *jaticá,* a spear with a detachable head, as they surface to feed; or to lob an arrow with a detachable point in a parabolic curve above the turtle's limited lateral vision, so that it will land on and penetrate the carapace—a method that requires considerable skill. The easiest way to catch them, of course, is to surprise them on land and to flip them on their backs, a predicament from which they are unable to extricate themselves.

Turtles are in many ways an ideal source of food, as they are rich in protein, and an adult turtle, turned on its back, can survive up to sixty days without food or water. The supply seemed inexhaustible. In 1800, Humboldt estimated the number of females who nested on the shores of the Orinoco River at "little short of a million," while Bates, half a century later, reported that 6,000 pots of turtle oil were being exported annually from the upper Amazon and Madeira rivers, while another 2,000 pots were consumed locally. Each pot contained the whites of 6,000 eggs. So forty-eight million eggs, the fruitless effort of some 400,000 females, were being crushed annually.

The hundreds of thousands of turtles which once swarmed over the sandbars of Amazonia have been reduced to a trickle of hundreds. The three *Podocnemidae* are now officially protected, but rural Amazonians do not hesitate to catch them or to dig up their nests whenever they have the chance. They are too good a windfall. IBDF, the agency charged somewhat schizophrenically with planning both the exploitation and the conservation of Brazil's natural resources, has only forty-seven employees and two boats to police the extensive poaching of *tartarugas,* spotted cats, otters, and other protected animals throughout Amazonas, Roraima, and Rondônia. I wanted to take one of the boats and witness the operation. The colonel of IBDF at Manaus read through my letter of introduction from his superiors in Brasília several times, looking for mistakes in punctuation or spelling or some other irregularity that would give him an excuse to deny me passage. At length, finding nothing amiss, he told me to report at the Porto at 18:00 hours. He was reluctant to have a foreign observer aboard, perhaps, because the IBDF was not doing all that it could to ensure the conservation of Amazonia.

There are four turtle beaches on the Rio Branco—Santa Fe, Mandulão, Aricuna, and Anta. During the three-month laying season IBDF posts guards on Anta, which receives the most eggs. The *Flora and Fauna II,* a *motor* somewhat smaller tyan the one we had taken from Santarem to Manaus, was heading up to Anta that evening to relieve the guards. It would take four days to get there. On the way we would do a little *fiscalização,* stopping boats and relieving them of any turtles. We were seven: Chagas the pilot, Agenor the bookkeeper, Saba the cook, Manuel the mechanic, and Paolo, Santarem, and Edivaus the guards. With a gap between his incisors, slicked down hair that was parted in the middle, and a thin, immaculately trimmed moustache, Chagas bore a resemblance to Count Dracula. He had the longest thumbnails I'd ever seen (the better to pick things up with), which he filed with a *pirarucú* scale, and had been a pilot for thirteen years. "The Rio Branco is low," he said. "We will have to tie up at night."

It was twenty-four hours to the mouth of the Rio Branco, the principal tributary of the Rio Negro. The prow of *Flora and Fauna II* sliced big, slate-colored waves. In a short while we had left the city of Manaus and were threading through a maze of forested islands. The Rio Negro offers a classic example of "braided drainage," and is studded, like the St. Lawrence River, with a thousand islands. The braided drainage makes for perfect conditions for the poachers, who run the goods into Manaus at night, laying low behind an island during the day. "A big adult *tartaruga*," Agenor told me, "goes for 1000 to 1500 [almost $100] cruzeiros in Manaus. Everybody buys them. The word goes out when a boat is coming in. You can get a medium-sized turtle for 200-400 cruzeiros on the beach and for a thousand from the man who brings them to your door."

The big thing to watch out for on the Rio Negro, Chagas said, were the hidden rocks. "But I have been running this river *longos anos, senhor,* and I know where the rocks are." On one of the gemlike islands a little *motor* had stopped, and three men were loading it up with the pink, mafic rocks strewn along its shores. There are no rocks to build with in Manaus proper. A little further we passed an abandoned fisherman's hut smothered with a flaming vine in the *Convolvulaceae* family. Because it is a blackwater river, the Rio Negro has few fish, and there are therefore few people along it. From this point I will let my notebook tell the story.

"The Rio Negro might be called the Dead River —I never saw such a deserted region," Richard Spruce exclaimed 120 years ago. And so it is today. Not a soul along its banks. The swarming mass of vegetation presses to the water's edge, tree-domes of different height and greenness, between and behind them —darkness. Farther up the Rio Negro I understand it is more populated. The inhabitants speak the Indian dialect, lingua geral. *A blowgun is a* grawatana. *Life has changed little since Spruce passed through except for the introduction of the internal combustion engine.*

. . . it is pitch-black now on the river. Shore and water are

cloaked in darkness. Light-crazed mariposas, *dobsonflies, are landing in our food. I stare at the white foam that boils against the boat. The temperature of the Rio Negro is now hotter than that of the air.*

Fiscalisação #1   *Ten a.m. the next morning.*
The boys tuck .38 revolvers into their waists, and we're off in the voadeira, *a fiberglass outboard, headed for three fishing boats. The men are seining for cardinal tetras, the bright red-and-green-striped minnows half the length of a matchstick who live at the mouths of the creeks that flow into the Rio Negro. Millions of cardinal fish destined for aquaria around the world, particularly in the United States, are netted along the Rio Negro every year. They are a major source of income for the* caboclos, *who get twenty-five cruzeiros per hundred from the middlemen who run them into Manaus, where the fish fetch four times as much. The problem is that less than twenty percent of the cardinal fish make it to Manaus alive. The* caboclos *and the middlemen pour the fish into twenty-liter cans. They feed them bread but don't change the water so most of the fish eventually run out of oxygen and die.*

There are no turtles in the boats. We board the voadeira. *A toucan screams. A* jacaretinga, *the ubiquitous small cayman, thrashes in the water.*

Back on the Flora *and* Fauna II *time passes cleaning guns, drinking* caipirinhas *(a drink made of* cachaça, *lemon, and sugar), and playing dominoes—a more popular sport on motors than cards because the slabs don't blow away. The score is tallied with red and black* tenta *beans. Chagas waves to the pilot of a beer boat on its way to Roraima, then switches to the outer bank, where the current is deeper, and there are fewer snags and sandbars.*

Fiscalisação #2   *1 p.m.*
This is a three-boat complex—a motor *pushing an* alvarenga, *a barge with a Quonset hut on the deck and bags of cement in the hull, and towing a third open boat in which a man with a radio to his ear is lying in a hammock. No turtles.*

We passed Ilha do Paricá—a solid mass of waterworn purple sandstone and at my insistence stop at a little sitio *to ask if there are any strangely carved rocks in the vicinity. We should be near the ones Spruce found a hundred years ago. The old* caboclo *is making a fiddle out of* jasmina *wood with a formica top and an* abiurana-

wood fretboard. His two grandchildren are out paddling in a dugout. His pretty mameluca* *daughter is in the hut making pants on a sewing machine. They live here year round. "No,* senhor," *he says. "there are no rock carvings near here. But five days up the river, at Boa Jardim, there is a huge rock with a church carved on it."*

Tonight, precisely twenty-four hours out of Manaus, we reach the meeting with the Rio Branco. The rocks are black, the sand is orange, and the water is café-au-lait and very low. Our keel scrapes a sandbar. Chagas curses.

Fiscalisação #3   *Next morning.*
A two-story motor, *the wheel and crates of empty beer bottles on the top deck. Brahma cattle on the bottom, destined for the savannahs of Boa Vista. But no turtles.*

Somewhat upstream a battered old motor *called the Deus Meu. Agenor and I climb on the roof. Two cases of beer, six watermelons, several dirty white blocks of* sorva, *the gum from which chicle is made, also used for caulking boats and, mixed with the latex of the*

---

*Brazil abounds with racial hybrids and terms for them that its people use with complete lack of self-consciousness. One of the best things about the country is the absence of the racial discrimination that blights our country; although the social classes in Brazil *do* tend to be divided along color lines, with the rich tending to be light and the poor dark-skinned. Brazil is basically a dark-skinned country. Some are *moreno escuro,* dark brunette; others *moreno claro,* light brunette; some *moreno cabo verde,* brunette with straight black hair; others *moreno sarara,* brunette with auburn hair (other terms for this type are *moreno jambo* or *cinamon* or *cor de canela);* and still others *brancinho* or *negrinho,* white-skinned with frizzy red hair, thick lips, and freckles. Some are *mulatto,* a mixture of white and black; some *mameluco,* part white and part Indian; and some *cafuso,* part black and part Indian. Some are a mixture of all three races, and many aren't sure what they are.

Another racial term is *caboclo,* which comes from a Tupi-Guarani word meaning "naked savage." *Caboclo* usually refers to the copper-colored native of Amazonia (the Brazilian equivalent of the Mexican *chicano),* but can also mean a person with dark black skin but straight hair. *Caboclos* are sometimes called *mestiços,* which can also mean part white and part black, as well as a peasant, or backwoodsman, regardless of his ethnic configuration. There are few full-blooded *negros, creoles,* or *pretos legitimos* any more, except in Bahia and Rio de Janeiro.

maçaranduba *tree, for shoe soles. Next to the* sorva, *in a red plastic bowl, maybe forty wriggling* filhotes. *With olive-green shells and gray heads, they are* iaçá *hatchlings. They are considered a delicacy. Down below Edivaus and Manuel are pulling up the floorboards. The owner and his two sons stand by glumly. "Ta chea," Manuel says. "This boat is full of turtles." There are twenty-eight* tracajás *and one* tartaruga *in all. From the bank above us a curious family looks down as we transfer the turtles to the* voadeira. *The* tartaruga *is a* capitari, *a big male who would have fetched a thousand cruzeiros in Manaus. He weighs 26.5 kilos. His carapace is sixty-nine by sixty-four centimeters and has a harpoon puncture in it. The* tracajás *are smaller, but there are a few good-sized* zepregos, *as the males are called. One has the letter W carved on its back. It is very weak and will probably not live much longer. The iris is black against a green background. The expression of the eyes is unreadable. They blink like the shutter of a camera, clicking, a fold of skin called the nictitating membrane coming up from below. The carapace is brown and yellow green, the plastron motley burnt-umber to reddish brown. Manuel weighs and measures each turtle, calling the number out to Agenor, then clamps an aluminum tag on the edge of the carapace. The first tag says IBDF Dec '76 RB 0I—the RB standing for Rio Branco. Santarem and Paolo kid around, thrusting turtles at each other. When they are all tagged and recorded, they are returned to the river.*

Fiscalização #4
A flock of roseate spoonbills with necks extended flap in front of a rainbow. At the mouth of an igarape, *four aquarium fishermen show me their catch: an* araya (stingray), *a* cardiso, pacupena, bararua, acari, tucunaré, traira, aruna *(which one is fileting on a log),* piranha *(whose teeth another bares obligingly for my camera), and a little aquarium fish called the* rose à ciel. *Bank swallows swoop low over the water. From what North American riverbank, I wonder, have they made the long haul to winter on the Rio Branco? But no turtles.*

    "Jose!" Chagas calls to the pilot of a passing barge. "The river," he says to me, "is still the best way to get goods to Roraima."

Fiscalização #5
Motor *with two* voadeiras *in tow, a pickup truck, a sedan, bags of flour, and 800 empty crates for the mayor of Boa Vista. Clean. Further on four* mariscadores *in three dugout canoes. They have* jaticás,

harpoons with detachable heads attached to buoys, and forked spears for throwing at jandia, surubim, *and* filhotes de piraibá. *They have five* iaçás *and four small* tracajás *on the floor of their canoes. "It's alright to have them if you're going to eat them yourselves,"* Agenor says, *"As long as you don't sell them."*

Two houseboats with thatched roofs have docked at the next sandbar. Chickens turned loose are scratching the sand. A slight barefoot woman in a pink flower-print dress says, "There are some who catch them and sell them in Manaus. But I'm a good Brazilian. Si, senhor. I wouldn't think of catching turtles except to eat them." Her speech is impassioned, but Agenor thinks the men with her are probably out digging up turtle eggs. Many birds are standing on the bar—white-winged swallows, a black caracara, trumpeters, white-necked herons. We follow the meandering tracks of a tartaruga *up a steep bank to a flat place where a dozen nests had been dug up today or yesterday. Some of the turtles had only reconnoitered and gone back, without laying. At the end of the bar another houseboat with a pinwheel has stopped to dig up eggs.* "Só para comer, *just to eat,"* a *shifty-eyed man assures us.* Aruana *and* surubim *drying on the roof. A little bit off, a* jacaretinga, *five feet long, lies sphinxlike with its neck up in the alert position, and its tail draped like a cat's over the sand bar.*

Jacaretingas, *which don't get much longer than five feet, are common throughout Amazonia.* Jacaré-uassus, *the black caymans, who can reach twenty feet, once plentiful, are now close to extinction. "During a journey of five days which I made in the Upper Amazon steamer,"* Bates reported, *"alligators were seen along the coast almost every step of the way, and the passengers amused themselves, from morning until night, by firing at them with rifle and ball. They were numerous in the still bays, where the huddled crowds jostled together, to the great rattling of their coats of mail, as the steamer passed." The black caymans were despised and feared for their cunning in sneaking up on people drunk or asleep on the bank and making quick work of them. Later, in the twentieth century, their skin acquired commercial value. Theodore Roosevelt speaks well for the general attitude toward* jacaré-uassus *in his book,* Through the Brazilian Wilderness: *"Caymans were becoming plentiful. The ugly brutes lay on the sand-flats and mud-banks like logs, always with the head raised, sometimes with the jaws open. They are often dangerous to domestic animals, and are always destructive to fish, and it is good to shoot them. I killed half a dozen and missed nearly as many more—a throbbing boat does not improve one's aim."*

Fiscalisação #6

Two motors *pulling two cattle barges. Seven* tracajás *and one* tartaruga *in the toilet. The pilot is angry and argues about the sense of
the law. "Look, everybody sells turtles and eats their eggs. There's
nothing you can do about it, so why try?" The man refuses to give
them up. Agenor bargains. He will take only four, leaving four.
"We'll be flexible," he says diplomatically, "if you are flexible." Four
flame-red arara parrots, raucous but in tight formation, fly toward
the sunset.*

*Fifty-three hours out of Manaus we arrive at Anta. This is the
end of the road for me and the three replacement guards. The previous guards report that 432 tartarugas have nested since November
8. The last one was on December 13, six days ago. The season is
over.*

With less than 500 turtles on one of the most productive
beaches in Amazonia, the status of the reptile, like that of the
pirarucú and the *peixe-boi,* is a cause for immediate alarm. Because
of its slow maturation rate of about six years the *tartaruga* is not a
good candidate for aquaculture, though it is raised in small ponds
in some places. But farming of the fast-growing fish—an untapped
resource of almost unlimited potential—seems by far the best way
of providing the Amazonian with protein. It is surely less destructive than the massive clearing required to raise beef cattle, and it
might take some of the pressure off the turtles.

10

Peruano's River

The *Flora and Fauna II* chugged away downstream, and I was on my own, midway up the Rio Branco in the middle of December.

I had two weeks or so to spend in Roraima, the northernmost part of the Brazilian Amazon, and no program. Maybe I would go up the Agua Boa, a clearwater river that empties into the Rio Branco not far from where we were, and was said to be a good place to see manatees; I had promised the scientists at INPA to keep a look out for manatees and monkeys and to ask everyone I ran into about them. If that didn't work out I would hitch a barge to Caracarai, where there was a road to Boa Vista, the capital of the territory. From there I could take a bush plane to the mountains, where I stood a chance of meeting some diamond prospectors.

After putting their food in ant-proof chests the new guards and I got into a *voadeira* and went visiting the neighbors, who lived on an island about a mile away. We moored next to several *lanchas* with palm-thatch roofs in front of a series of steps that had been chopped out of the ten-foot clay bank. The hut to which they led was filled with about a dozen people who were dancing to a record called *Os Pumas 18 Hits Nacionais* that was spinning on a small battery-powered phonograph. One of them introduced himself as José Peruano, and we fell into conversation. Peruano was fifty, several inches shy of five feet, with high cheekbones and lower teeth jutting out over his upper lip conveniently for cracking open bottles of *cachaça,* on which, by eleven in the morning, he was already thoroughly skunked. His mother was a Tucano Indian, and his father had come from Iquitos, Peru, hence his name — the Peruvian. He had come to the Rio Branco in 1942 to tap rubber — during the war, when the United States was cut off from its rubber sources in the Far East, the Amazon revived as a producer. After the war the rubber business fell off again, but Peruano stayed on the Rio Branco gathering Brazil nuts and *sorva,* the gum from which chicle is made; he reckoned he had done just about everything there was for a man to do in the backwoods of Roraima. For the last thirteen years he had been living with the Aika Indians a hundred miles up the Catrimani River and selling spotted cat skins to the illegal trade in Manaus. The Catrimani is a 400-mile whitewater river that comes tumbling down from the crystalline highlands of Venezuela to meet the Rio Branco just south of the Agua Boa. Glowing with pride and *cachaça,* Peruano grew eloquent about the abundance of game in the woods and the fish in the river and the richness of his *roça,* or plantation, a hundred miles up the Catrimani. He was just laying in some provisions and would be returning in a few days. My ears pricked up. How had he come? I asked. "By *canoa,*" he said. Did he want another paddler? "I would be honored if you visited my house," he said.

I explained that I was a *pesquisador,* a free-lance investigator studying monkeys and manatees and how people live in Amazonia, and I would even pay him to take me up the Catrimani and teach me about the river. Peruano said that five days upriver from his house there was a mission for the Indians and a road with trucks going to Boa Vista all the time. It was hard work after his house; there were twenty *cachoeiras,* cataracts to portage, but I was young and strong, and he knew the river, and the two of us could make it to the mission in — he counted his fingers — fifteen days. "How much do you want?" I said. We studied each other carefully, he wondering how much to ask, I wondering if I could trust him. If I decided to go with him, I realized I would be placing my life in his hands. That he was a good talker, I already knew; but there were basic qualities like good will and competence which I still couldn't make out. "800 cruzeiros," he finally decided. I entrusted myself to Peruano, to the river, to what happened. "Let's go."

Taking the money in advance, he shook the 100-cruzeiro notes and grinned. "With this we can forget about going by canoe. I think I'll just make a down payment on one of the *lanchas* below," and after considerable negotiation with the white-haired *caboclo* who owned it, and swearing up and down that he'd be back in a month with the rest of the money, we were off, chugging downriver with three bottles of *Creoula cachaça* and a full tank of gas. Peruano was in great spirits, swigging the *cachaça,* elated at his sudden rise in status to owner of a boat with a motor. He was just explaining how it would now take only three days to reach his house instead of the usual ten by canoe, when the motor sputtered, gagged, then gave out completely. Suddenly we were adrift on the Rio Branco, spinning round and round in the swift, silent current. Peruano succeeded in getting the boat pointed downstream while I fiddled around with the throttle and a switch that seemed to control the fuel's richness, and after turning it over several dozen times finally got the cranky old motor going again. We were just opening a second bottle of *cachaça* to celebrate when the motor conked out again. In the silence we could hear dolphins snorting as they circled curiously a dozen yards away, and the wind rattling the thatchwork of *coroa* palm. Peruano steered between two islands, across another channel of the Rio Branco, and into the mouth of the Agua Boa. I tied to a branch while Peruano struggled with the starter cord. After many yanks the engine fired. We chugged limply upstream. The water grew clear. The bank was riddled with the holes of *acari*, walking catfish. In larger holes slept nighthawks, and one vast cavity, under some roots, showed signs of a struggle; the sand was stained with blood. "Two days ago," Peruano explained, "I found an anaconda sleeping there and killed it with my harpoon. It was four *bracos*, armlengths, long." We passed a dozen or so 50-kilo blocks of *sorva* gum floating in a makeshift corral, to keep them from drying up and breaking. The going rate for *sorva* in Roraima was four cruzeiros a kilo. We paused to shoot the breeze with a man in a cedar dugout with mycosis scabs on his back and shriveled fleshless calves like those of a polio victim. A startled *tangara*, red-capped cardinal, with black back and white belly, cried at the tip of an overhanging branch. Half a mile up the Agua Boa we found two boats like our own tied to a sandbar. They belonged to an intinerant river-merchant Peruano knew and was hoping would sell us some gas. In the absence of stores throughout most of rural Amazonia it is the river merchants who keep the *caboclos* supplied with ammunition, bolts of cloth, fishhooks and line, batteries, swapping the goods for *sorva, farinha,* jaguar hides, or turtles. Their boats are called *regatãos*.

Peruano hailed the merchant, and his extraordinarily beautiful *mameluco* wife came out of the cabin and sat at the bow. Five of them, she said, were down with malaria. Then the merchant himself came out and asked what he could do for us. He had no gas. Would he take a look at the engine? He fell to, announcing after several minutes that there was water in the carburetor, which he proceeded to clean. I gave him my cloroquine tablets, keeping only a curing dose for myself and hoping that the merchant's family had *Malaria vivax*.

Peruano was staying with a woman named Didi who lived on an island opposite the mouth of the Catrimani River. Didi's hut and the two others on the mile-long island comprise the settlement of Catrimani which manages to appear on most good-sized maps of South America by virtue of the fact that there are no other candidates a hundred miles in any direction. We arrived just in time for dinner—a catfish called *peixe liso* or *piracatinga,* also known as the *urubú d'agua,* the vulture of the water, because of his scavenging habits. Didi's house was immaculate, and we ate sitting on the floor. There were four tartarugas on their backs under the kitchen table; all sixty-pounders at least. Didi's husband had gone to the head of the island to fish for more turtles with *palmito,* palm-hearts; the turtles also take hooks baited with the yellow fruit of the *carapari* tree, whose branches droop over the water. A *morena clara* of thirty-three, Didi had already produced eight children. Some were caucasoid, some negroid with kinky blond hair. Didi had a sentence for keeping them in line. Something about taking wood to them. But she never would have. There was a deep womanly calm, a clarity and a simplicity about Didi that I had already noticed in other riverine *caboclos.* Perhaps the river imposes its own quiet, steady flow on the lives of the people who live on it. Certainly their lives are completely oriented to it. They drink it, swim in it, fish in it, wash in it, urinate in it, throw their refuse in it, salvage crates from it, spend most of their time on it. The sound of a motor brings them to the bank just as surely as it brings country folk to the window on a back road.

The sun sank fast and early. The sky was bloody for five minutes. A little bird called *batative,* all black with a white head and a black eye-ring, sang briefly in a bush by the back porch, and it was pitch dark by six. The kerosene lamps went on in Didi's house and so did Peruano's radio. I picked up my guitar and traced a few weird and fanciful chords across the strings. The Indian girl who had been playing with Didi's children fell into rapt silence. I had been trying without much luck to break the ice with her. When I had asked her name she had been so paralyzed with shyness that she had pulled her dress up over her face. But thereafter her eyes had never left me. Once, after I had failed to light a cigarette after several tries, she had burst into wild laughter. Later in the evening when she was outside I asked Peruano who she was. "My wife," he said. "When my *civilizado* wife died nine years ago, the Aika gave her to me. She was only eight years old at the time and was named after some animal. I have taught her to wear clothes and to speak

Portuguese, and given her a *civilizado* name, Maria." It hadn't occurred to me that anyone so childlike could be married, especially to a man of fifty. I asked Peruano why she had been so shy when I asked her name, and he explained, "The Aika believe that when you know their name it gives you a power over them."

In the morning we went to the main channel of the Rio Branco, tied to a tree with small white flowers, and waited for a barge from which we could buy gas. The current babbled through snags. A silver fish with a broad tail jumped over the prow. Curious *bôtos* circled and snorted. Peruano shaved and cleaned his gun. I watched a *pium* mosquito on my left wrist fill its transparent abdomen with my blood. The *pium* were swarming at our wrists, ankles and elbows, where there was good feeding and we couldn't see them. "*Muito pium,*" I remarked to Peruano, passing my hand across my face and staring at the palm, which had come away bloody with their gorged bodies. "*Si senhor,*" Peruano agreed. "*Muito pium.*" The flies left a small red dot like a blood blister wherever they had drunk, and within an hour I was covered with bites. The insects are a phenomenon of whitewater rivers; there had been none on the Rios Negro or Tapajós. During the first five days of canoeing up the Catrimani, Peruano told me, the *pium* were thick; thereafter they would be less noticeable except for occasional pockets of intense activity. Largely because of the insects, the Catrimani was still virgin territory, inhabited for the first hundred miles by only three *caboclo* families. Bates gave the insects a good description. "The *pium,*" he wrote, "relieves the mosquito at sunrise" and occurs in "such dense swarms as to resemble thin clouds of smoke.... They alight almost imperceptibly and squatting close, fall at once to work, stretching forward their long front legs, which are in constant motion and seem to act as feelers, and then applying their short broad snouts to the skin. Their abdomens soon become distended and red with blood, and then, their thirst satisfied, they move off, so stupefied with their potations that they can scarcely fly." I was determined this time not to succumb to "jungle ulcers" and had brought a quart of alcohol to cleanse the *pium* bites and to reduce their itch. Each evening I washed myself down, and this proved very effective.

At midday a barge finally came into view, but we could not get the motor started to go forth and meet it. Try as we might we couldn't get even a rise out of the motor. Lacking tools we had no alternative but to pole ignominiously back to Didi's. "Forget the *lancha,*" I said to Peruano. "Let's set out in the canoe tomorrow."

Peruano was reluctant. He wanted to spend Christmas at Catrimani. It was four days away. There would be a *festa.*

But Peruano relented, and early the next morning we loaded the canoe with sugar, salt, *farinha,* gun powder, kerosene, cooking oil, machetes, cloth, presents for Peruano's Aika friends, and Maria's three-month-old hound, Truvão (Thunder). Didi asked if I had any tetrex, an all-purpose antibiotic not easy for her to come by, so I gave her a handful of the red-and-yellow capsules. Then she wanted me to take a picture of her family. Realizing that it was a rare chance for them to have their existence documented, I lined them up in front of their house and snapped a few shots. Maria got into the twelve-foot dugout and, with Truvao on her lap, made a place for herself astern among the mounds of provisions. I took the middle seat. Peruano shoved off and jumped into the prow. The canoe rode only six inches above the water.

"This river is full of fish," Peruano remarked as we entered the mouth of the Catrimani. He shook his harpoon at a murky purple form. There was an explosion in the water, and the fish disappeared. Peruano laughed. We soon picked up an escort of several hundred *pium* and two *bôtos,* who kept arching in formation, fifteen feet ahead of us. Against the *pium* I spread drops of Cutter's repellent over my skin, but I was sweating so profusely that it did little good. Against the humid heat I wore a broad-brimmed straw hat that Peruano had sold me. We were dead on the equator, half a degree north of it, to be precise, and I had never felt the sun so close before. Scores of inch-long water-striding insects called *piulis d'agua,* in the family *Gerridae* jumped off a protruding snag as we approached. Eight *tracajá* turtles, sunning as we rounded a point, scuttled instantly into the water. In back, Maria was singing to herself a ditty that went, "There is a stranger paddling in the canoe in front of me."

Sitting at the prow with his legs tucked under him, digging his broad, heart-shaped cedar blade into the water, Peruano was a master paddler. The Indian, I had noticed, seemed to do everything in short, quick movements. Peruano put his paddle into the water about every two seconds, and pushed it behind him in less than one; his fast, fluid strokes reminded me of Eketi walking or Bebgogti lapping water from the Rasgado with his hand. Sometimes he held the paddle still and at an angle as a rudder to steer around a snag or a rock, while I kept paddling behind him. By good luck he preferred to paddle to the left, and I to the right, so we generally kept to those sides. My paddle, however, was narrow and scalpel-shaped; it had less than half the surface of Peruano's and I had, the first few days, probably less than half of Peruano's strength as a mover of water; so my contribution to the progress of the canoe was, until I could match Peruano stroke for stroke, negligible. In the beginning I could only insert the paddle in the water once for Peruano's every two times, and the canoe would gradually veer to the right, which Peruano would correct with a quick slice across the front of the canoe, ending with a flick of the wrist that sent the boat turning sharply. His most radical move was to lean out to one side and, putting his entire weight over the paddle, plunge it deep into the water and literally pull the boat toward him. He was able to do this because the canoe was made out of dense, black, rock-hard *itaúba* wood and virtually impossible to capsize. He had bought it three years before for 300 cruzeiros. Its shell was the hollowed half of an *itaúba* bole to which two additional side planks had been nailed. At home he had another dugout, the same size and made entirely out of a single *itaúba* tree which had taken him two weeks to burn out with heated rocks. This canoe was lighter, but its disadvantage was that it had seams, and now that we were riding so low, the seams were well below the water-line. The seams had been caulked with *sorva* gum but in places the caulking had washed away, and the water was streaming in. Peruano stopped the more serious leaks by stuffing rags into the cracks with a carving knife. The minor ones were allowed slowly to trickle until the bottom of the canoe was filled with enough water for Maria to scoop out with a bowl made from the husk of a *cuilba* fruit. She bailed the leaky craft several times an hour. One third of the floor was covered with planks that could be raised, lowered, advanced, or set back. The dugout handled completely differently from a North American bark canoe. For one thing the lone paddler sat up front. Theodore Roosevelt, who canoed with the natives on both American continents, declared heartily that, for strength and skill with their paddles, the Amazonian watermen had no equal. I had certainly never encountered anyone the likes of Peruano.

It was the dry season, and the river was ten feet lower than it would be in July. It ran through long, straight trenches lined with the soaring, densely packed trees of the rain forest. We would stay close to the sheer clay wall of one of the banks, paddling under dangling roots, low-hanging vines and branches. Then there would be a broad, sweeping bend as the river doubled back, and we would cross over to keep in the shade. On the lower Catrimani at this time of year there were many *praias,* exposed sandbars along

147

which we could walk, towing the canoe with the cord to Peruano's harpoon. Maria, Truvao, and I would jump out. Peruano would wrap the cord once around my seat, hooking it securely to the barb of his harpoon point, and I would start walking along the *praia* with the cord over my shoulder and the wooden buoy clutched to my belly. With Peruano still in the canoe, steering with his rigidly held paddle, the half-ton of dead weight moved upstream at about four miles per hour, twice the rate we achieved paddling and with far less effort. Iron and other minerals carried in suspension down from the Guyana Shield had settled out in orange and opaline swirls in the shallows where *arraias,* stingrays, with shells two and three feet in diameter, lay half-buried in the sand. Fortunately the rays always became aware of me before I was within two yards of them, and shot off into the pea-green depths, leaving mushroom clouds of disturbed mud. Maria and Truvao would run ahead, gaily flushing out whatever animals remained on the *praia* and studying the tracks. *"Onça,"* she shouted one time. "Jaguar." Peruano debarked and came over. The large feline prints were mint, he said, not more than five minutes old. The cat must have bounded into the thicket just as we rounded the bend. Peruano growled menacingly for the benefit of the jaguar, who was probably watching us. Maria was mainly interested in turtle and tern tracks, and with Peruano shouting directions from the boat, she dug up, the first afternoon, one speckled *gaivota,* or tern egg, a bit larger than those of domestic chickens, and ninety-seven *tartaruga* eggs, putting them in her hat and running to show them to Peruano. He was pleased. *"E nossa jantar,"* he said. "That's our dinner. Sometimes you get as many as 200 in a nest." I said something about how if everybody dug up all the turtle eggs, pretty soon there weren't going to be any turtles left any more, and that was why IBDF stationed guards at Anta. Peruano laughed. "You know the guards at Anta?" he asked. "They dig up the eggs themselves and sell them to all comers." I was shocked. "But don't worry, *senhor.* I never dig up more eggs than I need, and there are many that I miss." Further along the *praia,* Maria sneaked up on a foot-and-a-half-long catfish with a leopard-spotted back and an orange tail sitting in an inch of water. Gently stirring up the mud from behind it to confuse it, she came down on it with a decisive machete blow that chopped it in half. The catfish was called a *pirarara* because of its wild, *arara*-like colors. On the next *praia* she clubbed two more catfish—a *braco de morça* and a *surubim*—as they lay half way out of the water, probably to avoid being eaten by dolphins.

For three days we saw no trace of man, our only company the

teeming wildlife that came into view at each bend. Maria would call "Chico, Chico" to the squirrel monkeys which would walk out to the end of branches to get a better look at us, and, curling and uncurling their long, black-tipped tails, they would squeak back excitedly. Once I counted six of them in an *apuí* tree. The last, smaller and with a slightly grayer coat, was apparently the junior member of the troop. He ventured closest and stayed the longest, with his head cocked in puzzlement and swiveling back and forth from shoulder to shoulder. His agitated movements loosened a fruit from the tree. It fell and was eaten in a flash by a fish which Peruano identified as a *cayarara*. A perfect example of opportunistic feeding.

From the canoe we could approach the animals silently and get much nearer than if we had been on foot. *Bemtevi* flycatchers followed us, hopping from shrub to shrub and calling out their name, and the *tangara* cardinals were as daring, especially the brown-headed juveniles. Once we passed beneath the languid coils of a ten-foot non-poisonous black snake with a yellow belly called a *papaova*. Often we disturbed on the dark undersides of leaning logs small, slumbering bats who would scatter frantically in every direction, only to return seconds later to the same position, fastened together in a tight mosaic that was indistinguishable from the wood as the sunlight, reflected from the water, danced over them. While individually insignificant in weight and in size, the *morcegas,* or bats, of Amazonia have the largest number of species—about one hundred—and the largest biomass of any mammal.

Every so often the demented cacophony of a flock of horned screamers would erupt in a treetop, and we would look up and see a flurry of vast black wings with white edges like the sails of airborne galleons. The toucans who shouted down to us came in three sizes; the largest, black with a white collar, was called the yellow-ridged toucan. Three sizes of kingfishers—the belted, the Amazon, and the pygmy—rattled and swooped down from branches. Pairs of flame-pink *arara* macaws, of blue-and-gold *ararayas,* of solid green *papagaios,* and emerald-and-cadmium yellow *araras amarelhos* would cross the sky with strong, shallow wingbeats, long tails streaming behind, and calls whose raucous freedom expressed, as well as anything, the undiluted wildness of the habitat. The macaws always traveled in twos and in tight formation. The Orinoco geese, with tan heads and necks and dark bodies, flew in swift, disciplined wedges, veering in concert, like a school of startled minnows, at a sudden decision by their leader. Peruano called them *marecas,* as opposed to the smaller, black *marequinhas,* which had higher-pitched honks and were equally abundant. He would like to get a shot at them as they sat in the water, but they always took off before we got within shooting range. He also would like to shoot one of the curassows which lowed like cattle in the bushes but never came into the open. The Portuguese name for these creatures, *mutum,* is onomatopoetic. The awkward, flightless hoatzins, who looked something like pheasants, stumbled and squawked in easy firing range, seeming to know their flesh was not desirable. The rufous-tailed jacamars which stood their perch fearlessly were too small. So were the tiny brown hummingbirds with dark eyelines called woodstars; they were no larger than the giant Amazonian bumblebee.

The *várzea,* where the bank would overflow, was dominated by palms, cecropias, and a strange, treelike aroid called *Montrichardia arborescens.* The shrubs were a dull, muddy color except on the branch-tips where new green leaves had sprouted since the last flooding. Many of the leaves, however, were down, giving the *várzea* a gray, skeletal appearance during the dry season. The cecropias were favorite nesting sites for the garrulous colonies of *japòs,* oropendulas, which took over a tree until it dripped with thirty or more of their four-foot, socklike nests. The *japòs* chose cecropias and *Tachi* trees because they are likely to harbor wasps, the birds' main food. The *japòs* have red tails, black bodies, and thick, creamy bills. Their call is like a door creaking open, followed by a cuckoo, exactly like the production of a Swiss clock. They are closely related to *japís,* the yellow-rumped caciques. Both are orioles and both inhabit cecropia and *Tachi* trees. The *japí* nest, however, is more massive and not so pendulous.

In elevated places soaring Brazil-nut trees and other *terra firme* species grew near the river, and the lavender or white flowers of *Lecythidaceae,* which I recognized thanks to Dr. Prance, often came drifting, as delicate as lotus petals, from some high spot up-river. The *terra firme* forests were spooky and silent in comparison with the swarming, sunlit life along the river—*urubús* flaring their wings threateningly as we glided past; jabiru and maguiri storks striding down the strand and lifting themselves slowly, heavily, into the air; caymans and iguanas charging into the water, dragging their slick tails through the sand. Occasionally we would glimpse a whispering ibis or a capped heron, white with a cobalt face and plumes on its crest, feeding in a quiet lagoon that opened off the main stream. Hawks and kites stood on branches, motionless except for their eyes; and the trees were full of stripe-backed bitterns who had probably just arrived from the south. They were so numerous and apathetic I thought that they must have been part of a migration.

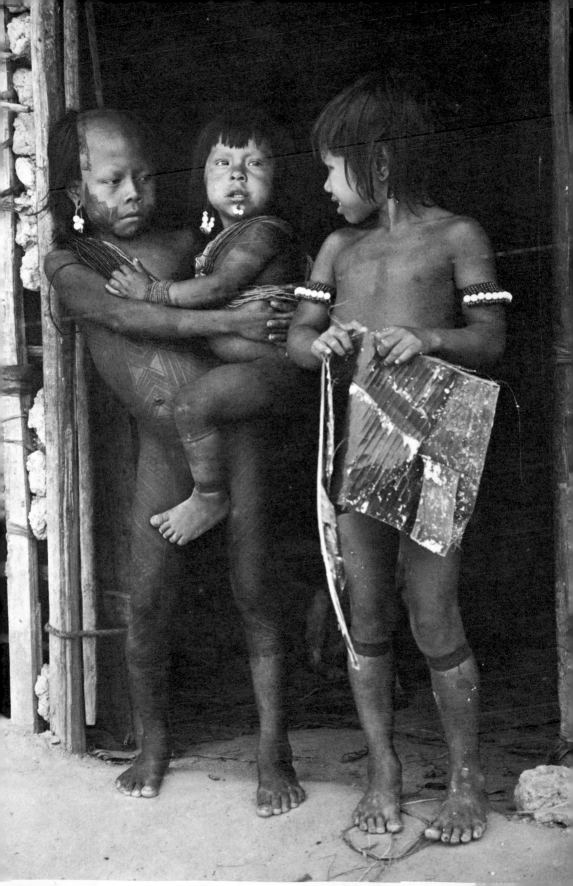

Overleaf *Cayapo boys standing in a doorway, Menkranoti. By Alex Shoumatoff.*

Left *Benmoti, the white captive, Menkranoti. By Danny Delaney.*

Right *Quechua man, Antapallpa. By Alex Shoumatoff.*

Facing Page *Quechua child grinding millet, on the road to Livitaca. By Alex Shoumatoff.*

Quechua women with llamas on the road to Berhinouilh. By Alex Shoumatoff.

Quechua women washing in a brook, Antapallpa. By Alex Shoumatoff.

Building a lean-to, Menkranoti. By Danny Delaney.

Left *Peruano with a* surubim *catfish on the Rio Catrimani. By Alex Shoumatoff.*

Right *Peruano cleaning a piranha on a side-stream of the Rio Catrimani. By Alex Shoumatoff.*

Overleaf *Caboclo man with homemade fiddle, on the Rio Branco. By Alex Shoumatoff.*

We passed a den of *lontras,* giant river otters, on the bank, well-concealed behind a curtain of vines. No one was there, but there were big, fresh tracks. No one knows how many others are left in the Amazon; because they are prized in the European fur market, *caboclo* hunters like Peruano usually kill them on sight. On almost every *praia* there were one or two capybara; if not the animals themselves, then their tracks or scat. About the size of a mastiff, the capybara is the largest rodent in the world—another item in the long list of Amazonian superlatives. With their strange, rectangular muzzles, bathing or drinking at the water's edge, trundling nonchalantly into the thicket when we had approached within fifty yards, the capybara seemed more like inventions or caricatures than real animals, like creatures from the imagination of Lewis Carroll. When there was no land cover immediately at hand, the capybara took to the water, remaining submerged for long periods of time. They had probably evolved this strategy as a way of escaping from their main predators, jaguars. Once, on foot, I surprised two of them, around the bend of a sandbar, only thirty yards away. They jumped in the river immediately and vanished from sight. Several minutes later one of them crawled out on the opposite bank, a hundred yards away, shook himself free of water, and slunk into the bushes. I never did see the other one again. It happened again several days later. A big capybara charged out of the bushes and into the water fifty yards ahead of us, and that was the last we saw of him. We looked for five minutes along the other side, but he had absolutely disappeared. Maybe, Peruano suggested, he had a secret hole on the bottom of the river, or maybe he had been eaten by piranha.* Later the same day a dead capybara came floating along, cause of death unknown. The part that was above the water was intact, and we did not turn it over. I thought of the National Geographic Society's film about the Amazon, which shows a wounded capybara being savaged by hundreds of piranha. It seemed odd that the piranhas of the Rio Catrimani would pass up a windfall like a floating dead capybara; I had already learned that the river was full of the fish.

At dusk we would pull into one of the small subsidiary creeks, beach the canoe, hack out a clearing with machetes, and sling our

---

*Back in the U.S.A. I was given two explanations for the capybara's vanishing act. One zoologist claimed that the rodents can hold their breath for up to thirty minutes, while another said they hide among the plants, with only the tip of their noses above water.

hammocks. Maria would start a small fire with wood shavings, expertly adding larger sticks until the stack was soon blazing bright enough to keep the jaguars away and hot enough to keep us warm as the ground cooled. We dined on smoked fish, an *arabú* (as the dish is called) of turtle eggs and *farinha,* washed down with sweet black coffee—it was delicious. After dinner Peruano would stretch an antenna wire up to a branch, recline in his hammock, and turn on the radio. We listened mostly to Christmas carols whose familiar tunes and foreign words accentuated, for me, the strangeness and loneliness of the surroundings. Every so often the caroling would be interrupted by an important local announcement, to which Peruano would listen with rapt attention. He was hoping to hear news of Nick, the river merchant, who was coming up the Catrimani sometime this month to buy his hides and the *fantasias,* costumes made by his Indian friends.

One evening Peruano picked up the Voice of America, and we listened for a while to a man in slow, easily understood English saying nasty things about the Soviet Union. Then Peruano turned the dial to Radio Cuba where a man was making equally disparaging statements about the United States in Russian.

"How many days away is America by canoe?" Maria asked.

"Oh, about four years," I answered.

"America is a big city, *senhor,* isn't it?"

"No, it's a big country like Brazil, with many big cities."

"America is completely covered with houses," Peruano explained to Maria. "Every place is owned. You don't have free land like here in the territory of Roraima where anybody can come and plant his own *roça* of bananas and pawpaws and lemons and live there as long as he wants. You don't have endless forests and Indians who go where they please, building their *maloccas* (roundhouses) and living off the land."

Peruano switched off the radio. "You may not think so, *senhor,* but this is a rich country. Açai palms you just cut down and eat. Fish, curassow, *porcos gordos de uma beleza* (fat wild pigs of a beauty)—" Peruano finished the sentence by smacking his lips. "They're all here, and it doesn't cost a thing."

Then he fell silent. Stars blazed behind the trees, and the darkness was full of sounds, the cascading roars of howler monkeys, which sounded like wind rushing out of the portals of Hades; the five sharp barks of the *cora* rat; the occasional click of a *jequitiranoboia,* a winged insect in the genus *Lanternaria* which Peruano erroneously considered to be *venenosíssimo,* and called "the flying snake"; and various loud crashes, piercing screams, clangs as if an iron bar were being smacked against a hollow tree, and other sounds yet to be explained by science but which the people of the region attribute to *Curupira,* the bogey man.

After several days, our pattern was established. Get up at 3:30, off by 4:30. Knock off the first long stretch by dawn. "Ten more of these today," Peruano would say as we looked back in the spreading light over the two miles of river we had just put behind us. Peruano knew the river by heart. To give an idea of the section that was coming up, a long, straight section, he let out, in a drawn-out falsetto, the word "eeecccceeeeeeeeeeeúp," punctuated by slamming one palm into the other. It ended at the mouth of a creek called Igarapé Morto, he said, where many years ago a man had died. Peruano preferred to take the river by starlight. No wind, no sun, no *pium.*

The mornings usually passed with little incident. Once we got out and checked an old *tapiri,* a hut abandoned years before by some Brazil-nut gatherers. Peruano was looking for *cuilha* fruit, whose husk is used for bowls; but the only plant of interest we discovered was an exquisite carmine wild lily which he said was called *burababa do mato.* Another time I looked up at the thin white track a jet plane was making across the sky. It was probably the Tuesday night flight from Rio to Miami. They're probably unwrapping the cellophane from their styrofoam trays and digging into their filet mignon, I thought to myself. I felt very far in time from that plane. Forty thousand feet overhead, and getting farther with each stroke of the paddle. While Maria amused herself behind me, singing snatches from the radio, talking to herself, and painting her toenails, I made up verses of my own:

The point is not how long you live.
Time is only relative.

One morning we discovered that Maria's two new dresses, which Didi had made for her on her sewing machine with flower-printed cloth bought from a river merchant, had fallen out of the canoe. We turned around and paddled quickly back to the beach where it must have happened. The dresses were not there. The river had carried them off. Peruano cursed Maria for her carelessness and she wept, sobbing softly and steadily with her head in her hands. We headed back upstream, having lost two hours. Morale was not good. "Here are 200 cruzeiros for new dresses," I said to Maria. "My Christmas present."

About 11:30 we would pull into one of the creeks and rest for several hours. The sun was too strong on the water. The creeks were usually choked with small fish and catching them was simply a matter of throwing the harpoon in their midst, with a fifty percent chance of success, or of baiting a hook with the small green winged berry of a *camapou* shrub, or with a slice of fish itself. Maria would get the fire going and lash three branches together with strips of bark into a pyramid, inside which there were two tiers. Peruano would clean the fish on his paddle and hand them to Maria, and she would lay them on the tiers to smoke. The fish were pan-sized, disc-shaped, and elongated. Some were *acara, traira, tucunaré, jacuanda* (also known as the *peixe sabão* or soapfish because it is so slippery), *acarãoaçu,* and *araçu.* But most were piranha: *piranha pacu, piranha sidaua* (the least dangerous type, sometimes called *piranzinha) piranha folha, piranha muura, piranha cajú, piranha cocama, piranha preta.* They were bony but not bad. Peruano said that the Catrimani was not safe for swimming, not only because of the piranha, but because of the *candiru* and the *piraibás.* He also warned about putting my foot in the water before I had carefully checked it out. Once I placed my foot in a creek and it was attacked by dozens of three-inch *madín* catfish. They wanted to eat me but did not have well-developed teeth. Another time, I tried my hand with the harpoon. Two yard-long, opal-green *aruana* were doubling back and forth in and out of amber sunspots at the mouth of a creek. But they were too fast and cagey. Long before the harpoon reached the water they had darted out of the way. Along the water's edge several *traira* were sleeping like logs. I could have caught them with my hands, but behind them, in the shadow of an overhanging bush, the four-foot form of a *pouraquê,* electric fish, rippled sluggishly.

On Christmas Eve we kept paddling until after dark. Peruano wanted to spend the night at the house of his friend Eugenio. About an hour away we saw a bonfire crackling on the shore of a lake to the right and made for it. There were Eugenio and his family, spit-roasting a great catfish called a *jandia,* the preferred fish of the territory. There were greetings and hugs. The fish was divided, seasoned with lemon and pimento, placed in *cuilha* bowls, and passed around. It was superb. Then we all got in our canoes and, shivering the glassy water with our paddles, glided along in the moonlight to Eugenio's *roça*. Neck to neck in their separate canoes, Peruano and Eugenio talked about the price of things.

P. If I was rich, I'd buy a new *motor* for seventeen thousand.

E. What make?

P. I heard on the radio that gas has gone up 100 percent.

E. Outrageous, the prices of the river merchants.

P. *Cuidada pau.* (watch out for the snag).

Eugenio's smile, I discovered the next morning, was beautiful, bristling with pride and crazy humor. The eyes laughed, the upper lip curled to reveal both corners of the mouth and the lower teeth while keeping the upper ones covered. The teeth were splendid; he brushed religiously. "I am a hundred percent pure undiluted Amazonian *caboclo,*" he told me. "I have no money but a lot of credit." Eugenio was about fifty. Five years before he had been collecting Brazil nuts when he had seen this place and decided to live there. "In the federal territory of Roraima," he explained, "you just move in and start living and the land is yours." He and Carolina, his wife of twenty-seven years, had done just that. "In five years, when the soil gives out, I will move back to Manaus where I am from." He was also concerned for his wife, who had diabetes and had recently had a serious operation in Boa Vista. They had lost their first child at birth and there had been none since. But a boy named Francisco lived with them. He was the son of an old man who had died in the house two years before and was buried with a wooden cross in the garden. "Nobody knows how old he is, but we figure he's about seven because he's losing his teeth." Sensing he was being talked about, Francisco looked up and grinned. He was sitting on the front stoop, splitting and bending the sides of a matchbox into the shape of a bird. *"Ninguem ensinou. Ele sabe,"* Eugenio said. "No one taught him that. He knows." Francisco came up and gave me the matchbox bird, saying it was a *bemtevi*.

Francisco was too young to be much help on the *roça*, and Carolina too weak to do much more than keep house, so Eugenio had imported Raimundo, a seventeen-year-old from Manaus, to help out. Raimundo had gone off fishing early in the morning and hadn't been back since. He returned about noon with his straw hat, torn shirt and jeans, bare feet, shotgun over his shoulder, and a string of fish in the other hand, looking like Huck Finn. "I saw this thing in the lake," he told us excitedly, "swerving back and forth under the water, and thinking it was a fish was about to pitch my harpoon when the head and then the whole body of a *sucurijú* (anaconda)

155

surfaced. It must have been twenty feet long." Eugenio laughed and showed me a scar on his right thumb where he had been bitten by a fourteen-palm anaconda. "The biggest *sucurijú* I ever saw was thirty-five palms," he said. We walked to a lemon-orange tree that stood in the front yard dripping with fruit, some golden ripe and some green. Eugenio selected from the pile of harpoons, paddles, shovels, axes, and mattocks that had been propped against the tree a long harpoon and coaxed several lemon-oranges to the ground. Squeezing them into our glasses of *cachaça* we sat on the bank and watched the green river gliding. It seemed to be going in two directions, upstream in the foreground, and downstream along the far bank. "There are gold and crystals in the river," Eugenio said. From inside the house we could hear Peruano snoring in his hammock, and across the river, about a mile away, *guaribas* (howler monkeys) roaring. "The *touchaua* (the leader) is growling. He must be upset about something."

Eugenio's income was mainly from *farinha,* and he spent most of his time pressing, grating, and roasting manioc roots. The river merchants paid him eighty cruzeiros for each forty-liter *paneira* or basket of *farinha,* and three months out of the year, when the crop was full, he could produce a hundred *paneiras* a month with his gas-powered grater. This income—24,000 cruzeiros, or about two thousand dollars, a year—enabled him to buy from the river merchant the goods he needed, with some left over for outstanding expenses like his wife's operation and trip to Boa Vista. In terms of food he was completely self-sufficient—manioc, bananas, citrus, pineapples, papaws, sugar cane, and cashews. *Inga* and *mari (Poraqueiba sericea)* trees (with edible fruit) grew in his *roça*. He had sixty chickens, and the fish and wild game—pigs, tapirs, and monkeys—were plentiful. From manioc he made his own glue, called *gomma da maça de mandioca,* and dry, white pellets of *tapioca.* He also had a charcoal pit and a press like an old hand-turned washing machine for squeezing juice out of cane stalks; it was only a few steps further (which he had not yet taken) to brewing one's own *cachaça.* Eugenio handed me a cashew fruit. The pulp was warm and sweet. *Gustoso,* I ejaculated—delicious. Then I made the big mistake of biting into the husk of the nut, which is highly toxic. My mouth was excoriated as if by acid. Cashew nuts must be roasted and shelled before they are edible. The taste of the raw husk stayed with me for the rest of the day.

After Peruano revived from his siesta the three of us played "31," a *caboclo* version of "21." The values of the cards reflected the male chauvinism of the region. The jack was worth more than the queen "because he is a man," Eugenio explained. "In Amazonia, the woman is dominated by the man. A woman must obey her husband. A married woman who runs around with another man is worth nothing." Carolina said nothing to this, but went on preparing supper. As we played cards in her immaculate kitchen, Francisco and Maria sat on the stoop, playing a game that consisted of naming all the animals they could think of. I heard the name of *tamandua,* the giant anteater, who is said to be able to kill a jaguar by crushing it in his arms; and of *tatú,* the nine-banded armadillo. After the card game was over I picked up the guitar and extemporized a song about our journey:

Vamos pelo Catrimani	Let's go on the Catrimani
À casa de Peruano	To the house of Peruano
Cinco dias mais andando	Five more days' journey
Para chegar à missão	To reach the mission
Oito dias remando	Eight days of paddling
Àte a cachoeira	Until the cataract
Là commence a terra	There begins the land
dos Indios Aika	Of the Aika Indians
Andando na praia	Walking along the sand bar
Cuidade araia	Watch out for the stingray
Là teng muito capybara	There are many capybara
Caindo na agua	Falling into the water
À noite Maria faz fogo	At night Maria makes a fire
E nos tomamos ovos	And we eat eggs
Oito dias remando	Eight days of paddling
Bunda doente	Buttocks aching
Contra a corrente	Against the current

Without warning, Maria began to dance in the dooryard, raising one foot, then snapping her torso down in time with the beat, her face lost in hair, her hands outspread. Although gourd-shaped and no more than four feet tall, she moved with the wild grace of a cat. After this letting go, we were fast friends.

That night I fell asleep in my hammock to the travels of Richard Spruce. Spruce is as rich as Thoreau, and I could not digest more than ten pages of him at a time. The last sentence I remembered was: "You who go of nights to geographical societies' meetings and other long-faced reunions, will perhaps despise our mode of passing the time."

On the morning of December 26 we left Boa Ilha, as Eugenio's *roça* was appropriately called. We had ahead of us three days of steady paddling before we reached any beaches—the hard, straight middle part. Peruano's back was killing him, and he was becoming short-tempered. He did not look well. "I look older than fifty," he admitted, "because I have had a lot of sickness and not much sleep." In places the current was so strong that we paddled furiously, barely advancing. Going upstream, he cursed, was *ruim,* ruinous. We passed two abandoned *roças* whose owners had left the year before. Late in the morning we called at the house of the only other people still on the river besides Eugenio, Peruano, and the Indians. The house had a roof of *inajà* palm and no walls. Inside a black woman and two children were eating *batatas.* A *tipiti,* used for expressing the prussic acid from manioc roots, hung from the ceiling. It was invented by the Indians, and its principle was that of the Mexican finger-snapper: the harder you pulled, the tighter the woven straw cylinder closed around the object placed inside. The house, less than half-constructed, was not well kept. The baby was crying. It was not a happy household. The woman's man had left her, Peruano explained later. She lived here along with her father, who was hunting. In the garden was a grave with a wooden cross, as at Eugenio's, and several bird traps, called *rapacas,* consisting of woven tiers of sticks propped up with another stick, had been placed in strategic locations. The woman handed us some slabs of wild pork that had been drying in the sun. *"Queixada,"* Peruano exclaimed, "the best meat there is." She brewed a delicious tea from a lemon-scented cespitose grass called *capim santo,* and we drank it gratefully.

That afternoon we entered São Sebastião, a long, straight trench fifty *braços* (armlengths) deep, according to Peruano. "In the *inverno,"* he said, "the water comes through so fast you can't get up it in a canoe. This is where the *cobra grande* lives." The *cobra grande* is a monster in Amazonian folklore which eats people, sinks canoes, and gets to be a hundred feet long. "I have never seen the *cobra grande,"* Peruano said, "but I have heard people who say they have seen it. They say it has *azulado* eyes, the color of fireflies." I asked him what other creatures there were to worry about, and he told me about *Mapinguari,* the giant cyclops, who lives in the *centro,* the deepest part of the forest. His footprint is as large as an upside-down *pinguari* (sloth). Peruano hadn't seen the Amazonian big-foot, either, but he believed firmly in his existence.

Shortly after passing Igarapé Putada (Whore's Creek), so named because three women had set up a house there in the days of the rubber boom, we heard the *tok-tok* and snorting of a large herd of wild pigs on the right bank. Peruano beached the canoe, grabbed his shotgun, and went to investigate. Maria and I followed. Crawling on our bellies into a bramble thicket, we were soon covered with mud and sweat. Palm thorns pierced our palms, and thorny vines tore the flesh of our backs. Ahead, Peruano, with the stealth of a jaguar, was sneaking up to the *queixada,* who were stomping, grunting, and making *tok* sounds and other noises whose rise and fall in intonation were almost human as they ate the fallen fruit of the *cocadioari* palm. There were about ninety pigs in the herd; "it was *black* with pigs," Peruano was later to report. He got to within fifteen feet of them, raised his rifle, and drew a bead on one of the pigs. Maria and I climbed trees in case the animals came our way; *queixada* stampedes are a not uncommon cause of death to hunters in the Amazon. Peruano squeezed the trigger. Misfire. The loud click alerted the *queixada* to his presence, and they bolted with a thunder of hoofs and a frenzy of squealing in the opposite direction. Peruano had had it for the day. We camped then and there, even though there was still a good hour of daylight. To add insult to injury, his hammock had fallen into the water.

Gradually I got into the rhythm of it, and when I was finally able to match Peruano stroke for stroke, one every three seconds, for twelve hours a day, we began to move much faster. Toward the end of the trip I was even able to converse while paddling. Most of my questions were about the Indians I was soon to meet. Peruano had first met the Aika on the Agua Boa in 1948, when he was tapping rubber. They numbered about 200. But in the late fifties, when a "portion" of them, including Touchaua João, the chief, died of flu introduced by a *caboclo* living among them, they moved to the Catrimani. In 1960, Peruano came up the river with an Italian missionary, Padre Jean Caleri, who wanted to found a mission for the Indians of the upper Catrimani. He met the Aika again; at that time Maria's mother was pregnant with her. Peruano lived with Caleri for three years at Cujubim Falls, helping him clear an airstrip and put in a *roça*. In 1969, Caleri left the Catrimani and went up the Rio Alalalu to contact the Waimiri-Atroares, who killed him and twelve of his thirteen companions. "They killed Padre Jean Caleri for his plate," Peruano related in disgust. "He said I can't give it to you because it's the only plate I have. *O indio é bichu, ne?* The Indian is a beast, no?"

Peruano had heard that shortly after the massacre, two airplanes of FABE, the Brazilian Air Force, flew over the villages of the Waimiri-Atroaris and dropped bombs on them. I had heard a simi-

lar story in Brasília about the dropping of napalm on their villages, which President Ismarth of FUNAI had dismissed as ridicu-
lous. On the upper Catrimani Padre Jean Caleri had treated the Indians as equals. He would call them in when it was time to eat, and
serve them coffee. His successor, Padre Giovanni Saffirio, didn't give
them food or clothes, which they wanted because of the *pium,* but
only medicine, machetes, and axes. The Jauari, Pouari, and Parahori
Indians lived at the mission, but they didn't like the new padre because he made them work hard. The Parahori were not acculturated, but were friendly, and the sixty or so Jauari were *"brutes."* The
Aika, with whom he began to live after leaving the mission, were
"civilized, and they have learned respect for people." Three families
lived with Peruano at Castanha Creek, another thirty or so lived up
on a mountain six hours away, and there were three more families
on the Pacú River, a tributary of the Catrimani, five days from
Peruano's house. They got together for festivals. Whenever a monkey or a deer was killed they inhaled a hallucinogenic snuff made
from the powdered bark of a tree. "É pinga deles," Peruano explained. "It's their *cachaça.*" They all lived together in a big round
house called a *malocca* with a high ceiling that sloped up toward
an opening in the center. They were a light-hearted people who
would lie in their hammocks and tell jokes all night long. Maybe
one of them would stand in the center and do a dance or tell a
story, and everyone would listen. "They will like you," Peruano said.
"It will be the first time they have heard a guitar." There was an
American who came up the river two years ago. He was working for
FUNAI, distributing medicine to the Indians. Then there was a
German padre who stayed here in the early 1960s, but nobody
liked him and he left." I was, it seemed, the third *estrangero* to have
come up the Catrimani in recent times.

Thursday, December 30. Peruano outlined the day's *igarapés*
and trenches, tracing with a meandering finger the course of the
river: *"Marara* aieeee *Caju* aieee *Mutum* aieee *Taboka* aieee
Tabatinga aieee *Castanha.*" *Taboka* was a new cut through about
fifty feet of land, shortening the river by about a mile and cutting off
an oxbow. About 150 feet wide, the water rushed through it, although some continued along the old course, the long way around
what was now an island. *Taboka* means the bamboo from which
large projectile points, used to penetrate the hides of wild pigs and
tapirs, are made. It took five minutes of furious paddling to ascend
Taboka. The river was swollen with yesterday's rain. It had fallen in
big hot pellets, enveloping us in its deafening noise. The birds had

taken refuge, and we had thrown wild banana leaves over the cargo. But now the river was like glass as we passed Tabatinga, a small red clay beach. After eight days our feet burned from the constant exposure to sun, water, and sand. The spaces between Peruano's toes were red and raw. But now the end was in sight. With his *casa* just a few bends away Peruano broke out his bottle of *cachaça* again. At two p.m., the weary paddlers reached Castanha Creek. Peruano let out a whoop as his hut came into view, and three Aika men came running to the bank. And when the paddle had been placed in the water for the last time and we stepped ashore, I shook Peruano's hand heartily, as I would that of a mountain guide who had brought me to the top of an alpine peak.

11

Out of Time

"You know," Peruano was saying, "I don't think I'll be going to the mission right away, as I had planned. In fact I don't think I'll be going anywhere for a while. My back hurts and I want to plant some manioc. We're almost out of *farinha.*" We were swinging in hammocks in the main room of Peruano's elevated hut. He had distributed presents—shorts, *cachaça,* and a handful of shotgun shells—to his three hunters, and we were all chewing on slivers of dried wild pork and listening to the radio. Their names—the ones, that is, Peruano had given them—were Ruby, Manoel, and Pedrinho. Peruano and I were *napeu,* strangers, while they and Maria were *Xirima,* fellow Indians. Ruby, Manoel, and Pedrinho were their *napeu* names.

I had seen this coming and controlled myself. "Well, when do you think you might be going to the mission?"

"Oh, *amanha,*" he said. One of the most important words in the Amazonian vocabulary, *amanha* literally means tomorrow, but it could be anywhere between tomorrow and next year.

"Do you think you could be a little more specific? I mean, when do you really think you might be heading for the mission?"

"Oh, two, three months."

I was still in control. "You know if I don't get back pretty soon, the people in America are going to start worrying about me." Peruano remarked that he didn't see how, if America was four years off by canoe as I had been telling him, two or three months were going to make that much difference. I just couldn't get him to understand my sense of urgency, and I sensed, besides, that my haste was in bad taste, as far as he was concerned. I should stay awhile and enjoy his hospitality. But I found Castanha Creek physically depressing in the extreme. With Maria gone downstream, the house and yard hadn't been swept in over a month. They were infested with enormous cockroaches and pervaded with the smell of rotten meat. All the pineapples and papayas that Peruano had promised were in his *roça* had been eaten by Ruby, Manoel, and Pedrinho. There was no *farinha;* only flat, brittle, white cakes of manioc flour called *beiju* by the *caboclos* and *nashi-kika* by the Aika, were baking in the sun.

"Well how am I going to get out of here?" I blurted at last.

"Maybe the boys will take you." By land, over the Serra Tabatinga, it was seven days to the mission.

"Won't you come with me?"

"No, it's too far for me to walk," Peruano said. "Give them something, and they will be happy to take you." I opened my pack and extracted a few items. Manoel examined carefully the shorts I handed him, discovered a hole in the crotch, and passed them back without a word. He was about eighteen, over six feet tall, with immense feet and a bowl-shaped haircut. A few curly black hairs had sprouted around his mouth. His father, also Manoel, had been chief after Touchaua João, but he, too, had died a few years before of a mysterious fever. Manoel's older brother, Chagas, was the acting chief. The role of the *touchaua* was not to tell anyone what to do; all decisions were group decisions, and the Aika, who were often scattered for weeks at a time on hunting treks, put a high value on their personal freedom. The role of the *touchaua,* rather, was to be a good orator and to have a deep knowledge of Aika culture.

Manoel wanted my flashlight. Ruby took my new machete and case, and Pedrinho settled for a shortsleeved shirt. Both Ruby and Pedrinho were orphans; their families had been wiped out by the same fever. Ruby's only relative was an aunt. He was a puckish-looking seventeen-year-old who spoke about as much Portuguese as I did. Earlier in the afternoon I had watched him skinning a *maracajá,* an ocelot he had shot that morning. His eyes had a flat, unresponsive quality that was scary. Pedrinho was completely different from the coldly pragmatic Ruby; very gentle, even effeminate, he spoke with a high falsetto and was not very effective as a hunter. He had been brought up by his mother; perhaps that explained his feyness. Manoel, Ruby, and Pedrinho were unmarried, which was not normal for Indians in their late teens. But there were no women of their age left in the village for them to marry. "We have no *wamani,*" Manoel said. *Wamani* were women. The convergence of two totally different languages upon the same sound for the same idea was uncanny. "Where are you going to find some *wamani?*" I asked.

"Nobody knows," he said.

The payment negotiated, Peruano gave them instructions. "Him you don't kill. He is a very important person, and if you kill him the planes will come and drop bombs on you, just as they did on the Indians who killed Padre Jean Caleri. I want you to take him as far as Pacú. The Indians there will take him to the mission." Peruano did not want them to go to the mission. My earlier impression, that Peruano and the present padre did not get along, was confirmed. He had probably had no intention of taking me to the mission in the first place.

The boys had never been exposed to a tape recorder, and I astounded them that night by playing back to them the songs they had sung for me and the animal sounds they had imitated. They were superb mimics. They had to be. At night when they hunted along the river they called the jaguars within range with a sharp nasal "hnnn ... hnnn ... hnnn." I recorded twelve animal imitations, three deep bass chants, and three of Maria's breathless work songs for passing the time while sewing or grating manioc.

In the morning the four of us set out through fifteen-foot-tall grass. My three guides' lower lips bulged with rolled-up cylinders of tobacco leaf. Manoel carried with a headstrap a basket containing *farinha,* two of my nylon bags, and the guitar, with a loaded shotgun over his shoulder. Ruby carried a shotgun, too, and my rucksack upside down, using the waist belt as a head strap; he refused to pin back his arms with straps. I carried a sidebag full of notebooks, photo and recording equipment. Pedrinho carried a cooking pot and a bunch of plantains. Peruano clasped my hand warmly and asked me once more to stay longer. With an enchanting smile Maria squeezed my hand, and I kissed hers. They sat on the stoop of their house on the high bluff overlooking the river and watched us disappear into the forest. Soon we emerged on a savannah, a sandy grassland sparsely flecked with low, twisted trees. On the far horizon, perhaps fifty miles away, stood the jagged crags of the Serra Tabatinga, clearly of volcanic origin, the tallest one a perfect isosceles triangle. Under the mountain was the *malocca.* "How far is it to the *malocca?*" I asked. Pedrinho held his hand out to where the sun would be at five o'clock.

The trail across the savannah was a thin white line only six inches wide, about the width of a *saúba* ant trail. The reason for this is that the Indians put one foot directly in front of the other. Moving at a trot, grabbing the ground with their spread toes, with no wasted lateral motion, they covered forty miles a day. In the jungle, as they slipped between vines and branches along a dim path that was often invisible to me, their sense of balance was uncanny. It is the same habit of putting one foot directly in front of the other that gives the Mohawk Indian steelworkers, as Edward Wilson observed, their extraordinary equilibrium. I was repeatedly strangled by the vines, many of which had barbs at thoughtful intervals, and tripped by the roots. By the time I had gotten up again the Indians had disappeared, and I couldn't see the path. I would have to coo like a dove until they returned the call, then echolocate them. They would be standing impatiently with hands on their hips; anyone so clumsy as I would have perished long ago in their world. And the people back home had always complained that I walked too fast.

At the other end of the savannah we entered the forest and began to climb into the serra, passing old *tapiris,* lean-tos. Pedrinho picked yellow *okwashik* berries, which tasted like orange-flavored hard candy. Manoel climbed a cacao tree and plucked some of the soft, spiny, green cauliflorous fruit; the species was different from the one at Menkranoti, but the white flesh was as delicious. Two of us had foot problems. Plunging in and out of creeks in canvas-and-rubber jungle boots I was wearing for the first time, I developed a blister on my right heel. I found my "Nam boots," as they are called—highly touted as the best footgear for slogging around in the rain forest—quite worthless. They were too clumsy and slippery for negotiating single-log bridges, they filled quickly with water and became heavy. I found my leather tennis shoes vastly superior. Manoel, who had no shoes, stepped on one of the black spines of an *Astrocarium* palm that littered the floor. I dug most of it out with a needle, but the tip remained imbedded and made walking increasingly painful for him with each day.

At five that afternoon we reached the *malocca.* It was deserted. Everyone was out at the plantations. It was a magnificent structure of palm fronds woven on a skeleton of poles, maybe fifty yards in diameter and forty feet high at the center. It had begun with each family weaving a shelter for themselves along the edge of a circle until the shelters had grown together into a great dome like a beehive with a small opening at the center to let out smoke and a door, five feet high, at each major point of the compass. Eight men, six women, and six children—all that were left of the Aika—lived in it together. Each family had its own territory, shaped like a slice of pie, with its own fire and posts for hanging hammocks, food, and possessions. Two jaguar hides, for trade to Peruano, were stretching to dry on taut strings; around a few of the fires were metal pots acquired from him, the only visible foreign artifacts. Manoel swarmed one of the high center posts, brought down the bamboo cylinder in which he kept his prized feather collection, took out several two-and-a-half-foot long flaming *arara* feathers, and stroked them lovingly. Pedrinho built a fire and placed several plantains to roast in it. Ruby took out the shotgun shells from his home-made rubber pouch (he had extracted the latex from a tree, cooked it, and moulded it into a pouch) that he wore around his waist, and placed them near the fire to dry. One of the cartridges went off, and he quickly gathered up the rest.

After dark, in the full moonlight, the Aika returned. The men were tall, with gleaming teeth, bowl-shaped haircuts, and low-slung buttocks. They wore strands of small white beads around their necks and upper arms, and carried eight-foot bows and arrows. Their foreskins were tucked under a waist-string. The women were shy and short and wore fiber mini-skirts. The children had clusters of toucan feathers in their earlobes and around their upper arms. One girl carried a pet *cayarara* monkey over her shoulders. Five emaciated dogs completed the entourage.

Chagas, Manoel's older brother, greeted me warmly. I felt an immediate kinship with him although his Portuguese was almost nonexistent. After a long struggle for words he managed to communicate that the population of the Aika had been 120 only three years before; everyone had died of *febre,* fever. He called for his wife to come over, and I placed a hand on her forehead. She was definitely running a fever. But what it was she had—malaria, flu, or tuberculosis—I had no way of knowing; I could only give her veganin. With my lack of medical training, I felt angry and helpless. Here were gentle, fine-looking people dying like flies, and they didn't even know what was wiping them out. "But you Indians have good medicine," I said. "You know the plants and have the cure for everything."

"No *senhor,*" Chagas said sadly. "If a Xirima has the *febre,* he dies. We have no medicine for the *febre.*" Later at the mission I would learn that Peruano had tuberculosis. Unknown to the Aika, and probably to himself, it was probably he who was responsible for the deaths of a hundred of the Indians who regarded him as their benefactor.

It was New Year's Eve and I was determined to have a good time, even if my companions didn't appreciate the occasion. I imagined my friends on the next continent raising their glasses to me, wherever I was, and suddenly felt very alone. I started playing the guitar. The men gathered round and started singing along, following my lips and adlibbing the words a split-second after they came out of my mouth. I sang "If I Could Put Time in a Bottle" by the late Jim Croce. They were such good mimics that it seemed as if I was with a group of friends who knew the song by heart. I asked Chagas if there had ever been an *estrangero* in the *malocca,* and he said no; neither Peruano nor the padre had ever been here, although he and the other Aika had been many times to the mission and to Peruano's.

In the morning Chagas showed me his garden. He had planted banana, manioc, *macaxeira* (sweet manioc), *cará* (a brown-skinned, purplish yam), *batata* (sweet potato), *mamão* (pawpaw), *girimum* (squash), tobacco, sugar cane, *umambi (Clibadium,* a fish poison from the daisy family), *abacaxi* (pineapple), and *coroa* (unidentified). The Aika plantations were much less elaborate than the ones at Menkranoti; the Aika, I read later in the *Handbook of South American Indians,* had progressed little beyond the hunting and gathering stage. The work habits of such a people are more sporadic than those of agriculturists, who put in a certain amount of work each day. The hunter-gatherer will mount a tremendous effort for twenty-four hours at a time, resulting in the killing of, say, a wild pig or a tapir. Then he will do nothing for a few days but eat and rest up for the next expedition. It is for this reason that the Yaguas, for instance, forest hunter-gatherers who have moved to the main river near Leticia, Colombia, are incapable of steady work and are considered lazy by the *caboclos,* while the riverine-agricultural Ticunas get the jobs. Today, for the Aika, was a day of rest. I spent the morning visiting with the different family groups. One old man, sitting in a vine hammock, was making twine, rolling together two separate strands of fiber made from a terrestrial bromeliad called *uyama,* back and forth across the top of his thigh, then, with a final snap of the wrist, finishing off another foot-long section. The maneuver was deceptively simple. I watched him do it over and over, but never fully understood how it resulted in the manufacture of twine strong enough to be used as a bowstring. The old man was blind in one eye, and his cheek was wet with the fluid that streamed down from the useless organ. Probably onchocerciasis, African river blindness, in which a microfilarium injected by the bite of a black fly multiplies in the bloodstream. A certain number migrate to the eye, where they die, causing blindness. Many of the forest Indians in Roraima and southern Venezuela have it. It is being studied by INPA scientists in the Yanomamo village of Tototobi. Three species of black fly have been identified as possible vectors. The disease is also found in Panama, Mexico, and Guatemala. The only known treatment is an expensive French drug whose side effects are sometimes fatal.

That afternoon a man named Leonça returned from a solitary sojourn in the forest. One of the most respected shamans in the region, he was about forty, with the wide-open face of a child and the perfectly toned body of a dancer. Leonça laid down the bow and arrows that dwarfed him by a foot and pulled the pigskin cover from his quiver, a bamboo cylinder about a foot and a half long and decorated down the sides with wavering lines. The seal was airtight and a loud pop ensued. Inside were three kinds of arrow points: the broad bamboo tip for killing pigs and tapirs, a barbed monkey-bone tip for killing *mutum* and other birds, and a straight wooden needlelike point for killing monkeys. The needlelike points were coated with the powdered resin of a tree whose active ingredient, triptamine (dmt), makes the monkey, after he has been shot, relax his muscles, release the branch he is gripping, and fall to the ground. Leonça took out several of the points and began to rub them against each other over a banana leaf until a small pile of reddish-brown powder had collected beneath them. He raised the powder to his nose and snorted it, four times into each nostril. Then he retired to his hammock. Fifteen minutes later he got up and started to chant, then spat, and moaned, and danced with great sweeping movements of his arms and imploring looks to the sky. The chanting was in a beautiful minor key like a spiritual. Long strings of strange syllables cascaded from his mouth. "Only he knows what he's saying," Ruby told me.

Washaharua, as the Aika called the snuff, was taken only by the men and particularly by the shamans. "It puts you in *um outro mundo* (in another world)," as Ruby put it. "You see anacondas swimming across the sky and jaguar eyes gleaming through the foliage." Death or illness is never accidental, the Aika believe, but caused by an evil spirit cast by some malevolent spirit or human enemy. To find out who the guilty party is, the shaman inhales *washaharua,* which puts him in another world.

The Aika also believe that each person has a *rishi* or alter ego—perhaps a hawk, a jaguar, a tortoise, or a rock—living an existence parallel to his own. Leonça's *rishi* was a hawk, which explained the flapping motions of his dance. After he had come down from his trance, I presented him with my Caldor's T-shirt and underpants, and he reciprocated with a necklace, whose white beads had been woven with wondrous subtlety in a pattern of 2-1-2-1. Ruby and Manoel explained that they were heading for the mission and talked him into coming along. Pedrinho, who was not up for a ten-day trek, would stay. We left immediately. Leonça soon demonstrated his prowess with the bow and arrow. Hearing the lowing of a *mutum* (curassow) in a group of trees he chose an arrow, threaded it, and moved toward the sound quickly, soundlessly, with long strides at a half-crouch and, before the bird had noticed that he was upon him, let fly. Plump black curassow, shot through the neck, and arrow fell to the ground. Later he shot a big fish called a *taida* in a clear stream, aiming well below to compensate for the refraction. Fetching the fish he found a quartz pebble and gave it to me. Leonça would think nothing of swarming a sixty-foot*warok* *(Pourouma)* tree, and hacking down the delicious blue berries, or of gathering, thirty feet from the ground, a tasty yellow fruit called *maco*. Once he stood below a tree and shot an arrow eighty feet straight into the air, knocking down a *jacami* (pale-winged trumpeter).

Another time as we sat resting he became fascinated with a column of *saúba* ants. The ants are probably the most abundant insects in Amazonia. They were everywhere. Hardly a branch or a tree had fallen over that the ants hadn't recruited; I had to step over an ant-ramp every fifteen feet, it seemed. The Portuguese called the ants "the king of Brazil," and later travelers referred to them as "the actual owners of the Amazon valley," and "the real conquerors of Brazil." In the tropics ants replace earthworms as the chief movers of earth, while the termites are the chief decomposers of wood. Their social organization, as Edward O. Wilson, the Harvard sociobiologist, points out, is less than man's because of their feeble intellect and absence of culture, but greater in terms of cohesion, caste specialization, and individual altruism. Of the probable number of 12,000 species of ants, 7,600 have been described, and many of them inhabit the Amazon. A close relative of the African driver ant, who will eat big mammals but moves only one meter every three minutes, is the *soldado* or army ant, *Eciton burchelli*. They are "swarm raiders," as opposed to other species, which are "column raiders"; in other words the foraging workers spread out in a fan-shaped swarm with a broad front. Their huge sorties bring disaster to practically all animal life in their path—tarantulas, scorpions, beetles, roaches, grasshoppers, snakes, lizards, and birds. They cannot, however, bring down vertebrate prey. At night the *soldados* bivouac between root buttresses or beneath a fallen trunk, linking their legs and bodies with strong tarsal claws,

> "forming chains and nets of their own bodies that accumulate layer upon interlocking layer until finally the entire worker force comprises a solid cylindrical or ellipsoidal mass up to a meter across. About 150,000 to 700,000 workers are present. Toward the center of the mass are found thousands of immature forms, a single mother queen, and, for a brief interval in the dry season, a thousand or so males and several virgin queens. The entire dark-brown conglomerate exudes a musky, somewhat fetid odor. [At dawn] when the light level around the ants exceeds .05 foot candle power, the bivouac begins to dissolve. A raiding column grows away from the bivouac at 20 miles per hour."

But the most common species of ant in the Amazon is the *saúba* (genus *Attini,* also known as *portadores, carregadores,* porter ants, and leaf-cutters). With his profound intuitive understanding Leonça recognized their ecological dominance over the land, and his attitude, as he squatted over the busy column, was one of utmost humility. "Look at these ants," he exclaimed. Thousands of them were hurrying back and forth along a long, clean, four-inch-wide highway they had cleared in the leaf litter. Some were coming down from a big tree carrying shredded leaf flakes many times their size to a mound of red earth several yards high and maybe thirty yards in circumference. Others were returning from the mound and going back up the tree. "They have their own roads," Leonça laughed. "Maybe they will take you to Boa Vista."

The *saúbas* excavate deep galleries and shafts into the soil, sometimes six meters or more. Henry Walter Bates suggested that the ants used the leaves "to thatch the domes which cover the entrances to their subterranean dwellings, thereby protecting from the deluging rains the young broods in the nests beneath." It is now known that the shredded leaves are used as mulch to grow a certain fungus that is the food of the ant larvae. "Different species," Wilson explains, "grow different species of fungus on a substrate of corpses of other anthropods, chiefly ants, insect feces, pieces of fruit, caterpillar feces, insect corpses, fragments of dead wood, fresh leaves, stems, and flowers."

The first night we ate Leonça's *mutum,* the *taida,* and the *warok* berries. The next night it was *jaboti* tortoise. Ruby ripped off the animal's plastron. The heart was still jumping. The tortoise was still alive, but the idea that it might have been in pain was not something that would have occurred to Ruby, conditioned since childbirth to ignore pain in himself. While I could feel through Leonça's gentle radiance his sense of oneness with all the living things around him, Ruby seemed remarkably lacking in compassion. He poked the tortoise's penis, almost human in length and form, and laughed cruelly. The night after that it was *jacaretinga*. Ruby hacked off the small alligator's tail and put it on the fire. The tail twitched and thrashed in the flames, though disengaged from the reptile's body. "God," I thought to myself, "I can't eat any more of these animals." I asked Ruby if there was anything the Aika didn't eat. "We don't eat deer, black panther, or jaguar," he said, "because they are sacred. The spirits of the dead live in them. We do eat cougar, however."

That night, as I lay in my hammock, I felt as if I had accomplished my mission in coming to the Amazon: I had found in Leonça the natural man I had wanted to meet. I had certainly left my civilization. No one knew where I was, and if anything had happened, they wouldn't have known where to begin looking for me. I was in another, earlier time, where people were still an integral part of nature and not living in an artificial world apart from it. As I swallowed the half-raw flesh of the alligator, I realized I was for the first time experiencing the world in a primeval, wild state, cut off from any of the cultural referents I was familiar with. I picked up my guitar and started singing the words of Bob Dylan's song "Like a Rolling Stone."

An *inambu* (tinamou) was calling in the night, and Leonça identified the low sounds, almost like a purr, of a nearby *queixada*. To the northwest, Ruby said, there was a tribe called the Inambu and beyond them another tribe called the Caxão, who ate people. Our hammocks were stretched like a circle of covered wagons around the protective fire. As I dozed off, the three of them engaged in a rhythmic dialogue called *wayamu,* which lasted for hours. They were not simply conversing, but answering each other in set metric responses. It sounded like a traditional form of storytelling. No one knows enough of the Aika tongue to have learned much about their legends; perhaps epics as grand as Homer's are waiting to be transcribed. At dawn the next morning the Indians rolled tobacco leaves in the ashes of the fire, stuck them under their lower lips, and took off.

Leonça shot at a *jacú* (guan) and missed. The arrow stuck high in a tree and Leonça had to swarm it. His second arrow broke off in the *jacú,* so he took the bird point off the first arrow and threaded it on the second. Now he had only one functioning bird arrow. Ruby plucked one of the *jacú*'s curled crest-feathers and stuck it in a small hole under his lower lip.

We stopped for lunch at a stream. Manoel climbed a *buriti* palm tree and made us a cold, protein-rich soup from the nuts. As we rested he pointed to a tree that looked little different from the others and said that it was the *washaharua* tree. I asked him to show me how *washaharua* was made. He chopped a circle around the base of the tree with his machete and began to pull up, tearing off twenty-foot strips of bark which he cut in three-foot sections. Then he made a fire and held a section over the flames until the blood-red sap bubbled out of the inner bark, and scraped the sap with his finger into the metal pot. He did this with each section until the pot contained a pint or so of sap which he kept boiling down until all the liquid had evaporated and only the rusty-brown crystalline residue remained. This he crushed into a fine powder which we transferred carefully into one of my empty vitamin C cannisters. I collected a specimen of the leaves which was later identified by Dr. William Rodriguez at INPA as *Virola elongata,* sometimes called *Virola theiodora.* The use of *Virola,* of which there are thirty species, as a hallucinogen and arrow poison, is widespread among the Indians of northern Amazonia. The Yano-mamo call it *epena.* The Jauari at the mission, Manoel told me, called it *yecuana,* while other Indians call it *niopo* and *yupa.* The name *washaharua* has never been reported, but it refers to the same tree. Sometimes the *Virola* is mixed with the powdered leaves of the aromatic weedy plant *Justicia pectoralis,* and sometimes it is taken alone internally, which is dangerous as the triptamines and beta-carbolines in *Virola* can be highly toxic. Under its influence the eyes take on a special brilliance. One feels a sense of freedom from time and a desire to scream and move around as the drug has a contracting effect on the lungs. Some Yanomamo men blow the snuff into each other's nostrils by means of a long tube. As they come on to the drug they squat before each other and, clasping each other's shoulders, shout into each other's faces at the top of their lungs. Then they take turns beating each other over the head with clubs, hard enough to send the recipient of the blows reeling, but not enough to kill him. In the exhilaration of his *washaharua* trance the recipient feels little or no pain. The bloody dents in their crowns are a source of such pride that the men keep the tops of their heads shaven to display them. Anthropologists continue to argue whether such ritualized outlets for violence help control outbreaks of violence in the society at large. To judge from what has been written about the Yanomami, the skull-bashing sessions would seem to make little difference. "Close on half of the male population," Thomas Sterling reports, "end their lives violently, most of them in tribal warfare."

We came to an abandoned *tapiri* which Manoel and Ruby had built and lived in for a spell several years before; high above, a band of *coata* monkeys was moving through the trees. Then we emerged on a brown ledge with a view for miles of the treetops and the tip of a very steep peak in the background. It was the first we had seen of the sun in three days, and its brightness hurt our eyes. Leonça found a monkey bone and chipped himself a new bird point. Two huge parrots flew by. We descended again into the dark jungle. It began to rain. We ran through the rain for an hour, and when it stopped we stopped and made camp. "After the rain," Ruby explained, "the snakes come out. *Mordeu, morreu,*" he added. "If you are bitten, you die."

It was two o'clock. My three companions had gone off hunting, as they usually did after we had stopped for the day. I opened the cannister of *washaharua* and snorted a few pinches, then lay back and waited to see what would happen. Was the snuff really hallucinogenic, I wondered, or only eidetic (consciousness-altering)? As the first rush came on I began to feel a great sense of well-being accompanied by vague sexual longings and an ecstatic sense of light and color as the sun sifted down, lighting a leaf here and there, and the blue strands of a great spider web rose and fell and glinted in the soft breeze. The Aika had names for five different kinds of wind. You wouldn't think wind would be so important to people in a forest, but that was just an index of the degree of their awareness, which I could hardly understand. To me the rain forest was still an undifferentiated mass, but to Manoel, Ruby, and Leonça it had dimensions and was imbued with a strong sense of place. Each stream, each slight change in contour, and each big tree were distinctive.

My ruminations were interrupted by an awareness of my unpleasantly clogged and burning nasal passages, of the dryness of my mouth and of a wave of nausea which I quickly alleviated with a few swallows from my canteen. In a nearby tree some small birds were screaming hysterically. A snake was among them. I saw the bright emerald ribbon of the *cobra pópagaio,* Shlegel's tree viper, slipping along the branch toward their nest. The shrieking grew louder and then stopped altogether. At the same time the exaggerated sense of self-importance that the drug had induced was replaced by a feeling of the utter insignificance of my individual being in the face of this seething verdure. I recalled that I was writing a book that would be coming out on another continent, in another tongue, in another time, 'but as a raison d'etre it did not seem very convincing. In the present context my life was no more significant or secure than that of the *carapana* mosquito I was about to crush on my forearm. In a sudden wave of empathy, I shooed the insect away instead of killing it. The only difference between me and the *carapana* was that I had culture. My mind was more evolved, but my senses were atrophied.

I began to feel the stir-craziness which the jungle, with its constant humidity, its apparently monotonous sameness, and its claustrophobic lack of open space, can impose. I hadn't conversed with anyone in my own language or with anyone who understood where I was coming from, in over a month. The cabin-fever and sense of isolation which can easily get to you in the rain forest is well described by Bates. After more than a year in Ega (now Téfé), with only a single issue of *Punch* magazine for company, he found that he had committed to memory even the small print of the advertisements. "I was obliged to conclude, at last," he wrote with marvelous understatement, "that the contemplation of Nature alone is not sufficient to fill the human heart and mind." And the condition of intellectual deprivation, he discovered, worsens instead of deadens with time. I found myself falling into the same pattern. I had wanted to "experience the jungle" as fully as I could, but try as I might, I could never stop the internal monologue, the broken thoughts of a thousand shapes, none of which had anything to do with where I was, that raced through my mind as I struggled to keep up with Ruby, Manoel, and Leonça. My mind was becoming a screen on which incoherent fragments of early childhood and vivid reruns of ancient scandals were being projected, and, as the trip wore on, the trappings of civility became more important than they had ever been for me. Perhaps I fell back on them as a defense against the overwhelming wildness with which I was surrounded. I became obsessed with keeping my fingernails clean and my face shaven, and I lived for the period in the afternoon when the others went hunting and I could curl up in my hammock with my one precious book, Richard Spruce's *The Notes of a Botanist in the*

Amazon and the Andes. It came as a bitter disappointment when I realized that even here, deep in the Amazon, I was a prisoner of my own culture. My notebook during this period reflected my disillusionment: "You realize how everything that streams through your head is learned from the schools you went to, the books you read, the people you associated with, and that it has no bearing on any culture but your own." And "I got news for all you who figure on going native. It can't be done. There will always be a part of you you aren't facing, a part you tried to bury."

Ruby had killed a *caracoro* (whispering ibis) and my eyes were mesmerized by the iridescent black and green feathers and the long, pale green decurved bill. Overhead the heavy wingbeats of an oropendula. Our camp was near a good-sized stream, and the birds like to be near water. Slowly I came back to where I was. The *washaharua* was beginning to wear off. As Ruby squatted beside me, plucking the ibis, I felt the gratitude to find oneself again among the living and the catharsis that often characterize the return from a psychedelic experience. "There — where you live," he was asking — "How many days does it take to get there?"

"Oh, about four years." The figure was gaining credibility with each new recital.

"You live on a big river?"

"When are you coming back to live with us? I want you to bring me a guitar and a watch. . . ."

The next day Manoel left his cooking pot and machete along the path in anticipation of our arrival that afternoon at Pacú, where other Indians would take me to the mission. We came to a small plantation and stopped to gorge ourselves with pawpaws. Several bushes of *urucú, Bixa orellana,* were in fruit with both red and green pods. The bright orange berries within are both edible and good as body paint. Manoel slipped a few pods into his pack basket. Further along Leonça shot a *cujubim,* a black guan with a blue face and golden-red crest feathers. It was a blustery clear day like the northeastern fall, the air having been cleared of moisture the day before. Manoel plucked a small feather, black on one side of the shaft, white on the other, from the guan's shoulder and stuck it into his pierced earlobe. We were nearing the top of a rise on the other side of which I could feel there was something exciting. It was the Pacú River, a torrent about fifty yards wide racing through enormous smooth black boulders glistening with spray, some covered with moss and podostemons, others with islands of fantastic foliage. A rickety one-log bridge with a handrail, the only way across during the wet season, spanned the river at the narrowest place. For the first time in days we washed our filthy, sweat-soaked clothes, slapping them against the rocks, and sunbathed as they dried. The biggest butterfly I had ever seen, light brown with dark stripes, much larger than a morpho, with a wingspan of nine inches, came winging down the riverbed, riding the wind. I think it was a *Brassolidae*. After half an hour Ruby, Manoel, and Leonça prepared new *banhus,* as the wads of tobacco were called, and set out at their merciless pace. Reeling with exhaustion—I had been up all night with diarrhea from *warok* berries—I ran behind like a drunkard. Suddenly Leonça froze. A two-and-a-half-foot *jararaca,* fer-de-lance, lay in the path. The most common venomous snake in Amazonia, the *jararaca* (genus *Bothrops,* six species) injects an extraordinary amount of yellow venom and is responsible for most of the deaths by snakebite in the region. It has a reputation for being extremely mean-tempered, but this snake was not living up to it. Perhaps it had just eaten. In any case it was totally lethargic and made no sign of resistance as Leonça picked it up gently with the tip of his arrow, placed it to the side of the path, and we went on our way. This was the only venomous snake I encountered during eight months. The reputation the rain forest has for dripping with snakes is, I think, like the aggression of the snakes themselves, greatly exaggerated. As Theodore Roosevelt points out, "If vipers and rattlesnakes had such a disposition for offence as is usually supposed, the human race could not have resisted in some parts of America." The Amazon is quite safe, I discovered, as long as you don't cross some predator-prey chain, and the animal erects defenses that were developed thousands of years before humans trod in their path. "In the poisonous snakes," Roosevelt explains, "a highly peculiar specialization has been carried out to the highest point. They rely for attack and defense purely on their poison-fangs. All other means and methods for attack and defense have atrophied. They neither crush nor tear with their teeth nor constrict with their bodies. The poison-fangs are slender and delicate and, save for the poison, the wound inflicted is of a trivial character. In consequence, they are utterly helpless in the presence of any animal which the poison does not affect."

Besides the six *jararacas,* the *Crotalidae* of Amazonia include the smaller *urutu (Bothrops alternatus);* the much larger *surucucu* or bushmaster, which reaches eight feet; and the *cascavel,* or rattler, which has many species but inhabits only the cerrado and the savannah and is not a problem in the *hylaea*. The *cobras-corais,* or corals, boast at least eleven species, with numerous harmless mimics. They are nocturnal, extremely docile, and rear-fanged: if you should have the extraordinary misfortune of being struck by one, there would still be time—a few seconds—to pull the snake away before it could enlarge its mouth and chew on you sufficiently to puncture the skin. Once the skin has been punctured, however, the victim is usually a dead person, unless the bite is a "dry" one; if, that is, the snake has recently struck and not had time to manufacture more venom. For the Crotalids I had borrowed from INPA four phials of polyvalent antivenin, almost two ounces each, and an enormous syringe with which to inject them. All four had to be injected within fifteen minutes; with these, plus the ingestion of an antihistamine for shock, plus cutting and vigorous suction of the wound, one's chances of surviving a *jararaca* bite were about fifty-fifty. Still a day from the mission, I would have given my chances for surviving the bite of this snake as considerably less. I probably owed my life to Leonça. If Leonça had not been just ahead of me and spotted the fer-de-lance, I probably would have stepped on it. I never would have picked it out from the olive-brown decomposing leaves with which it blended so closely. Several hundred yards later—I was now on the look-out for snakes—we passed another black-and-green one; but it did not have the ace-of-spades-shaped head of a viper. At the mission I learned that several snakes killed in the immediate area had been sent for identification to Dr. Paolo Vanzolini in São Paulo, and he had pronounced them new species. As with practically every other field, the herpetology of Amazonia has been studied only superficially.

Several hours later we arrived at the Aika settlement of Pacú. It consisted of four or five *tapiris* in the middle of a banana garden, in one of which a beautifully woven basket hung from the ceiling. No one was around; evidently they were all at the mission. The trio went hunting. They came back an hour later with no meat, only some *macaxeira* roots. The morale of the group was not high. In the last two days we had eaten just about nothing, and tonight there would be only roots and a small *jacú* for the three of us. Ruby announced that they were tired; their feet were aching and they were going back to Peruano's in the morning. I would have to find my own way to the mission. "How am I going to do that when I have never been there and have no idea where it is?" I asked. Panic seized me.

"You will have to find your way there," Ruby said simply, "or starve to death."

My fear turned into indignation. If they weren't going to live up to their bargain of delivering me safely to the mission I wouldn't give them the flashlight, the machete, and the other things I had promised them. I did not pursue this argument further, however, as there was really nothing to stop them from killing me and taking the items themselves. I had just been reading, in fact, about Spruce's narrow escape from his guides' attempt to murder him in his sleep. Fortunately he had overheard the plan. Ruby and Leonça were quite resolute about not going to the mission; Peruano had told Ruby not to go there and Ruby, who spoke the best Portuguese, was the spokesman in all negotiations with the *estrangero*. Manoel, however, had a brother at the mission, and did not seem so violently opposed to going. Maybe someone there, I pointed out, would take care of his foot. He had no hammock, and had been sleeping in a sling of inner bark strips. "Suppose I give you my hammock," I suggested, "and we go there in the morning?" He agreed.

The mission turned out to be only three hours away. I probably could have found my way, as the path was well worn. By ten o'clock we could hear trucks on the road in the valley below, and we descended into vast plantations of bananas and manioc. Manoel stopped to put on his best shorts and shirt, to slap some *urucú* on his face, and to stick a feather in either ear. *"Xirima muito là,"* he explained. "And there are a lot of *wamani* from far-off *maloccas*. Maybe I will find one for me." Soon we met a pretty one in the path, with an orange, *urucú*-stained grass skirt, armlets of many colored vertical beads, white bead slings across either shoulder, black circles like jaguar spots on her face and body, and three wooden spokes, each about five inches long, protruding from around her mouth, one from either jowl, the third from under the lower lip. I realized, having seen photographs of identically decorated women in Brasília, that she was a Yanomamo. "She's a Yanomamo, isn't she?" I asked Manoel. He said "MM-mmm," with the inflection that means no in our language but yes in his. I became very excited at the thought that I was in a Yanomamo village. As the largest primitive group in South America, the Yanomamo number about 15,000, and their *maloccas* are scattered in the remote forests of Roraima and southernmost Venezuela. They are the best known Amazonian tribe, largely because of the work of anthropologist Napoleon Chagnon at the University of Pennsylvania. I had applied to FUNAI to visit a Yanomamo village on Rio Auaris, right on the Venezuelan border, but my authorization was good only for April. I started to remember that the Yanomamo had many names. Sometimes they called themselves Waika or Uiaka. Could it be that the Aika—Ruby, Manoel, Leonça, even Maria—were in fact Yanomamo? "You're a Yanomamo, too?" I asked Manoel.

"MM-mm," he replied. How stupid of me!

We came to an enormous *malocca,* with a seventy-five-foot ceiling and room for maybe a hundred. Inside some men with paddles were stirring hot banana sludge in a great hollowed-out log. Their faces lit up with excitement at the arrival of visitors. The name of the village was Wakatauteri. Wakatau was the Yanomamo name for the Catrimani, and Wakatauteri were the people of the Wakatau. Beyond the *malocca* were the buildings of the mission. The Indians led me to the hospital where a white woman of about forty was giving an injection to an old woman. Her name was Claudia Andujar. I had heard of her: one of Brazil's most famous Indian photographers. She introduced me to a bearded Italian named Carlo Zaquini, who had been living at Wakatauteri for eight years, attending to their medical needs and trying to unravel their mythology. Both were startled to see me. One didn't just walk into the Catrimani mission: it was at kilometer 143 of the Perimetral Norte, the new highway that would eventually skirt the northern boundary of the Brazilian Amazon. At kilometer 49, FUNAI had a roadblock, beyond which unauthorized personnel were not allowed. Before the roadblock had been set up, there had been an invasion of prospectors following a rumor of uranium, and twenty Yanomamo had died of measles. Some 250 kilometers of the road had been built; it would be completed "next year" (a variant of *amanha*). Peruano, who said it had been a road belonging to some company, had either been ignorant that it was the Perimetral Norte or had deliberately misinformed me. I was in an awkward situation: as an unauthorized visitor on FUNAI lands I could be deported from the country immediately. I told Carlo I would like to leave as soon as possible, and he said that would be a good idea. But as long as I was here, I should know the rules. "Never give them anything," he said, "except in exchange for work or for something they have made." This was to keep them from turning beggars (as was starting to happen at Menkranoti) and losing their culture. Carlo gave them cards with different-colored dots that were exchangeable for knives, mirrors, fishing lines and hooks, and aluminum pots. The only thing that was free was medical treament, which he and Claudia spent most of the day administering. He was violently opposed to giving them clothes. "Dirty clothes are a vehicle of disease," he said, "and bad-fitting clothes are horrible." He was totally opposed to the violent and haphazard sort of acculturization that Peruano represented, in which Indians like Manoel and Ruby left off the basic chores of their culture like tending their gardens to hunt jaguar for a pair of shorts. The reward system at the mission, he realized, would collapse once the Perimetral Norte was open. *Caboclos* would start to homestead along it, and the introduction of *cachaça,* clothing, shotguns, and diseases would begin. But by then he hoped the Indians, through exposure to the dotted-card system, would understand "the value of money," a concept that was missing from their culture. Maybe by the time the *caboclos* arrived, the Indian would see that he was in many ways spiritually superior and would not slip into the degraded and helpless self-image that so often happens when contact comes. But Carlo was not optimistic. The Yanomamo were in a world that was so different that, even after eight years, he had hardly begun to penetrate it, and the introduction of something like a shotgun, which made obsolete skills developed over millennia, depleted game, and left the Indian with long stretches of time in which to brood upon his technological inferiority, could be devastating. When the road opened to colonization, Carlo would move elsewhere, taking with him the lessons he had learned.

An hour later I was digging into my first sit-down meal in almost a month, with rice, *farinha,* salad, assorted vegetables, and even cold beer from the refrigerator. The dining room windows were covered with chickenwire, against which many curious faces were pressed; the Indians were not allowed inside. One of the faces belonged to Manoel. In our week together we had become friends, equals. Now he was on the other side of the chickenwire. I smiled at him quietly, feeling guilty that he could not taste this meal. While the work of Claudia and Carlo to preserve the Yanomamo's cultural integrity was inspiring, the system at the mission had certain flaws. The dotted cards reminded me of giving grades. When a culture is institutionalized, I thought to myself, it becomes a caricature of itself. The very presence of people with trucks, guns, cameras, and other incomprehensible equipment creates problems for the Indians' self-esteem, especially when the differences are reinforced by chickenwire. But having been driven nearly crazy by begging Indians at Menkranoti, I knew how hard it was to create a space for oneself. And the Yanomamo, I understood, were even more materialistic than the Cayapo. Although it was accentuated by our presence, the materialism was there before, in their own culture, which placed great importance on the exchange of goods, marriage

contracts, and other worldly transactions. The Yanomamo themselves were scared of envy, and therefore extremely generous with
their own possessions. The worst thing you could call someone was
xiimi, a miser.

For Claudia it was not the meticulous cataloguing of the
Yanomamo's material culture—the shape, color, and function of
each item—that interested her, but the other world of their minds,
one that would take years of gradually learning their extremely difficult language, which was neither Tupi-Guarani, Carib, or Gê, but a
tongue of its own; of fathoming their complex belief in witchcraft
and myth, which took hours of patient recording from the storytell-
ers, transcribing, then translating; and ultimately learning to convey
or suggest this other world through her own medium, photography.
Claudia had a grant from the Guggenheim Foundation to record the
Yanomamo's spiritual life before it disappeared, as was sure to happen before much longer. She showed me some of her extraordinary portraits. They had been taken with a combination of time
exposure and flash; lucid Indian faces frozen against a backdrop of
swirling smoke.

The Yanomamo cosmos, Carlo explained, had three levels:
earth, earth above, and earth below. Everything had started on
hutumus, the upper level; a part had fallen to *yano,* the earth, leaving a big hole; another part had fallen through the earth to *hekura,*
the world of the unconscious. At death some of the spirits, called
poré, returned to *hutumus* by means of a vine ladder; it was a
happy place, with plenty of food and attractive women, a place of
reunion for parted families. Other *poré* were transformed into animals for their misdeeds. The Yanomamo had a whole different way
of looking at animals. The night, they believed, came from the
mutum, or carrasow. You didn't kill a deer or a jaguar because you
would be killing a former person. Their food taboos were extremely complicated. Some of them were related to age grade: old
people didn't eat tapir because it was tough to chew and gave indigestion and kidney trouble. The deer taboo was local; maybe a
hundred years before, Carlo conjectured, someone had gotten ill
from eating a deer and had attributed it to spiritual causes. But the
hawk taboo was universal among all Yanomamo. If you killed a
hawk you had to go through the same ritual of purification as if you
had killed a man. It was called *unokaimu.* You had to lie in your
hammock for a week without speaking to anyone. There were several dietary restrictions and you couldn't touch your own body. If
you itched, you had to scratch yourself with a stick.

The Yanomamo, he went on, were hysterical about witchcraft. All sorts of bad spirits were thought to live in animals, plants, in rocks, and in the center of the mountains; there was no chief spirit, however, either good or bad. All sickness and death was connected with witchcraft. There was no physical illness, except for what they now said came from the whites. They called themselves Waika, the fierce ones, and their enemies Jauaris (evidently Ruby regarded the Indians at Wakatauteri as enemies). The Ucap were a special group of Jauaris who came early in the morning or late at night and sent through blowguns a magic powder called *aroari* that killed you. Since sickness was caused by magic, its cure primarily involved magic. If you were slightly ill you went to Carlo's clinic. If you were very sick you went to the shaman. If you died, you were cremated and your ashes were ground to a powder and, mixed sometimes with banana pulp, eaten by your relatives. It was their duty to liberate your spirit.

The first man was Omama. He copulated with another man who got pregnant in the leg. The first woman was either fished from a river or came out of a rock. In Yanomamo culture, women seem to be an afterthought. Their function is to carry bananas and firewood and to be stolen. The seed of life resides in the *man's* spine. "It is not uncommon," Chagnon writes, "for a man to injure his errant wife seriously; and some have even killed their wives. . . . Some of them chop their wives with the sharp edge of a machete or axe, or shoot them with a barbed arrow in some non-vital area, such as the buttocks or leg. Many men are given over to punishing their wives by holding the hot end of a glowing stick against them, resulting in serious burns. . . . Women expect this kind of treatment and many of them measure their husband's concern in terms of the frequency of minor beatings they sustain . . . . By the time a woman is thirty years old she has "lost her shape" and has developed a rather unpleasant disposition. Women tend to seek refuge and consolation in each other's company, sharing their misery with their peers." At puberty, in a ceremony called *ruhumasi,* three holes for the three sticks are made in the girl's face with needles of *inajá* palm. At the time of her first menstruation a girl goes into isolation. Thereafter she can program her maternity with *manacase,* a contraceptive potato. The *manacase* is dried, grated, and drunk in soup, and its powder is passed over the belly and vagina. Ideally a Yanomamo woman wants only one child every three years, so that the infant can be breast-fed during that period. The breast-feeding itself acts as an imperfect contraceptive; it is difficult for a woman to conceive while her milk is still flowing. Sometimes, though, it does happen, and the second child is generally killed so as not to jeopardize the first's supply of milk. Twins are always killed. When a woman begins labor, she goes into the jungle alone, gives birth in a squatting position, cuts the umbilical cord with a bamboo knife, returns to the village, and stays in her hammock for three days. Then she bathes the child in the river. A week later she begins carrying the baby in a sling.

Most of the Yanomamo's wars are over women. This is true of all the forest tribes. Adrian Cowell, author of *The Tribe That Hides From Man,* explains the importance of periodically introducing fresh women into one's village: "In the jungle, women are the deciding factor in war. If you capture the wives, you not only eliminate your enemies' battalions of the future but, with a little application, can double your own force in a generation. And so most Indian raids are for women, and this serves the unconscious purposes of bringing new genes into an isolated group." At Wakatauteri, as in most villages with access to western medicine, there was a surplus of women, which meant the group was expanding. One man had three wives. Just a few days before, Carlo told me, a fight had broken out over the women at Wakatauteri. But at the Aika *malocca* in the mountains, there was a shortage of females, and the population was dangerously low.

There are about a hundred Yanomamo *yanos,* or *maloccas,* in Roraima; only about half have been visited by *estrangeros.* The average size of a *yano* is about sixty. The small size is optimal for democracy and personal freedom. One rises and works, or doesn't work, at will. One is absent hunting, communicating with the spirits, or visiting another *yano,* as long as one wishes to be. The logistics of food-gathering for a group larger than sixty requires more social organization, and rather than subject themselves to that, the *yano* "fissions": a portion goes off and starts a new village. The Yanomamo visit a lot. Every visit represents the reaffirmation of an alliance. One is either a friend or an enemy; there can be no neutrals. Messengers go from one village to another and extend an invitation. Three or four days later the visitors arrive. On the first night the two groups line up on each side of the *yano* and simulate combat. There is a formal exchange of news and requests for material goods. Carlo described the immediate political climate: "The Opikteris, who live a few hours away, and the Wakatauteris tolerate each other because the mission is here. But the Raitaushiteris were raided by the Opikteris three years ago. They live a day away. The time is ripe for revenge."

The spirit of this sort of warfare is well conveyed by Cowell: "To the Indians, war is a sport, with trophies for the victor. They spy on an enemy for years, then attack and kill, capture, and marry his women. Even when the arrows are flying there is an almost game-like intimacy between the opponents, and they shout each other's names, learnt from captives or from spying on the enemy. Often periods of war are interrupted by periods of festival when the enemies dance in each other's villages.... Where ... miles of jungle isolate the tribes from each other, war is one human group reaching out to another in the excitement of death."

I did not mingle with the Wakatauteri, as I was not supposed to be there. The next morning a plane landed with a group of Italian prelates who were making a tour of their installations in South America. One of their padres, the head of the group told me, had been in jail in Argentina for the last two years. "The order has been having trouble recruiting from Europe, the United States, and the more advanced countries people who are willing to dedicate their lives to spreading the gospel." As we dined under the portrait of the Pope it was clear that Carlo was under fire because in the eight years he had been at Wakatauteri he had not even attempted to preach the Gospel. Siding with Carlo, I explained that the Christian message was totally irrelevant to the Yanomamo's sort of spirituality; they didn't need it and wouldn't understand it. The only meaning it had among the Cayapo, I told them, was as a status symbol: if one could go to another village dressed in western clothing and sing "Glory, Glory Halleluia," one had a better chance of impressing the women. The visiting prelates were not interested in hearing such blasphemy. Nor did they even try to meet a Yanomamo Indian, but after a lengthy siesta returned to their plane. I flew out with them. Two hours later I was nursing a cold beer in a sleezy hotel in Boa Vista. Having come up the Rio Branco by boat, the beer had cost a dollar; frontier prices. Already the magic of the Yanomamo seemed eons away. Two men were sitting at the bar, and I caught the drift of their conversation. One was complaining about how the Indians, protected by FUNAI, were sitting on mineral wealth that could make Brazil a rich country. "If I was in charge," he remarked, "I'd blow them all to kingdom come." The other agreed solemnly and brought up the massacre of Father Jean Caleri. "Padres make good eating," he joked, and both broke into laughter.

12

Vanishing Animals

The next part of the expedition involved a series of flights: Boa Vista to Manaus, Manaus to Téfé, Téfé to Iquitos, Iquitos to Lima, Lima to Arequipa, and from there to the alleged source of the Amazon. The plane to Manaus flew over the Catrimani; I caught a glimpse of it far below, beneath several cloud layers, meandering extravagantly through the forest. In Manaus I filed a story about the canoe trip for the *Washington Post.* With their photographs syndicated in 500 U.S. papers and the Paris edition of the *Herald Tribune,* Peruano and Maria made a brief appearance in a world they would never see.

Téfé, Brazil, is just downriver from the little wedge of Colombia that comes to a point on the Amazon's left bank at the city of Leticia. Leticia is the focus of drug and animal skin traffic for the upper Amazon. Most of the coca grown in the high jungle of Peru passes through Leticia in the form of a white paste, on the way to further refinement in the "kitchens" of Bogotá and eventual distribution as cocaine to customers in the United States. As I walked up the main street of Leticia I passed several German tourists carrying a stack of jaguar and otter skins back to their cruise ship. The United States and most European countries—with the notable exception of Germany—now forbid the import of the skins of endangered animals. Their sale is illegal, too, in Brazil, Peru, and Colombia, but this does not stop their being sold openly in Leticia.

I was on my way to see Mike Tsalickis, probably the most famous gringo in western Amazonia and certainly in Leticia. He owns a bungalow hotel and a snake farm in which postcards of himself wrestling an anaconda are for sale. He also runs hunting safaris and tourist expeditions to a village of utterly demoralized Yagua Indians. Up until a few years ago he was the major exporter of live animals from the Amazon. I met him in his office. A soft-spoken, dark-skinned Floridian of Greek extraction, he was about fifty, with quick-darting eyes and languid, lanky movements like the snakes he

187

had loved to catch as a boy and came to admire above all other creatures. He began his career in Florida as an alligator hunter, moving to Leticia in 1953. "In the beginning," he told me, "the prices for exported animals were so little that there was no money in it, but gradually they got to be in demand." Tsalickis shipped animals to a distributor in Tarpon Springs: squirrel monkeys for cancer research, night monkeys for malaria, woollies for pets and virus study, capuchins for heart transplants, white-lipped marmosets for hepatitis; jaguars, ocelots, pumas, and jacarundis (a lead-colored cat about the size of an ocelot) for zoos. When the Colombian government banned in 1974 the export of any animals, live, dead, or parts thereof (like skins or plumes), Tsalickis had hundreds of Indian hunters in his employ and was supplying "ninety-some-odd laboratories. "I produced ninety percent of the small laboratory animals from South America," he reckoned. "I was shipping 8,000 monkeys a year, mostly squirrels because they're docile and live good in captivity. I held the animals in Leticia for thirty days, then flew them out in my own plane. I packed them lightly—six monkeys to a box—and had the best percentage of live arrivals of any of the twenty-five animal dealers in Leticia. I never shipped an illegal animal." In 1974, nine kilos of cocaine, with a street value of millions of dollars, were found on Tsalickis' plane. The mechanic was imprisoned, but Tsalickis, himself, was never implicated. Acquaintances confirmed his vigorous assertion that he had no knowledge that his plane was being used for drug dealing.

I asked about the illegal skin trade in Leticia and he said:

"Skins move—jaguar, ocelot, cayman. You just pay off the police, and they look the other way." What was the status of the wildlife in Amazonia? "Not so bad as the conservationists make it out to be. What we lack to destroy the animals is population. As long as you have the jungle you will have the animals, but clear it and that's the end. The effect of the people living in the jungle is slight. It's when you have civilization that the wildlife starts to disappear. The only hunters are the Indians, and not all of them hunt: the Ticunas, for instance, mainly fish, and will only kill an animal that's on top of them. Now the Indian only kills for his daily needs, and he won't hunt in a radius of more than ten kilometers from his hut because he's a lazy person. He'll only hunt four to five kilometers in from a river because if he kills an animal twenty miles in, how's he going to drag it out? So you have all that area between the rivers that isn't ever hunted; all those back creeks and lakes that still have manatees and otters, both the giant and the little one, in them. There will still be plenty of wildlife as long as we don't get back in there with the roads."

In 1967, Tsalickis released 1,000 male and 4,000 female squirrel monkeys on Santa Sophia Island, in the main Amazon River near Leticia. Several years later Bob Bailey, a high school classmate of mine who was in his early twenties and had dropped out of Wall Street, was traveling around South America and got a job with Tsalickis. He became so fascinated with the monkeys on Santa Sophia that he ended up spending two years on the island observing them, corresponding with scientists, and becoming in the process a first-rate primatologist. Today he is an authority on the platyrrhines, or New World monkeys, at Harvard, where, after my trip was over, I contacted him. Bailey agreed with Tsalickis that habitat destruction poses the greatest threat to the Amazonian fauna, and said that many of the animals officially listed as endangered may not in fact be; the truth is that their status is simply not known. But he disagreed with Tsalickis about the abundance of game around Leticia. "You can go five days from Leticia in any direction and have difficulty finding an animal." Tsalickis's statement that the interfluvial areas were teeming with life was misleading, as the great concentrations of animals are always along the riverbank—unfortunately where people, too, congregate. "The big monkeys—howlers, spiders, and woollies—are probably endangered and are now extremely hard to see. Because they are pure vegetarians, spiders and woollies are the tastiest. A big howler can weigh twenty-five pounds. A hunter doesn't pass one up. The only restricting factor is the price of the shotgun shell. The quarry has to be worth the shell. A hunter doesn't bother with squirrel monkeys or marmosets, and that's why they're not endangered. He wouldn't kill a jaguar, either, unless there was a market for its skin. Unfortunately there is."

Compared with the African and Asian species, the primates in the New World are relatively unstudied. There are several reasons for this, Bailey explained. First, living conditions for researchers in Latin American rain forests tend to be particularly primitive; secondly, since humans are thought to have evolved in Africa, the primates on that continent have been thought deserving of special attention. "Howlers are by far the best studied of the platyrrhines mostly because they don't move around very much, but also because they are among the largest, the most common, and the most accessible. They have very large and specialized stomachs in order to process the large amounts of leaves and fruit that they must eat in order to maintain themselves. They are the most sedentary of all the New World primates because they have to sit still to let their digestive system absorb all the vegetation they eat—quite similar to a cow chewing its cud. A man named Kenneth Glander has seen howlers just keel over and fall dead to the ground, apparently because they had eaten too much of one kind of leaf that had toxic substances in it. They are usually able to avoid such poisonous foods, but sometimes they make a fatal error, much like kids eating mistletoe at Christmas or lead paint. From 1931—when Clarence R. Carpenter made his pioneer study of howlers in Panama—until the mid 1960s, they were virtually the only arboreal monkey that had been studied—baboons had of course been studied in the 1950s in East Africa. Yet, compared to baboons in Africa and macaques in Asia, relatively little is known about the howlers' social behavior. Only recently, for example, has it been discovered that they do not have fixed territories, as Carpenter thought, but occupy home ranges that are not stable. Their unearthly choruses serve to maintain group integrity and to warn other groups to stay away. A group consists of one large adult male, several younger adult males, up to seven or eight females, and their offspring.

"The Amazon," Bailey went on, "is flat and wet, and most of the nutrients are in the trees. Therefore most of the animals are adapted to procuring energy from the trees: the monkeys are all arboreal, and many are equipped with prehensile tails. The arboreal anteaters and the cats are at home in the trees, and even the ground animals—the pacas, agoutis, and coatimundis—mainly feed on the things that fall from the trees. To a lesser extent, so do the tapirs and peccaries. Few Amazonian animals are neither arboreal nor dependent on the trees for energy."

Bailey's own work focuses on body size as a determinant of ecological behavior. Since the daily energy requirement of a primate is a function of its body weight, smaller-bodied species require more energy per day per unit of body weight than larger-bodied ones. The smaller monkeys, therefore, must eat high-energy food like arthropods and sap, while the larger species, with less intense metabolisms, can eat fruits, leaves, and other foods with higher fiber and lower protein content. The diminutive marmosets take the niche that squirrels occupy in Africa: they run along branches, eating insects and sap. They have claws instead of fingers, with padded toes; they are not graspers, but clingers. Their procumbent lower incisors are specially adapted for gouging holes in trees; after a pygmy marmoset has finished with a tree it looks like an apple tree riddled by a yellow-bellied sapsucker, except that the holes are larger. Because their food occurs only in small packets, the marmosets are highly territorial. They are also monogamous, mating for life and usually producing twins. The father helps raise the young, which is very rare in the animal world. Gibbons are the only other monogamous primate, and they are an ape.

Because their size makes them more vulnerable, the smaller primates favor larger group size; "more eyes, better detection," as Bailey puts it. Too small to confront their predators — cats, tayras (a weasel-like carnivore), birds of prey, and snakes — they have adopted a hiding strategy, with reduced auditory signals and cryptic coloration. One species is mostly nocturnal. Most sleep and nest in tree-holes, move noiselessly, flee to thick cover, or remain motionless upon detection. The larger monkeys, like the howlers, the woollies, and the spiders, are not territorial. They will occupy a fig tree until they have disencumbered it of its fruit, then move on to the next tree. Ranging over a large area of jungle, they are obstreperous and polygynous. "As a species' food resources become more widely dispersed," Bailey explains, "a male becomes less able to expel other males from the foraging sites of his females and offspring. He can best maximize his own reproductive success by inseminating as many females as possible." Since the males of large species must spend much of their time defending their group females from other males, they do not take part in child-rearing. The female howlers help each other — the phenomenon is known as "aunting" — while coalitions of male spiders defend areas occupied by scattered mothers with their young.

There are forty-one species of New World monkey, belonging to sixteen genera, with much subspecific polymorphism, or color variation. Thirty species primarily or exclusively inhabit Amazonia, and most of these the Brazilian part. Little is known about their behavior, ecology, or conservation status. Most of the knowledge stems from anecdotal accounts. I pieced together the following information about some of them from Bailey; Anthony Rylands, a British primatologist at INPA; a paper by Russell Mittermeier, another Harvard primatologist; and other sources.

Howlers. *Alouatta* sp. Prehensile. *A. seniculus* is *guariba vermelho,* the red howler. *A. beelzebub,* so named for its devilish appearance, is the black howler, with red hands and tip of tail. *A. caraya* comes no further north than Mato Grosso. The howlers' "cascading roar" acts as a spacing mechanism. The dominant male is called *capelao guariba* (father priest) by *caboclos.* Howlers will roar whether or not interlopers are in the vicinity. They swim and can live on seasonally flooded islands. Their choruses are heard traditionally before dawn, but often in the middle of night. They are very pacific and withdraw rather than confront. Mittermeier once surprised a female. With her infant clinging to her, she scrambled off through the branches, stopping every so often to look back. Howlers lack opposable thumbs, and their grooming bouts last less than one minute. The females are the most active groomers, spreading and combing each other's fur with their fingers to find objects which they remove with their mouths. They are scattered with relatively high density throughout the *hylaea,* though hunted near men. In some parts of the Brazilian Amazon drinking from a howler hyoid bone is thought to ease labor pains during birth.

Woollies. Prehensile. The *barigudo* (pot-belly), *Lagothrix,* species, has a coat that varies from café-au-lait to *vermelho* to gray to black. Young woollies are friendly and make nice pets, but an adult can become vicious, and it will attack, wrapping its strong prehensile tail around your neck and sinking its teeth into your skull. The adult male woolly is the largest monkey in the New World.

Spiders, *Ateles* sp., have long puzzled primatologists because their groups vary in size from two to forty. Recent field work in Colombia and Guatemala has revealed that the animals have a social structure virtually the same as that of our closest relatives, the chimpanzees. They do not occur in groups at all—at least in the sense that all the other New World primates do. Females are relatively solitary, coming together only at large fig trees and other concentrated food sources. Most of the time females travel alone with their offspring. Males, on the other hand, travel in communities consisting of relatives—brothers, sons, and nephews. They maintain a large, exclusive home range and expel intruding males. In this way they cooperate to monopolize a number of solitary females whose home ranges fall within the large male community.

They are a delight to watch traveling through the trees. Though large and heavy, they move with grace and speed, their long arms and legs and their well-developed prehensile tail allowing them to get to the very tips of small branches. It's common to see a mother use her body as a bridge over which her infant walks—otherwise the infant could not cross many large gaps in the canopy.

There is a great deal of variation in color among spiders. Just as in tamarinds *(Saguinus* species), a population on one side of a river may be very differently colored from one on the other side.

The spider monkey seems aptly named, with all five of its long "limbs" (tail included) going out in different directions, and its small head atop a large body that seems to consist mostly of a bloated stomach. They often whinny like horses and at times let out blood-curdling screams.

The woolly monkey is probably the "cutest" of all the New World monkeys because of its soft, furry coat. But the spider is the most endearing because of its playful, curious manners, its gangly acrobatics, and its small head with eyes outlined in white like targets. Its meat is prized by *caboclos* and Indians alike. A spider monkey in Tsalickis' zoo talked to me for fifteen minutes. His facial expressions and sounds were so human and familiar, that the barrier between mutual understanding seemed so slight I thought at any moment we would break it.

Capuchins and *Cairaras.* Semi-prehensile. *Cebus apella* is *macaco prego,* the tufted capuchin. *Cebus albifrons* is *Cairara branco,* the white-faced capuchin. *Cairara de serra, Cebus nigrivittatus,* is pale brown with pale red on the forearms and a dark line down the front of the forehead. *Cairaras* and squirrels sometimes travel together. The association is thought to be of mutual benefit: the hyperactive squirrels, whose group size ranges from ten to a hundred, stir up insects as they run along and jump up and down and leap from branch to branch, which the less energetic *cairaras* eat; while the *cairaras,* with their more powerful jaws, open fruits for the squirrels to eat.

Squirrel monkeys. *Sciureus,* species. Known locally as *chico-chico* or *beiju-beiju* (kiss-kiss) because of the sound they make with their lips; and as *macaco de cheiro* and *macaquinha.* These small, golden-green monkeys with black muzzles, golden forearms, and a long tail are uninhibited by humans and are the most easily seen species. Squirrel monkeys are the only primates whose *males* are seasonally spermatogenic—they are unable to breed during most of the year (this is common among *females* in many species but never males). Just prior to the breeding season (August and September in central Amazonia) the males become "fatted," gaining twenty percent in body weight and taking on the robust look of a bulldog. At this time they compete fiercely, frequently inflicting wounds on each other. As the females wean their previous year's young in May and June, they take advantage of the abundant food available at that time to return to breeding condition. By August their young are completely independent and they, like the males, have gained weight. Their coats are shiny, and they are in peak health to begin another breeding cycle. By the end of the breeding season, which is also the dry season and hard times for the monkeys, the males have lost all their fat. They have expended all their stored energy by competing with each other for access to the now-receptive females and have had little time to search for the few food sources available at that time of year. The mortality rate among males is very high because of the strenuous reproductive effort, and the sex ratio among adults therefore is one to four (males:females).

Females cooperate with each other to raise offspring. Very often a young female can be seen carrying and caring for a young sibling. Gestation: five-and-a-half months. The female matures at three years; the male at five years.

Uakaris. Locally known as *bicós* and *acaris. Cacajao melanocephalis* is the black-headed uakari. With long fur, a bald red face, and a nasty look, it inhabits the *várzea* and the *igapó,* has an apparent preference for blackwater rivers. It is very rare and probably endangered. Few have ever seen one and nothing is known about it except that it travels in bands of forty to fifty and it has practically no tail, while all the other platyrrhines have tails and depend on them. Why this particular group should be tail-less, no one knows. The black-headed uakari is localized in the Rio Negro basin; the white uakari lives north of Fonte Boa on the Solimoes; and the red uakari lives along the Rio Jura. Uakaris also have bald faces—the only such primate—and are called *macaco ingles* because they look like old Englishmen.

Titis. *Callicebus* sp., locally known as *zogi-zogi*. Good beard. Entirely green-black. *Callicebus torquatus* has a whitish face, white or yellow collar, yellow hands and feet; the rest is black. Titis are monogamous and pair for life. They become very morose in captivity. Separated, each will die of an apparent broken heart. They are very territorial; their vocalizations, a crescendo of "wa-wa-wa's," begin early in the morning.

There are two species of titis, *Callicebus moloch* and *Callicebus torquatus*. In some places in the Upper Amazon both species occur in the same place (sympatric). Their home ranges actually overlap which is puzzling because they are obviously closely related and appear to be virtually the same except for minor differences in coloration. If they follow Gause's Law—that no two species occupy the same niche—they must exploit their environment in different ways; but as yet it isn't understood how that may be.

Sakis. *Chiropotes satanas,* locally known as *cuchiu*. Crown and tail are hairy *(cabeludo)* in the extreme. *Caboclos* use the tail as a feather duster. Habits are as little-known as those of the uakari.

194

There are two species of sakis, *Pithecia pithecia* and *Pithecia monachus*. The former is polygynous and called the *poroacu*. The male *poroacu* has a white mask; the female is brindled *(pintado)*. Both species eat small fruits and berries and enjoy the upper canopy. They are extremely fast and shy and disappear as if by magic when aware of being observed.

Night monkeys. *Macaco da noite, Aotus* species, locally known as *jupara* and *kinkigu*. Monogamous, lives in tree-holes. *Caboclos* catch it by felling the tree and prying it out of its hole. Brownish with red or gray chest and white around eyes.

Like all nocturnal animals they have large eyes. They are the only nocturnal New World primate. *Aotus* was long thought to be primitive because it is nocturnal like the primitive prosimians, but anatomic study has revealed that it is a cebid, quite closely related to *Callicebus,* that took advantage of a vacant primate niche and became active at night.

Tamarins. *Saguinus* species, locally known as *shangui, sangui, soim, macaquinho,* or *micazinho*. Small, insectivorous clingers. The pied tamarin has a white chest and back, a woolly brown bottom half, black face, and big ears. Another species is café-au-lait.

There has been much speciation among the tamarins. In some cases species that appear very similar are separated by a mere narrow river and can be told apart only by a slight difference in the amount of white around the mouth. Other species, though, have evolved bizarre, colorful structures like long white manes or exaggerated moustaches.

Laboratory studies have shown that female tamarins must have experience in taking care of young—usually their young siblings—when they are juvenile. Without such experience they are inept in bringing up their own young.

The tamarins are sometimes called marmosets, but only *Cebuella* and *Callithrix* are true, sap-eating marmosets.

Marmosets. *Cebuella pygmaea,* the pygmy marmoset, is the world's smallest living monkey. It inhabits the western part of the Amazon basin. A full-grown adult can sit on your hand. Some Indians keep them as pets to pick lice out of their hair.

Armed with a list of questions prepared by Rylands, during my trip in Roraima I queried the local *caboclos* about monkeys: Which side of the river had they seen them on? What color were their coats? What size were their bands? Had they ever seen one species moving with another? What species did they have in their houses, and why? Besides the destruction of their habitat, and their being hunted for food, live capture still poses a serious threat to the monkeys, even though their wholesale export to laboratories, zoos, and pet shops has fallen off significantly in the last few years. Pets are generally taken by shooting a female who is with her young: if the young survive the shot and the fall from the tree, they are taken as pets.

Primate carcasses are also in demand as bait for fish, turtles, and especially spotted cats. After shooting a monkey, the *gateiro,* or cat hunter, drags it for several hundred yards through the forest to leave a scent trail, then places it in a crude wooden trap of *açaí* palm, bound together with vines. Ocelots and the smaller margay cats follow the scent into the trap, whose door closes or whose roof collapses as soon as the monkey is touched.

Bagging a jaguar, however, is a much more difficult matter. The cats are hunted at night. Nigel Smith of INPA describes the various devices used to bring them within range: "Jaguars can be lured by using an instrument designed to imitate the panting groan of this nocturnal cat, made from a tube of hollow wood, such as bamboo, covered at one end with stretched hide. Horse-tail or other tough hair is passed through a small hole punched in the covering; one end is tied and pulled through the hollow core. To coax a jaguar, the hunter wets his finger and repeatedly pulls on the hair, while his companion quietly rows up and down a stream, listening. If a jaguar comes to the water's edge to investigate, they spotlight it and shoot. Another method is to groan into a hollow gourd; the deep resonating sound can be heard by humans for several hundred meters and by jaguars probably even farther. Ocelots are attracted with whistles, made from the metal casing of a flashlight battery, that imitate the piercing cry of an agouti *(Dasyprocta* species). The metal is bent into a wedge shape with a small hole punched through the upper surface. The hunter puts the lower surface on his lower lip and blows over the pierced upper surface. With all calling methods the knack is to resist the temptation of calling too frequently."

Jaguars. Once in the rain forests of Guatemala, Bailey realized that he was being stalked by one. He had heard somewhere that in such circumstances it was a good idea to make a lot of noise, so he did. The jaguar escorted him to the edge of the jungle at a distance of thirty feet, but never pounced. Later Bailey realized that he had been singing "O Pray for the Peace of Jerusalem," our high-school theme song, which he had not thought of in a decade.

During the 1960s Smith estimates the annual kill of jaguars and ocelots in the Brazilian Amazon to have been about 15,000 and

80,000 respectively. Since 1967, when the government outlawed all commercial exploitation of wildlife, he estimates that the annual kill has dropped to half those numbers and is not seriously impairing the animals' reproductive capacity. Very little is known about any of the Amazonian spotted cats; the first systematic study of the ecology and behavior of the Brazilian jaguar, *Panthera onça palustris,* is now being conducted in Mato Grosso by George Schaller of the New York Zoological Society. The *onça*'s main prey seems to be tapir, capybara, cayman, and wild pig although the stomachs of some jaguars have been found to contain considerable amounts of fish. Its territorial requirement is believed to be about a hundred square kilometers. Within a few years, when the studies of Schaller and Mittermeier are finished, our knowledge about the jaguar and the monkeys should increase dramatically. Communication from Schaller indicates that he is much less optimistic about the status of the jaguar than Smith is. One of the United States' most respected zoologists, Schaller is also concerned for the otter and the black cayman. Many conservationists seem to take a dark view of the future of Amazonia. I disagree with the picture they give of the current extent of habitat and species destruction. I don't think the human density in Amazonia is sufficient yet to threaten with extinction any of the widely distributed, commercially exploitable species. But it is only a matter of time, and each day the picture grows darker. I do share the conservationists' foreboding about the future, and I join in their plea for an immediate stop to the slaughter of endangered species and for the protection of centers of endemism.

From Leticia to Iquitos, Peru, it was a short flight. We were now in Spanish-speaking Amazonia. The *mata* was now the *selva.* Iquitos was to me the most attractive Amazonian city I had seen so far, smaller than Belém or Manaus and without their sprawl or congestion. The most elegant section, where the hotels and jungle cruises were, boasted some handsome colonial architecture, including a wrought-iron structure designed by Eiffel of the famous tower. In this building I was hoping to find a Belgian who I had heard from Gustaaf was in touch with some of the unacculturated Peruvian Indians: the Augutero, who were remote but friendly and had ceramics; and the Auka, who had killed four missionaries a few years before but were no longer hostile—the widow of one of the missionaries was living among them. But the Belgian had just gone to Lima. I followed in the next plane. The first thing I noticed about Lima was the great number of vintage American automobiles. Every other car, it seemed, was a 1955 Chevie coupe or a Buick Roadmaster; I even spotted an Edsel. The next thing I noticed was that none of the cars had windshield wipers. Was Lima so infested with petty thieves that not a windshield was safe? No. The explanation was simple: It never rains in Lima, so there is no need for wipers. On the sere Peruvian coast, Lima is lucky to receive in a year one or two inches of rain, mostly from condensed fog during the winter months. That also explained why the roofs had no pitch; most of the buildings in the outskirts were adobe cubes, stacked up on each other. It was an old city, older than anything in North America, with many churches and a cultured, cosmopolitan appearance that I had not seen in a long time.

I tracked the Belgian to the Hotel Gran Bolívar. The country of the Auka, he said, had been penetrated by an oil company. One day they had up and vanished, and not been seen since. The Mayoruna were fine Indians. But I would need the cooperation of the Summer Institute of Linguistics, who had missionaries among them, and the ISL was indisposed at this point to helping other Americans get in to see the Indians, as it was uncertain whether its own contract with the Peruvian government would be renewed. I should try to visit the Mayairunas from Pucallpa. If I was unsuccessful I should continue to Iquitos, and he himself would arrange for me to visit a village of Jivaros who had contact with only a handful of outsiders. "The Jivaro still take heads," he said. "There are still territorial battles. But you have to be with them at least a month before they will show you one. Once they get a feeling for who you are they will even sell you one."

Two other experts on the Peruvian Amazon joined us at the bar: Nicholas Asheshov, editor of the *Lima Times,* "a rag for the local gringos," as he put it; and Tony Morrison, an English biologist who had recently written a Time-Life book about the Andes. Asheshov had mounted an expedition to pinpoint the exact source of the Apurimac River, the Amazon's longest tributary; Morrison had shot the Pongo de Mainique, the dreaded whirlpools of the Urubamba River. Both were on my ambitious itinerary. The pongo, Morrison said, was no joke. It was at the bottom of a sluice through which the Urubamba plunged from the Cordillera to the jungle, dropping 10,000 feet in fifty miles. It was best taken in a long dugout with a strong outboard motor; at the bottom of the sluice, where the whirlpool began, was a four-foot wall of water; behind it there was another. If I took the *pongo* in a *balsa,* a log raft, I could get stuck in the whirlpools for days. Peter Mathiessen had shot the Pongo de Mainique in a *balsa* some fifteen years before. He had told me, back in the United States, that it was the most foolish thing he had ever done. He had also warned against the *mestizos,* the half-breeds of the high jungle, who had little respect for property or human life. Matthiessen hadn't recommended the adventure; neither did Morrison, especially at this time of year, when the rainy season was beginning and the river was rising. I wouldn't find anyone to take me through the *pongo,* he said, unless I paid him handsomely. The Belgian's descriptions of the Machiguenga Indians, who live along the Urubamba, were no more encouraging. "The Machiguenga will play you false," he said. "They will kill you while you are sleeping. That is not Indian. An Indian will say, 'Wake up and defend yourself. I want to kill you.' I think they are hiding something. I think there is gold in their land and some white men behind them."

In 1971, Bob Nichols, a correspondent for Asheshov's paper, and two Frenchmen disappeared in the remote jungle several weeks east of the Urubamba; they had been looking for the lost Inca city of Paititi. In January, 1972, some Indians had drifted down and told of their being killed. "Later that year," Asheshov recounted, "a Tokyo law student on holiday found and photographed the Machiguengas who killed them, no trouble. Bobby Nichols and his companions were killed because the Indians said they were frightened and wanted the three men's knives and shirts. A jungle mugging, as it were. The Machiguenga trailed them for several days, waiting for the right moment to ambush. They finally jumped them as they were crossing a stream."

The next day I called on Felipe Benavides, who at fifty-eight is the leading figure of Peruvian wildlife conservation. With superb bearing and aquiline features, he belongs to one of Peru's oldest and most prominent families and lives in a sumptuous estate in the suburbs. It was said that he could have been president if he had wanted to be, but instead he had retired from diplomacy in the 1950s to devote himself to conservation, starting an organization called PRODENA, which is an arm of the World Wildlife Fund. During the 1960s he single-handedly turned a government that had been systematically obliterating its natural heritage into one of the most environmentally conscious regimes in Latin America. Three national parks stand as monuments to his determination: Paracas, the continent's first marine reserve; Pampas Galeras, at 4,500 meters, where the vicuña is recovering from near extinction; and the 22,000-square-kilometer Manu Park, the largest protected tract of rain forest in the world and the seventh largest park in the world. "It's a gem," Benavides declared. "Largely due to the difficulty of getting there it is totally virgin and unspoiled. All the rest of the

Amazon has been completely buggered. About 200 Machiguenga and some uncontacted Amahuaca Indians live there. The timber and oil people were moving in. It took two or three years of writing articles and—you know how it is—fighting one against the other before it was declared a national park. Now Manu has eleven guards."

Benavides knew about the massacre of Bob Nichols and the two Frenchmen, which had taken place in an area that is now the park. According to the version he had heard the Machiguenga killed them because they were eating from their gardens. He urged me to visit Manu, but it was in the valley of the Madre de Dios River and well out of my way. I mainly wanted to ask about vicuñas and condors, which I stood a chance of seeing in the Apurimac valley. "The vicuña," he declared, "is on the safe side. There are perhaps 35,000 of them, with 24,000 in the reserve. Poaching is still going on—a guard was recently killed—due to the fact that countries like France still allow the import of vicuña skins. I wrote to the president of France and said look you must stop the import of vicuña wool. The vicuñas are protected in Peru, and any wool that's sold in France is contraband. I got an answer back from some scientists, and they said we have made an investigation and have found that no vicuña wool is being sold in France, only alpaca and llama. So I wrote back and gave them the names of the stores.

"Why do they poach those vicuñas? It's not the fault of the poor South American. It's the market in Europe, the supposedly 'old stock' vicuña wool in Harrods and the shops on Regent Street, in Florence and Paris. 'Old stock' my eye—it was just smuggled in from Bolivia. It's the rich Arabs who buy vicuña wool. They don't need it. It's a luxury. It's your exporter—that gangster Tsalickis. Look at their names: they're all Greek, German, or Dutch." Benavides became emotional. "People say how are we going to educate the poor third world? I say how are we going to educate the rich industrial world? How much do you think they pay a man for a skin? Two machetes, and he risks his life. Do you know how much the skin is sold for in Europe? $3,000. The murder was committed in the Andes, but where's the body? In Frankfurt.

"Stop the demand, and you will stop poaching. Give us a chance to rebuild our herds and there will be plenty of vicuña wool for everybody." The World Wildlife Fund and The Frankfurt Zoological Society, he said, had sent radio equipment to monitor the poaching at Pampas Galeras. By 1980 he hoped that vicuña wool would be exported from the preserve.

Most of what is known about the Andean condor comes from the field study by Gerry and Libby McGahan made early in the 1970s. As the largest land bird on earth, it has a wingspan of up to twelve feet (only surpassed by the giant albatross). *Vultur gryphus* rides air currents to altitudes of more than 15,000 feet and sails at 35 miles per hour. "Males carry a flashy red or black crest," Gerry McGahan writes. "The adult female is smaller and has a red eye, while the adult male has a light brown iris. Immature birds are brown. . . . The nasal septums of condors are perforated, making a hole through the base of the bill. Feet are suitable for walking, or bracing while tugging against food, but not for grasping prey. Contrary to fanciful folk tales, the condor cannot fly off with young calves or lambs." The birds spend most of the year in the Cordillera Blanca; when the seals on the Cape of Paracas are breeding they descend to the sea to feed on the stillborn young. No one knows how many condors there are, but there are probably no more than several hundred in the entire range. Hunters used to shoot them at Paracas for sport; that has been stopped. "What also has to be stopped," Benavides said, "is the religious slaughter of the condors by the Quechua Indians of the Andes. For one festival they catch the condor and hang it by the legs while men on horseback go under the bird and hit it with their fists in front of the priest. In another festival the condor is pitted against a bull. The bird is tied to the bull's back. The condor pecks at the bull's ears and eyes, making the blood run and driving it into a frenzy while the bull tries to buck it off. The condor symbolizes the native Indian and the bull the Spanish oppressor. Eventually the condor is released, and a man finishes the kill, but by then there isn't much left of the bird."

A female condor lays only one egg every two years, and the ability of the species to recover from this sort of persecution is therefore very poor.

"But I'm not that worried about the condor," Benavides concluded, "because in Paracas in the month of July I've seen eleven in one day."

In lowland Amazonia the main threat to wildlife is habitat destruction. "The seemingly endless stretches of unexploited jungle you see are deceptive," Bailey wrote. "It is a very fragile environment that's disappearing at a dizzying rate." In the Andes the main threat to the wildlife is hunting and trapping. Conservation strategies for the two regions vary accordingly, with the emphasis in the former case on the preservation of entire ecosystems and in the latter on the protection of individual endangered species.

13

A Gringo in Quechualand

The source of the Amazon has been the source of a lot of argument. For years it was said that the Marañon, a long, strong river that comes down from the Peruvian Andes and joins the Ucayali, as the Amazon is called above Iquitos, was the source. At the confluence of the Marañon and the Ucayali, the Marañon is clearly the greater stream. Its annual discharge is 3.43 x 10^{11} cubic meters, while that of the Ucayali is 3.01 x 10^{11} cubic meters. Visually the Marañon is obviously the main trunk of the river; its geographic significance is greater, and its champions therefore argue that its headwaters—a lake called Lauricocha at an elevation of more than 4,300 meters—deserve to be regarded as the source. Sebastian Snow, a young Englishman who mapped the Lauricocha region in 1951, states the argument for the Marañon in his book, *My Amazon Adventure:*

> At about five o'clock we passed the confluence of the Marañon with the Ucayali. The junction of these two great rivers forms the crux of the whole controversy as to which river is the true source of the Amazon. . . . John Brown took aerial photographs of this confluence in the summer of 1951 which showed clearly that the waters of the larger tributary—the Ucayali—did not appreciably add to the waters of the shorter tributary—the Marañon. He could see clearly that the Ucayali only slightly widened the channel after its confluence. Now, as I passed this crucial point a year later, I saw for myself that the photographs told the truth and that the Ucayali does not appreciably influence the enormous body of water brought down by the Marañon.

On some maps of the Amazon system, in fact, the main river is called Marañon from its confluence with the Ucayali until the Brazilian border. Then it becomes the Solimoes until Manaus, and only then does it become the Amazonas.

Technically speaking, the source of a river system is generally considered to be that part of it which is farthest from its mouth, and the Apurimac, which with the Urubamba is the main tributary of the Ucayali, has the Marañon outdistanced by some hundred kilometers. The Apurimac is the river in Thornton Wilder's *The Bridge Over San Luis Rey,* and its gorge is one of the deepest in the Andes, and for that matter, the world. From its headwaters to the mouth of the Amazon it is some 5,600 kilometers; whether the distance is just shorter, or just longer, than the course of the Nile is a matter that has not been resolved to everyone's satisfaction. In Belém, Johnny Shaves explained the controversy: "If you go one way round Marajó Island it is ten miles shorter than the Nile. If you go the other way it's six miles longer. It's all a foolish bit of geographical hair-splitting, if you ask me, since the tide comes in both ways."

Even after one has accepted the Apurimac as the source river, the battle continues to rage over which of its five headwater brooks is longest and therefore the ultimate source. Few seriously argue any more that the source is Lake Vilafro, at 4,747 meters. On November 6, 1970, Nicholas Asheshov of the *Lima Times* reached a glacier on the side of Mt. Minaspata, right on the continental divide, at 18,150 feet, and declared it to be the source. On October 15, 1971, Loren McIntyre of the National Geographic Society scaled the ice-edged ridge of 18,200-foot Mt. Chocecoroa, above Corhausanta, one of the headwater brooks, and at 17,220 feet discovered a pond which he pronounced to be the source; in his honor, his colleagues called it Laguna McIntyre. In Lima, Asheshov belittled McIntyre's accomplishment: "He says it's a marshy lake one kilometer above the mine where everybody goes and has a pee. ... Ours was an elaborate route which at one point included having the brook flow through a tunnel for 2.5 kilometers." In Washington, McIntyre told me of a tunnel under construction further down the Apurimac which will divert the river and shorten its run by miles. When it is finished the Marañon will recapture the honor of being the source river, in terms of both length and volume.

The morning after my meeting with Felipe Benavides in Lima, I flew to Arequipa, Peru's second-largest city, at the foot of a snow-capped, 19,000-foot dormant volcano called Misti. Somewhere behind that mountain, up in the Cordillera Blanca, was the beginning of the Apurimac. In the market I haggled over the provisions I would need for my one-man assault on the source: a poncho, as both a coat and a blanket; a pointed llama-wool cap with ear flaps; a pair of stout hiking boots with Vibram soles; medicine for *soroche,* mountain sickness, which because of the electricity in the air, is more severe in the Andes than in any other high place; a bag of hard candy; six tins of sardines, of which I heard the mountain people were especially fond; a bottle of *pisco,* the local grape brandy; a supply of coca leaves; and a *yipta,* an ashy piece of lime-stone used to neutralize the juices of the coca. My plan was to get to Cailloma, the highest village in the Apurimac valley, staying in the houses of the Quechua Indians, whose life has changed little since Inca times, and getting a feeling for the desolate steppe on which they live. Few gringos have explored the upper reaches of the Apurimac. The three kayak expeditions I had heard of had resulted, collectively, in four deaths. The survivors, bringing their own food and tents, had had almost no contact with the native inhabitants. I had three maps of the Apurimac Valley, each of which showed villages with completely different names in completely different places, with completely different connecting roads, or none at all. In Arequipa I could get no information. There was no public transportation from Arequipa to Cailloma. From Cailloma to Paruro, a good-sized town 150 miles down the Apurimac, there was *"poca mobilidad";* from Paruro there was a bus to Cuzco. To go from Arequipa to Cuzco via the Apurimac Valley would take at least two weeks; the train was six hours. The people in Arequipa shook their heads as I described my journey. "I want to do a little *alpinismo,"* I explained.

"You mean *Andenismo,"* a shopkeeper corrected.

Arequipa is a white city under a blue sky, with Misti, the once-volcanic monadnock, looming nearby to give the citizens the proper attitude of humility. The buildings were made of a rock called *cillar.* I met someone who said he was going to Cailloma. "Wait at the gate of the Macon Tunnel Company. I'll be there in an hour." I dragged my gear to the appointed place, but never saw the man again. The gatekeeper, embarrassed for me, wanted to be helpful. His name was Carlos. He nodded toward a small yellow bus sitting in the tunnel company's yard. The bus was going to Chivay, he said. Chivay was several villages below Cailloma, but already in the mountains, most of the way there. The bus was beginning to fill with people who had come up the road, mostly single men, a few with wives and children. They were Indian in appearance, with high cheekbones, lashless eyelids; impassive, hairless, copper-colored faces with large crescent mouths and large, nobly decurved noses.

They wore ponchos or gray overalls, pointed woolen caps or black hats with battered rims. They were quiet, hardy, and perceptive-looking. When they spoke they spoke in Quechua, the ancient Inca tongue, now the official language of Peru, but in general use only in the mountains. Carlos and I had been communicating in Spanish, but he also knew Quechua. The bus was now full. Someone had gone for the key, and he would not reappear for several hours. In the interim Carlos dictated a few useful phrases in Quechua. I noticed that a few Spanish words had crept in.

maimanta — where are you from?
mihunata bendirewe — sell me some food
allohariwai waaikipi — do you have any lodging?
noka pagasaiki — I will pay you
mainintata risah Caillomata — show me the way to Cailloma
accompaniawe — will you go with me?
noka rereita munani bicuniata — I want to know the vicuna
noka — I
kang — you
ari — yes
manan — no
haika ora pitah chaiaimanh — how many hours does it take?
noka munakaiki kanta — I want you (to a woman. "She will say no if she doesn't want you," Carlos said. "If she does she will put up her hands and turn her head away shyly.")
I mang su ting kai — what is this?
kang tokai — do you play (a musical instrument)?
quena — a notched-end flute
pinculho — a long, horizontal, plug flute with five stops
manduria — a stringed instrument, often with an armadillo shell for the sounding box, and four sets of strings in groups of two or three or a mixture; sometimes called a *bandolin*
charango — five sets of strings with ten or twelve strings altogether, shaped like a ukelele but smaller
chillador — an instrument with twelve metal strings
mandolinata — mandolin
guitarata — guitar
antara — pan-pipes
bamba — name of a place
Urubamba — the spider's place
Apurimac — the great speaker
Minaspata — above a mine

The Quechua, Carlos said, were *"dulce,"* gentle, *"pero pobre en palabras."* They would be very hospitable.

mikur — food
ke su — cheese
tangtata — bread
tragoto — pisco or aguardiente
wasi — house
puniunata — bed
nina — fire
chiri — cold
wana — wind
maio — river
uru — mountain
hampe yervas — do you have medicinal plants?
ensegne me — show me
ya cha chive — for what sickness?
nynwita kousatiwan — snow blindness
laika — brujo, shaman

I waited in the cold, strong wind, burying my face in my poncho against the flying particles of sand. Carlos was an expert at lighting matches and cupping them in his hand so they would keep burning long enough to light a cigarette — an important skill in these parts. Late in the afternoon the man came back with the key and started up the bus. I got on. He said I couldn't go on it because I didn't work for the Macon Tunnel Company. None of my letters of introduction from important people in Lima impressed him in the slightest. It had been a wasted day but not entirely: I had gotten to know the Peruvians a little better. I would do a lot of waiting in Peru, and I might as well get used to it. "In what *departmento* of your country is the tallest building?" Carlos was asking. "Isn't it true that the whole population of the United States can be fitted into their cars?"

The next morning I was waiting at the beginning of the road to Chivay with a group of Quechuas. A gringo in a yellow truck stopped for me. He was a Swiss engineer for the tunnel company. The tunnel, he said, would divert water down from the Cordillera to irrigate the lower slopes of Mt. Misti, up which we were now steadily climbing. Only an occasional cluster of *wasis* — stone crofts with *ichu*-grass roofs — or an occasional gymnosperm on the bobbing curve of a foothill, bent by wind almost to the horizontal; or the wheeling form of an Andean gull — brought life to the moonscape. The hut style and the scenery reminded me of Connemara and the boulder-strewn wastes of Western Ireland. Six hours later and many thousands of feet higher we were in Chivay, drinking a farewell beer at a table on which a vase containing roses, carnations, and a cactus flower had been placed. I passed a man standing in an expressionless daze with his hand against a wall, probably drunk on *aguardiente,* then crossed an ancient bridge over the Culca River and watched women far below washing clothes, and boys casting for trout in the gray torrent. A flatbed truck picked me up and three villages later, after dark, deposited me at Sibayo, where there was a police checkpoint. I played the guitar and drank *aguardiente* with the policemen and then crashed on the rusty springs of a bedframe. It was 12,000 feet and below freezing. The dry cold was the opposite of the humid heat of the jungle to which my system had finally been growing accustomed. At five a.m., one of the policemen awoke me. A truck from the Arkata silver mine was going to Cailloma. Shivering, I got in. At seven a.m., we crossed a river about twenty feet wide. It was the Apurimac, the mother of the Amazon. Three neo-tropical cormorants stood on its edge looking for streaks of fins on the water. Then we pulled into the main square of Cailloma.

The doctor of Cailloma, whose name was Mikanon Ango, not only put me up in a stone outbuilding in his barnyard, but helped me get started on the first leg of my journey. He took me to see a man who had some horses, but the man said they were *"muy flacos,"* very skinny and too weak to travel. So we approached the majordomo, the custodian of the village hall, who was sitting up in the ruins of an old church, spinning wool. "Sorry, can't spare the time," he yelled down. Then we met a brickmason named Adrianchiti standing without expression in his yard sucking at a ball of coca leaves in his cheek. He agreed to take me to Berhinouilh, the next village. I gave him a downpayment, which he handed to his wife, and we shook on it.

After that exertion, I returned to my lodgings and slept for the rest of the day. Cailloma was at 13,800 feet. In the thin air, with little to act as a filter, the sun was brighter and nearer than it had been in the jungle. Consciousness, full alertness, was a hard thing to hold on to in this environment of bright red rock, bare ochre earth, and distant blue peaks. The square was full of women in coca stupors, with numb cheeks and blackened mouths. The difference between the sunny and the shady sides of the street was about forty degrees. One fried in the sun or froze in the shade; there was no in between. I took a few *soroche* tablets. Tourists arriving at Cuzco are advised to lie down for several hours. Many suffer from *soroche,* which can include vomiting and fainting. The better hotels keep a supply of oxygen tanks on hand.

Late in the afternoon I accompanied the doctor, who was making a call at the Arkata silver mine, five miles farther up the Apurimac. I asked about the diseases of the region. Tuberculosis, pneumonia, bronchitis, and colic were the main ones, he said, and silicosis, a chronic lung disease caused by the inhalation of silica dust, was a problem for the miners. Verrugas, a contagious disease characterized by large, virulent warts, is also a frequent complaint. I never saw it in Peru, but in Brazil, outside the capital, I saw a dog with verrugas. The area around his mouth was so infested with the growths that he was unable to eat, to judge by his emaciated condition. Sebastian Snow describes a victim he came across on the Marañon:

> Inside the shelter, with his head against a large earthenware cauldron, lay an Indian boy, his legs covered with verrugas, or warts. They were hardly distinguishable because they were so covered with blood and flies, with hundreds of mosquitoes circling above. The poor chap had been lying in the same position for weeks, letting Nature do its worst and getting weaker and weaker all the time. . . . I thought that some ointment I had might ease the dreadful sores, so I got to work, entirely covered his legs, and used the whole jar. The natives and Pacchioni would not help me, as they said verrugas was very contagious, but I considered the risk justifiable in the circumstances.

I asked the doctor about Quechua remedies; he mentioned *ahenho,* an infusion for stomach disorders; *ortiga,* stinging nettles, rubbed on the face for *soroche; chachacoma,* for colic and gas; *sasawi,* for pulmonie. All these remedies, he said, were derived from *"plantas sylvestres,"* woodland plants. Three streams converged into one that flowed through the canyon where the mine was. On the rim above the mine was Lake Vilafro, a forty-minute hike, which the doctor claimed was the source. But I could see some ten miles to a notch from which one of the streams came down, and the ultimate source was probably a good many miles beyond that. I took a picture of the stream with a boy holding a photograph of Swami Muktananda as I had promised a friend I would do when I reached the source of the Amazon, and left it at that.

Soon after dawn the next day Adrianchiti appeared at the door, wrapped my knapsack and duffel in his poncho, hoisted the load up over his shoulders, tied the two upper corners of the poncho in a square knot across his chest, and we set out. "Be careful in Berhinouilh," the doctor said as we looked into the kitchen. His daughter was playing on the floor with a small, furry guinea pig called a *cui*. "There may be some *bandidos* there, and they will slit your throat if they think you have money."

After forty-five minutes we sat down on a hilltop well above Cailloma. My heart was racing, and my brain was pounding against my skull. Physical movement was far more taxing than it had been on Swiss scrambles at the same altitude. I took out my bag of coca leaves and offered it to Adrianchiti. He eagerly helped himself to a large heap, transferring some of the leaves to his *wayaka,* or coca-bag, a colorful pouch which also contained a few coins, lucky pebbles, and a small mirror. The rest of the leaves he sorted through carefully, placing them one by one in his mouth. Then he bit off a small chunk of my *yipta.* I masticated several dozen of the leaves into a ball, but the coca didn't do much for me, either as an energy-giver or as a consciousness-raiser. After the pleasant-tasting juices had all been swallowed one was left with a mouthful of emulsified leaves. Recent tests, however, have shown that the coca's main value is not narcotic, as a deadener of hunger, but that the leaves themselves are more nutritious than almost anything else in the Quechua's diet.

Adrianchiti was dressed in Quechua fashion, with pants and a short jacket of homespun wool called *bayeta,* a short-brimmed black hat, and sandals called *hosokles* whose soles were made of tiretreads and whose straps had been cut from an inner tube. The skin of his face, bare feet, and hands was like cracked black leather, impervious to sun- and windburn and the constant glare of the naked rocks.

Far below us was a Quechua homestead, with circular corrals of stacked rock where the llamas and sheep spent the night, and two *wasis.* The land beyond them stretched for a hundred miles of nothing but sandy badlands and gleaming fingers of stream systems spreading over green *pampas* flecked with yellow clumps of *ichu* grass and the brown, black, and white pellets of grazing llamas. We could barely make out the dark form of a woman who had come out of one of the *wasis* and was moving quickly up the hillside, holding her skirts. A hundred miles away, a huge cloud was shadowing a snow peak. This barren vastness is known as the Altiplano, the *puna,* and the *pajonal,* and is found in Peru, Bolivia, and northwestern Argentina at 3,500 meters and above. It is an alpine grassland. The rest of the vegetation is sparse and insignificant. It is cespitose — cushion-forming — in order to retain moisture, or outrightly succulent. As in other alpine zones the most common wildflowers are *Compositae, Umbelliferae,* and *Cactaceae.* Lupines, clovers, and other *Leguminosae* are important as nitrogen-fixers. The isolated clumps of a large ground moss called *yareta* are used as fuel. So is the low shrub *tola.* So are the dried cakes of llama dung. So is almost anything else that burns.

Soon after we had started walking again we came face to face with twenty llamas. Some of the larger ones had red woolen tassles in their ears. They shied away from us, leaving the rest of the herd farther uphill. Behind them four women in their thirties and forties were nimbly picking their way through the rocks. They were barefoot and wore several layers of broad, brightly colored skirts, ponchos tied in front with bundles thrown over their shoulders (and in one case a baby), tan or black felt bowlers on their heads and their hair in two pigtails that reached their waists and were then connected in a complicated series of braids called *trensas.* One of the women was driving the llamas by cracking a sling called a *honda,* also used to stone tinamous and large, rabbit-sized rodents called *vischacas* or *tamas.* The other women were twirling drop spindles called *pushkas* in the air as they walked along, and winding wool on them — the perennial occupation of every Quechua man, woman, and child.

"*Maimanta?*" one of the women asked. "Where are you from?"

"*New York-manta,*" I answered, trying out my Quechua. "From New York."

The women laughed gaily, and we hadn't passed each other for more than a few minutes when one of them came running back and thrust a handful of *papas,* little high-altitude potatoes, at me. I took them and offered her a few soles in payment. She waved the money away, smiling and saying, "*Manan, manan.* No, No." Among the Quechua it is traditional for the women to do the herding of the sheep and the llamas. It has been so since Inca times, when the men were forbidden by law to be alone with the flocks, for fear of sodomy.

The llamas struck me as shrewd, wilful beasts, like the camels who are their Old World counterparts. The llama *(Llama glama),* however, seldom weighs more than 300 pounds, while a full-grown dromedary can weigh a ton. Llamas do not do well below 8,000 feet and can go three and four days without water. In the Apurimac valley the breeding, feeding, driving, and shearing of llamas is the

principal activity, and a llama is the Quechua's most valued posses-
sion. Some flocks number in the thousands. While llamas are motley, with up to a dozen shades of black, white, brown, yellow, and
orange on a single animal, their smaller domestic relative, the alpaca *(Llama pacos),* is usually brown, black, or pure white. Then
there are two wild llamoids: the guanaco *(Llama guanicoe)* and the
vicuña *(Vicugna vicugna).* The guanaco is slightly smaller and
slimmer than a llama, and its coat is generally tawny brown. The
vicuña is the smallest and most graceful of the four. Its hair is finer
than that of any animal, usually between six and eleven microns,
roughly seven times finer than human hair.

At noon we reached the summit of a pass called Chila, and I
collapsed on a large cushion plant with four-petaled purple flowers
that seemed to belong to the *Ranunculaceae* family. Nearby were
some small wooden crosses. Adrianchiti crossed himself. It was a
holy place. An Andean flicker was hopping around a white clump-
ing cactus called *wauraku.* *"Siempre* — up and down," I observed to
Adrianchiti. I don't think he understood, but he nodded anyway. We
shared the potatoes, which tasted like wool and took an effort to
swallow. I had a splitting headache from the glare and could feel
that my nose and lips were badly burned. I made a remark
to Adrianchiti to the effect that I didn't see how the Quechuas could
make it through without coca. I don't think he understood that
either, but he nodded and said, *"Claro."* We made stabs at conversation in monosyllabic Spanish. He was an *albanil,* he said, a brickmason. He would leave me at Berhinouilh and return tomorrow to
Cailloma to finish the house he was building.

A cluster of *wasis* between two steep canyon walls, Berhinouilh
was the perfect *bandido's* hideout. I did not see any *bandidos,*
however, because the woman who owned the only pension, or
place to eat, in Berhinouilh whisked me into the back room immediately after I arrived and whisked me out of Berhinouilh early
the following morning on a motorcycle operated by her fourteen-
year-old son.

Louis felt important with such an unusual passenger, and he
beeped his horn at everyone we passed. For several hours we rode
between sixty-foot cliffs which the still small Apurimac had carved
out of the steppe. At about twelve thousand feet a resinous, twisted,
broadleafed evergreen called *hewinha* began to grow in the cracks
of the canyon walls. We passed the Inca ruin of Maukayachta, a
round town with a series of concentric walls and an occasional tur-
ret. The bank was studded with flowers that looked no different

from our black-eyed Susans. Then we left the canyon and came up on a vast plain, much of which was under cultivation, quilted with orderly patches of corn, potatoes, barley, broadbeans, quinoa, and wheat. Fifty miles away, in the center of the plain, we could see a big town with a church on the highest point. This was Yauri, also called Espinar, the commercial capital of the upper Apurimac region. We sped through neat villages; the people had little to litter with, I reflected; but, too, mountain people are always neat: who could defile such crystalline purity of water and air? We passed pack-laden burros and the silhouette of a lone horseman on a rise, and a group of neotropic cormorants — brown with white bar across chest; shape of loon, stance of cormorant.

Yauri had some ten thousand souls and one paved street up which, shortly after our arrival, there came a funeral procession led by a man carrying the cross hooded with black velvet, then the coffin, borne by six men in ordinary clothes, followed by a disorganized and not particularly mournful-looking crowd.

I went down to the marketplace and as I was inspecting bags of medicinal plants which withered old women were selling, picked up a following of urchins who did not leave my side for the next two days. Many of the *yerbas,* herbs, like the coca, had been transported by llama train from the high jungle. I recognized the red seeds of *Bixa orellana,* the common *urucú* paint of the forest Indian; but here, under the name *achiote,* they were only eaten. Three *yerbas,* spread over the face, were for *kahaweira,* headache; another was for *riumba,* backache. A resin called *copal,* passed over the face, was refreshing, like a mentholated cream, and, burned as incense, dissolved into purgative smoke. I walked up to the chapel, which looked over rooftops, walled roads, and undulating rows of planted fields. Small groups of women were scattered over the landscape, sitting in the shadow of a building, in the middle of a corral or a field, winding yarn around their *pushkas,* and gossiping. The two bells above me pealed, and as their sound carried over the desolate *pampa,* the women looked up.

Even though Yauri is the biggest town in the valley, the sight of a gringo was for many of the inhabitants a first, and people with all sorts of questions approached my table at the pension where I kept waiting vainly for promised trucks that never came. One man asked me when the world was going to end. Another offered to sell me the Plaza de Armas, Yauri's main square, for $50,000. A woman handed me a scrap of paper that said, "Can you tell me something I can take to make my eyesight better?" An old man asked me if I wanted to buy a little girl cheap, and when I said no he said I could even have her for nothing. A young man asked if it was true what he'd heard on the radio that the U.S. was supplying arms to foment a conflict between Chile and Peru, and if he went to America what could he do there? How much did a bellhop make? There were many questions about the price of things in the United States; I had five offers for my guitar; a teen-age boy taught me a beautiful song, and an old man recited a poem in Quechua, declaiming the strong rhymes and lilting lines with such fierce pride that I could not help being moved even though I couldn't understand a word of it.

At six p.m. on my second day in Yauri a *tanque,* or gas truck, bound for the Katanga silver mine, pulled in. This was the nearest I would be able to get to Livitaca, the next town on my itinerary, so I climbed into the flatbed above the tank and waved good-bye to my well-wishers. "Watch out in Livitaca. They'll rob you blind," one of them shouted, and everyone laughed. This was exactly what the woman in Berhinouilh had said to me about Yauri. It seemed to be a running joke from town to town.

The truck rumbled across the plain, leaving long curls of dust. Behind us the sun was sinking over a range of luminous salt hills, and we were passing into a country of flat-topped mountains with velvet sides. We crossed an ancient arching stone bridge which spanned the Apurimac, far below. The river was twice as large as when I had last seen it, and it was gliding green now between the hundred-foot walls of gray rock that it had eaten out of the plain. Farther on it surfaced, spilling over the steppe, and I saw several *parihuanas* — flaming pink Andean flamingoes — stirring up the water with their feet. We stopped in the hamlet of Bumawasi, where they were having a *fiestaque,* a little festival. The couples were whirling around to waltzes and *huaynos* — the traditional Quechuan mountain music unparalleled for its melancholy purity in the world's folk music. A few women were holding out their arms, lowering their heads, then lifting them up quickly, as I had seen Maria doing at Eugenio's *roça.* It was a beautiful way to dance, like wild horses pawing the earth. A man handed me a bottle of *aguardiente,* the panacea of the Altiplano.

We moved on. In the middle of nowhere the man who had been riding next to me pounded on top of the cab for the driver to stop. In a distant hollow I could see a thin column of smoke rising from a small *wasi.* The man climbed down, and I handed him his bundle of belongings. A child was running through the tall *ichu* grass to meet him. The child's left arm was in a sling. He fell, dropped out of sight momentarily, got up, and kept running. The *aguardiente* tasted of the oil drum in which it had been kept.

Manuel, a young man who had been breaking rocks in a copper mine near Yauri for $2.50 a day, had loaded his wife and two kids, their bed, cooking pots, radio, and the rest of their worldly possessions into the flatbed of the "tankee" and was hoping to find a better job at the Katanga mine; they would live in his parents' *wasi,* which was near the mine. We rode together in the darkness, passing the *aguardiente* bottle against the cold. He strummed *huaynos,* and I marveled at the billions of stars stacked in blazing tiers over the mountains. I recognized the constellation Orion standing on the meridian (the north-south line across the sky), the three white stars of equal brightness that made his "belt," and the three others that trailed down to form the scabbard of his sword, the middle one — the Great Nebula — surrounded with glowing gas; new stars were being formed there, 1,600 light years away. I made out Betelgeuse and Aldebaran, great red stars; the blue-white Rigel; our celestial neighbors, the Pleiades; Sirius, in the constellation Canus Major; the constellations Vela and Argo Navis; and the two most famous sights of the southern sky: the Magellanic Clouds and the Southern Cross. Fading tails of meteors strayed across the sky. I rattled, semi-paralyzed with cold, in the flatbed of the "tankee," overwhelmed by this vision of the universe. The solicitations of the citizens of Yauri flooded back: "Take my son . . . take me to North America . . . write me for life."

It was past midnight when an enormous complex of illuminated ducts and conveyor belts and smokestacks and refineries, taking up an entire mountainside, appeared suddenly before us — an awesome piece of machinery anywhere, but doubly awesome and nearly surreal here in the bleak, wild Apurimac valley. It was like a great beehive, with hundreds of drones in white overalls and hard-hats swarming over the works; trucks and graders and other heavy equipment with tires twice the diameter of a human's height making their way from one level (there were five in all) to another. "Katanga," Manuel pronounced. The Japanese had installed the mine, and with wretchedly paid Quechua labor they were working night and day to extract the precious ores from the Altiplano, just as their floating fish factories were harvesting the anchovies, whales, and other marine animals in the plankton-rich Peruvian trench.

We unloaded Manuel's possessions, and, leaving everything on the side of the road except for the radio and my gear, walked for an hour in the starlight to his father's *wasi.* The door at which Manuel tapped was three feet high. It swung open, loosing a vicious blast of llama dung smoke. His father got up and showed me to a shed where I crashed on a pallet of sheepskins under a stack of ponchos. The next morning Bonifacio, Manuel's father, came to me with a cup of warm water to wash my mouth out, and we talked about going to Livitaca. After several bowls of potato and leek soup we set out. Bonifacio slipped a straight razor into his jacket pocket. I was intimidated by the gesture, but realized that if he had really meant me harm he would not have shown me that he was armed. He only wanted me to know, I think, that he was capable of defending himself. We soon left below us the pueblo of Fundición where Bonifacio lived and climbed to a pass between a Mt. Isabelle and another peak called Laguna because at its summit was a small lake held like a jewel in a setting of pointed rocks. At the summit of the pass the snowcapped peaks of Chile, two hundred miles to the south, were visible. Bonifacio told me about the spirits called Auki whose palaces are inside the mountains. "The condors are their chickens," he said, "and the vicuñas are their llamas."

"I would really like to see a vicuña," I said.

"Well look over there," he said, pointing to three brown animals trotting delicately along the crest of a ridge and occasionally stopping to look at us and bray nervously. Bigger than I thought they'd be, they were the epitome of natural grace, with their long necks held way forward and their feathery feet flying over the rocks. In a few minutes they descended to the moist *pampa* below where three horses were grazing. Hours later, we reached the place where we had seen them last. The meadow was called Pampita Kukairmum. I bathed in the icy brook; we shared a tin of sardines and Bonifacio's scallions. About two in the afternoon we went over a third pass and saw smoke some fifteen kilometers away. That was where Livitaca was, he said, beyond that smoke. There was no way we could get there today, so the old man whipped out some coca and *aguardiente,* and we sat there for an hour discussing the various things we could do. In an hour we would come to his parents' house. Maybe they would lend us a horse, and we wouldn't have to carry all this gear ourselves. Two *sierras* beyond the *sierra* on the horizon was the pueblo of Accha, considerably farther down the valley. If we headed directly for Accha, bypassing Livitaca, we could get there in two days. But at Livitaca there were some *cuevas,* caverns, which had been a preInca burial site. The ruins, called Warari, were one of the wonders of the valley, and I didn't want to miss them.

Arriving at Bonifacio's parents' *wasi,* we were told that they had gone to Livitaca for the day, so we lay in the dooryard wrapped in ponchos and napped until their return. A few hours later a woman came over the hill shooing some sheep; barefoot, sharp-tongued, suspicious. It became evident that the parents would not be returning that day. She said we could spend the night in a tiny cell four by five feet with one side open to the dooryard. There was no question of our being allowed to sleep in one of the houses. Considering that Bonifacio was the son of people who lived here, the lack of hospitality was startling. There was definite unfriendliness here; even Bonifacio kept his distance and acted like an outsider. It was only later, when I read Tony Morrison's *Land Above the Clouds,* that I got some perspective on this xenophobia. The Apurimac valley is in Chumbivillcas, one of the most primitive provinces in the Central Andes, where "Indian life continues almost unchanged by the approach of civilization. . . ." Morrison explains: "Territorial rights in Chumbivillcas have never been settled and each year some communities battle before the planting season: in the fights a serious injury or a death is heralded as a good omen for the harvest so the struggle is hard, without pulled punches." Bonifacio was from Fundición, three passes away but still close enough to be a threat to the hard-won subsistence of this *pueblito;* and who knew what danger I represented. As we huddled in our cell we could hear someone in the *wasi* on the other side of the yard playing a flute. On the *ichu* grass roof stood a wooden cross with a carved bird on either arm. After dark a boy brought us some potato soup. We slept fitfully with rocks in our backs, listening to the families calling to each other from *wasi* to *wasi.* In the morning the boy brought us some more potato soup. We said our farewells and set out.

At noon we reached Livitaca, a town of several hundred souls. The citizens were recovering from the Festival of San Sebastian, which they had celebrated the day before. There had been a bullfight—*la corrida tradicional.* An *alcamari*—the fierce Andean caracara—had been tied to the back of one of the bulls and allowed to rip apart its ears. In its frenzy the bull had killed a horse. Every red-blooded *macho* in the village had made passes at the bull with ponchos woven in the special colors of Livitaca.

I presented my letters of introduction to the governor of Livitaca, a man of some refinement who apologized for the drunken condition of the townspeople. "They think you are a mining engineer," he said, reading over my documents. "They don't realize you're a distinguished explorer." I was the first foreigner in the village, he told me, since two Frenchmen with backpacks had passed through the year before.

We stepped into a courtyard where the official band of Livitaca had passed out against a wall. The governor told them to get up. They jumped to their feet and began playing a rousing march in my honor. One man played a cornet, and two others blew on long flutes called *pitos*. There were two sizes of drums—a big one called a *bomba* and a little one called a *tambor.* I was then seated at a long table and served *kankacha,* a huge leg of roast lamb which is a specialty of Livitaca.

After a siesta I was provided with a horse and an escort of a dozen youths who took me to the caves of Warari. The entrance was guarded by a brown hummingbird who flew out angrily as we approached. The hummingbird's main food was the nectar of the little red wildflowers, *pamp hykchin,* which littered the mouth of the cave. Inside we discovered the nest with two eggs. We lit candles. They were real caverns, maybe twenty big rooms whose high ceilings dripped with stalactites and whose floors were bristling with stalagmites. The boys shined up the figures they had made out in the limestone—the elephant's head, the lion's mouth, the pulpit, the Sunday market, with everybody selling bread and sweets.

"And this is the *choca* where the Indians lived," one of the boys said, lighting up the floor of the fifth room to reveal a petrified skeleton—ribs, backbone, vertebrae, skull—unmistakably human. "Meester—*diente humano,*" another boy said, handing me what was said to be a thousand-year-old molar.

I found eleven more or less intact skeletons in the other rooms. In the last one there was a pool which the boys had called the Lagunella de los Pinnis because it was filled with calcareous needles with which they said the Indians had made necklaces. They made me stand on a rock in the middle of the pool, poured water on me, baptized me Piridewarari. "It's a tradition," they said.

The governor was waiting at the entrance, and he explained that the skeletons were those of the Chumbivillcas, who had lived around Livitaca until the Incas had wiped them out in a great conquest called the Maita Caapaac, which took place in the tenth century. The governor said he had found Chumbivillcas mummies in other caves, along with pottery, star-shaped bronze heads of clubs called *champas,* and stone idols of squatting monkeys. Lower in the valley on Chocquepillo, a 4,000-meter peak, the Chumbivillcas had erected a monkey idol of stone the height of several men. There Luis Marquez, a Chilean padre who had lived in Livitaca until 1975, had found arrowheads of smokey quartz, flint, and limestone, which he estimated to be 5,000 years old.

Livitaca itself, he told me, was at 3,780 meters. It had been founded in 1550 by the Spanish, who mined the region for gold and silver. *Lewis* were bolas, an Inca weapon consisting of two or three rocks wrapped in rawhide thongs, whirled around the head and thrown at horses, vicuñas, or even human enemies; Lewitaca was "the place where *lewis* are thrown." The pointed dolomitic peaks around Livitaca, similar in appearance and composition to those in the Austrian Tyrol, were full of precious ore. "I know of twenty rich gold mines around here," the governor said, "but no one has the capital to work them." Most of the formations in the area dated from the Eocene and Oligocene periods and were ferruginous, silicaceous, or calcareous. The gold was found in a cementlike quartz conglomerate. Copper was found at the points of contact between igneous intrusions and sedimentary calcerous rock. Silver and lead occurred in veins *(cuerpos)* running between the intrusions and the sediments.

That night, which I spent in the schoolteacher's house, I discovered that Livitaca was rich in other ways. The teacher's name was Hernan Molina Boza. He was a fine guitarist and the official songwriter of Livitaca. Each *pueblo* on the Altiplano has its own weaving style and its own songs. Hernan showed me an exquisitely embroidered poncho that his grandmother had woven of vicuña hair years before, and he played and sang one of Livitaca's *yaravis:*

A Livitaca mas abachito	A little below Livitaca
A e un punto natural	There is a natural bridge
Quero passar pero non puedo	I want to cross it but I can't.
Venga la muerte quero morer	Come, death; I want to die.

Yaravi comes from a Quechuan word, *harawek,* and means sad or melancholy. *Huaynos,* the other native form of music, are in 2/4 time and are the main dance music of the Altiplano. Before the arrival of the Spanish the Quechuas made music with pan-pipes in the ancient pentatonic scale, notched-end flutes, whistles, rattles, bells, trumpets, tambourines, and drums made of bamboo, pottery, bone, metal, shell, hide, gourd, and wood. The Spanish introduced stringed instruments, and the Spanish church music and military marches had a profound influence. Today's pan-pipes come in two rows of bamboo stalks tuned in diminished triads which, held together and blown alternately, produce a full eight-note diatonic scale. Hernan took his set down from the wall and rendered the most famous *huayno,* "El Condor Passa," which Paul Simon made a hit in our country.

The next morning, to cap the superb hospitality, I was sent on my way with two mules and the lieutenant governor of Livitaca, whose name was Javier, as my personal guide. I rode Plata, an old silver mule, into the magnificent gorges of Pocara. Javier pointed out the natural bridge that had been the subject of Hernan's song. In the afternoon we reached Sawasawa, a cooperative consisting of seventy-seven families, with a thousand cows and two thousand sheep who ranged over 20,000 hectares. Light-headed and dehydrated, I had little appetite for the dessicated potatoes, bread, and the three-inch ears of corn called *sora,* similar to the earliest maize domesticated in Mexico, that were offered. I asked for water, about a quart, and taking to bed, gently shivered under a pile of ponchos until I finally dropped off. I awoke in the middle of the night drenched in sweat. The next morning I was fine. We set out for Antapallpa. I attributed the fever to overexposure to the sun. Javier's diagnosis was interesting. "Maybe the sun is sick," he said. "When the sun is sick it contaminates the waters of the earth, and people get sick from drinking them." Javier had his own ideas about medicine. That morning he cut his toe on a rock, promptly washed the wound in his own urine, and wrapped it in a rag he had in his pocket. His pockets were filled with rags, string, and needles for such contingencies.

Antapallpa, which we reached that afternoon, was perched over the vertiginous Apurimac gorge, by now nearly the size of the Grand Canyon. I had not seen the river since leaving Yauri, and I could not see it now, as it was at least a mile below. Antapallpa was a truly depressed *pueblo* — no sugar, cheese, meat, or eggs to be had, only coca and *aguardiente,* under whose effects most of the people seemed to be. They had almost nothing and could muster up neither a smile nor a show of interest in anything, although I may well have been the first gringo to have set foot in the place. They seemed to be just going through the motions of living. Waiting for lodging to be prepared I began to feel feverish again. Soon I was overcome with shakes. I could not control them this time. They lasted several hours, with the same total cardiac and pulmonary involvement as if I were in a hundred-yard dash. I eventually came to, prostrate on rusty bedsprings to which I had no memory of being transferred. Javier was trying to make me drink some stuff called alcohol, and that was just what it tasted like. By morning I seemed better, but Javier suggested that we go to Pillpinto instead of Paruro, where I had originally intended to leave the Apurimac valley. It was a day to Accha, then three days up and down gorge walls to Paruro, and, meekly averting his eyes, Javier said he didn't think *the mules* could make it. From Pillpinto buses left daily for Cuzco, too. I realized now that I was probably not just suffering from heat exhaustion, but could be dangerously ill. If I bailed out of the valley at Pillpinto, I could get to Cuzco and a doctor in three days.

As we left Antapallpa we saw two condors circling Mt. Walitatelah above the village; their nest must have been somewhere up there in the crags. With hardly a beat of their six-foot wings they came gliding low over the rooftops of Antapallpa and down into the Apurimac gorge, where they disappeared.

By noon I was violently ill again; with malarialike periodicity, the fever and chills had struck again. Javier brought me to a Quechuan family who took us into their one-room *wasi* without any questions. Victoria Huwamani,* the woman of the house, immediately covered me with ponchos and kept me plied with delicious herbal teas. The *wasi* had two levels, a higher one for cooking and a lower one for sleeping. Beside the fireplace was a stack of wood that had taken Huanpukari, the man of the house, a day to bring up from the Apurimac gorge. A large rope basket called a *warawachu* hung from the ceiling to keep the cheese and meat out of reach of dogs and cats. In one corner were two large earthen jugs full of *chicha,* a nutritious beverage made from fermented corn. Huanpukari offered me some of the *chicha,* first spilling a little on the ground as an offering to the earth, which the Quechua believe is alive.

Built into one of the walls was a slightly concave stone on which Milchtura Huwamani, the oldest daughter, ground millet. In another corner Kaitana, the second daughter, spent the afternoon weaving a brightly colored blanket on a broad loom. Stuck in the thatch of the roof were *pushkas,* bottles, wooden spoons, spools of llama wool, and the silver skin of a *zorro,* the Andean fox. Victoria

---

*The ending *wamani* recalled the Yanomamo word for women. Certain Quechuan chants, too, (see John Cohen's recordings) are remarkably similar to the Yanomamo songs Maria sang for me. I have no explanation, except that all South American Indians were ultimately of the same cultural stock.

Huwamani had a son called Donepashiu, and Kaitana an infant daughter Loisa. Their husbands were out irrigating the potato fields.

Several times as I thrashed in semi-delirium I would open my eyes to find my host sitting upright in a cone of blankets, his position and expression unchanged, the firelight playing over his timeless Inca face. By about eight p.m., I realized that the worst was over; I had made it through another day. I picked up my guitar. My fingers settled into a familiar position and my feelings began to be translated into notes. I had no idea what I was playing; it just poured out of me like an oracle, uninhibited by any mental processes. The family just sat there, giving no indication that they were in a room in which music was being played. I played for a long time — maybe forty-five minutes, and maybe even sang, I don't remember. Everything I played felt right, transcending who I was, who they were, the unfathomable differences between us, the improbability of my being there. It all seemed to be transcended by the exchange between my music and their silence. At length I put down my guitar and said, "Well I hope you liked it." I said it in English because I didn't want an answer, and I didn't get one. Then I sank into blessed sleep.

"Bueno alojamiento, no?" Javier said as we set out the following morning.

"Yes," I said. "Those were fine accommodations."

14

Recovery

The walk to Pillpinto took six hours. During the first three we rode along a thin mountain rib with superb views of snowpeaks across the Apurimac gorge. During the last three, with the sun directly overhead, we descended into the steepest, hottest, driest, and deepest canyon I had ever encountered. The Grand Canyon has a nice level plateau halfway down, and the trail is so well-worn you can take it at a run, as I did some years ago. But the path down into the Apurimac gorge had switchbacks every twenty yards, each of them necessary. It was full of loose boulders and dizzying exposures. I walked with Plata in tow; the old mule was useless as a mount going downhill. After half an hour I was dizzy, my throat was dry and aching, and I stopped caring about anything. It was the fifth day in a row that my strength had been pushed to the limit. But somehow the limit seemed to be expanding; I suppose that is the reason for pushing it. We reached the river at about three o'clock, and though it had been one of the most brutal workouts of my life, a final statement by the Andes to those foolish gringos who would venture into them, I was not as tired as I had been the three previous days. We sat by the green torrent, waiting for a truck (which women were filling with sacks of limes and yuccas) to clear the middle of the bridge. A man who was also waiting was speaking to Javier. I didn't understand much of his Quechua, except for one question: "Why didn't you kill him?"

"Did I hear you right?" I interrupted.

The man was taken aback and replied nervously, "I was only joking, *señor.*"

"Well it wasn't very funny."

An hour later we finally crossed the river, and I was put up on the table in the front storeroom of Pillpinto's only pension. It was not very restful, but I was thirty feet from the bus that would leave at six in the morning for Cuzco. The room was full of live chickens, and the waitresses kept coming in and out. In the bar on the other side of the wall I could hear the clientele getting drunker and drunker until finally there were sounds of glass breaking, chairs and possibly tables overturning, and bodies being thrown about. The candles went out, and the fight spilled into the dooryard where the proprietor helped break it up by bringing the most battered combatant into my room, where he spent the night on the floor beside me. The *mestizos* down in the valley were a good deal coarser than the shy, gentle mountain Quechuas. My suffering on the storeroom table, as I shivered and glistened with sweat, evoked only derisive laughter. Javier had gone off with my pay to buy corn to take back to his family in Livitaca—there were eight children—and the only person in the pension who was not obnoxious was the policeman. He was a decent man, dedicated to defending "the honor of the public."

The eastern wall of the Apurimac gorge, which our packed bus climbed early the next day, received less direct sunlight, and its character was completely different from that of the arid, sunbaked western wall. The hillsides were lush with yuccas and century plants, whose spikes were as much as twenty feet tall, and with pine and cactus and eucalyptus. We drove past some elegant villas with elaborate gardens, probably the summer or weekend homes of wealthy Cuzcans. Flies and fleas (as I had learned the night before) abounded. There were no big trees; the primary forest in the valley had probably been cut down long ago. After several hours my daily attack came on, a little earlier than usual. Reaction in the bus to the gringo in distress was mixed. One man offered me *pisco* from his flask. The young *mestizos* laughed mercilessly. The women ignored me completely. I hung on, drinking orange soda after orange soda to replace the fluids I was losing. By the time we reached Cuzco, the attack had peaked. I took a taxi to the best hotel in town, the Hotel Cuzco—a dark wood-paneled Victorian building that reminded me of Claridge's—checked in, and asked for the house doctor. He came in a few hours, informed me that my temperature was 41 degrees Centigrade, or 104 degrees Fahrenheit—*maximum*—and that I had picked up a staph or streptococcal infection from water I had drunk or something I had eaten. Then he prescribed a strong antibiotic which, as it drained my liver, turned my urine the color of Coca Cola.

I was in bed for ten days. For five I could not eat anything. I got weaker and weaker while the attacks got stronger and stronger. There was no assurance I would make it through. After three days I began to wonder about the doctor's diagnosis. His examination had consisted of sticking a thermometer in my mouth and listening to my heart with his stethoscope. Maybe I was suffering from a delayed attack of *paludism,* as malaria is called in Peru. In the previous two months I had been twice exposed to known infestations — on the Agua Boa, to the river merchant's family, and on the Manaus-Caracarai highway, to the military engineers. I had stopped taking cloroquine prophylactically; maybe there was still enough of the drug in my system to delay the onset of the disease but not to quell it completely. The periodicity of the attacks was certainly a classic trait of malaria; but then again many diseases mimic malaria's recurrent fever and chills. *Paludism* would not occur to this doctor, because it is an illness of the *selva,* the lowland jungle, and unknown on the Altiplano. Just in case, I took the killing dosages of both cloroquine and fancidar. After two days there was a noticeable improvement. The attacks grew shorter and milder. Whatever I had — I never found out for sure — seemed to have run its course. Inexplicable high fevers are a frequent complaint with North American visitors to the Altiplano.

After the fifth day I knew I was on the mend, but I also knew the trip was over. The illness had destroyed my health and my morale. I would have to cancel my visit to the remote Jivaro headhunters and forget about shooting the Pongo de Mainique. I had been having premonitions about the Pongo anyway, nightmares about being smothered in green foam, and I was just as glad for an excuse not to have to go through with it. The fictitious depiction of shooting the Pongo that my writer friend Tim Ferris had composed in his New York apartment before I had come down would have to stand for the experience. I had stapled it to the beginning of my notebook and reading it over brought on bouts of laughter that were dangerous for a man in my condition. After his description, the real Pongo could only be an anticlimax:

"Damn this place! I don't know that we shall ever get out alive."

Watkins surveyed the slate-gray skies. He and his band of nine men had been trapped for nine weeks and two days in one of the giant whirlpools of the Urubamba River. Their two balsa rafts circled relentlessly in the vortex, tiny creatures caught in nature's claw.

"Ububububa. Uba! Uba!"

Jenks, riddled with malaria, was delirious again. Watkins calmed him with a boot toe to the temple. His terrible *Uba's,* which preyed upon the sanity of the men night and day, ceased for the moment.

The banks of the river glowed like emerald. The water was a cascade of azure blue and white, broken by occasional copies of the Lima *Evening Standard,* which drifted past, preserved in plastic bags for home delivery. By reading them the men had learned that *Evening Standard* delivery boys, in a job action, had taken to dumping thousands of the newspapers into the Urubamba River.

Just below the surface of the water Watkins and his men could see the glittering eyes of millions of deadly piranha, the dread fish that could clean a man's flesh to the skeleton in four one-hundredths of a second. The previous Tuesday, Saunders had made the mistake of allowing his hand to trail in the water while he was asleep. His fellow expeditionaries didn't notice until it was too late. The piranha cut Saunders' fingernails straight across, an unpleasant contrast to the semicircle cut that Saunders, a native of Liverpool, was accustomed to. The wretch had kept his hands in his pockets since.

On the tenth day I got out of bed and flew to Lima. "After so long a voyage," Richard Spruce wrote at the end of his Amazonian peregrinations, "I was much fallen in flesh." I was twenty pounds lighter, and my deep tan had turned a pale, sickly yellow; the people in Lima whom I had left only three weeks before hardly knew me. I stayed in the city long enough to file my story with the *Washington Post,* and then put into action Plan 2. There was one important biotic community in the Amazon system that I had yet to examine, and it is the richest one of all—the high jungle. As one descends from the Altiplano one encounters the first trees—*Alnus, Corullensis,* several species of *Weimannia*—at about 3,000 meters. Smaller than the trees in the *selva,* the lowland jungle, the trees are perpetually shrouded in mist and festooned with orchids, bromeliads, *Scrophularaceae,* and ferns, and encrusted with mosses and lichens; epiphytic plants thrive in the diffused light. This is the cloud forest; Peruvians call it the *céja de la selva,* the eyebrow of the jungle, and sometimes the *montaña* or the *céja de la montaña.* Farther down the mountainsides there is more light. Grasses, shrubs, cecropias, *Moraceae, Campanulaceae,* and bamboos start to appear. Along the rivers that rush by at the base of the mountains is a special community called the *monte ribereño,* which consists of trees, shrubs, lianas, cucurbits, passifloras, and bamboos. At 800 meters the *selva* proper takes over.

226

Plan 1 had been to descend the Urubamba valley; but now that I was a semi-invalid, I was in no position to take on the *pongos* or the *mestizos*. I could see the cloud forest just as well in the Huallaga valley, which was more civilized and easier to get around in. Plan 2 was to fly to Tingo Maria, the largest town along tne Huallaga, which I had heard was one of the most beautiful places in the world. The view from the plane, coming down from the snowpeaks and the arid Altiplano and over the lush *céja de montaña,* seemed to confirm this. The town was nestled among steamy crags dripping with vegetatior. Through the sensual, dreamlike valley the river ran red and swollen. Rainy season had started a few weeks before, and the Huallaga river was rising quickly. In a few more weeks it would be unnavigable. As we flew over the furious sluice I realized the folly of taking on the Urubamba, an even more violent stream, at this time of year, and felt oddly grateful for the illness which, by altering my itinerary, had probably saved me from a worse fate.

A taxi driver in Tingo Maria drove me around the town itself, a haphazard huddle of buildings mired in mud, and pointed out a few run-down hotels. Then he took me a mile out to a lodge built right on the river in the rustic style of an Adirondack camp. It was, in all, the nicest accommodations I found in my travels, and a perfect place to stay for a while and regain my strength. I checked in and asked if someone could direct me to a botanist. I was sent to the Universidad de la Selva (the University of the Jungle), but it was closed; the professors and students were on vacation. A janitor there told me about a man at the botanical garden whose family had been guiding visiting naturalists for three generations. But the man was on an expedition, I learned at the garden, so I wandered among hundred-foot stalks of *Gigantocloa* bamboo that were no less marvels of the vegetable kingdom for their having been imported from India. I passed a building called El Empresa Nacional de la Coca. The Huallaga valley produces some silver, coffee, and cacao, but coca is the mainstay of the economy. Some of the leaves travel by mule train to the Quechuas on the Altiplano. Some is processed by medical companies into pain-killing drugs; cocaine has long been used as a local anesthetic; and the Coca-Cola Company imports 500 tons of coca annually. A good deal ends up illicitly in Mexico and the United States, where it is processed into cocaine and sold for big money. The Empresa Nacional is supposed to keep an estimate of production and to make sure the product doesn't end up in the wrong hands. The Mafia controls much of the coca, a citizen told me. The other day four men had been killed for denouncing the traffic in Lima. This sort of thing happened all the time, he said.

Late in the afternoon I returned to the lodge. The man at the desk told me about a *gringa* who knew much about plants and lived nearby. I followed a road that ended at a Bavarian chalet fringed with gingerbread and sitting on the edge of the river in a lovely garden of bamboos and orchids and other radiant tropical flowers. At the gate a police dog sounded the alarm. "Quiet, Ruski," a small, silver-haired woman shouted down from the porch in German. Her name was Ruth. She was in her sixties and had the healthy glow of someone who lives close to nature. She was having tea on the porch with her grandson Lorenzo, a blonde-curled eight-year-old, and would I like to join her? Of course she knew my friend, Tim Plowman, the American botanist who studied *Erythroxylaceae* and came often to Tingo Maria. After tea, Ruth took Lorenzo, Ruski, and me to a gorge through which a clear green stream, the color of the river in Yosemite Valley, plunged in a series of small falls. The trees were all decked with ferns and orchids and aroids; they were not just freestanding expressions of their own vitality, but hangers and pedestals for hundreds of other plants. All the boulders in the stream were smothered, too. It was as lush a paradise as I'd ever hoped to see. I recognized some of the house-plants I had left at home growing in their natural habitat—deiffenbachia, philodendron, cingonium (the *Araceae* taking over my study), a pepper plant, the red-ribbed and white-speckled calathea. Across the stream stood a tree fern, a characteristic plant of the high jungle and one of the most primitive. There were no palms; it was too high for them to occur naturally.

At 7,000 feet, Tingo Maria is a very special place, with the feeling of both the mountains and the jungle. The Huallaga valley is a refugium, one of Amazonia's centers of endemism in which the number of plant and insect species is extraordinarily great. Peru has the world's richest butterfly fauna—about 4,000 species—and some 20,000 moths. About eighty percent are discovered. Some of the rarest and most spectacular butterflies and beetles on earth are found only around Tingo Maria. Most of the requirements for the unfettered proliferation of life are met here: wedged in mountains, Tingo Maria is protected, isolated, subject to a regime of heavy precipitation; there are many soil types and microclimates. By now much of the virgin forest is gone, surviving only on the crags and in the precipices. In the last ten years most of the big animals—the jaguars, ocelots, and monkeys—have been hunted out, too—but the butterflies are still so abundant that you can catch them with your hands, in spite of the fact that Tingo Maria is a mecca for collectors and that almost every shop in town sells trays and framed landscapes made from their wings. The local people work as guides for the butterfly collectors, just as they would be hunting or fishing guides in another part of the world.

I accompanied a French collector the following day. He had taken up butterfly collecting after he was married, he told me. Each year he would go by himself to some remote part of the world for a month or so and hunt butterflies. Back home he spent most evenings pinning and mounting and labeling specimens in a special room devoted to his hobby, and plotting his next escape. He was only interested in large butterflies, he told me. That day he must have caught a hundred of them.

In the morning the collector and I visited the Cueva de las Lechuzas, the cave of the owls. The entrance was halfway up a cliff and about eighty feet high. From it we looked down to a great pit about a hundred yards in diameter from whose ceiling loomed dirty, fantastically colored stalactites. The floor was covered with guano and a fine brown dust which, inhaled can cause histoplasmosis, a fungal disease that resembles tuberculosis in some ways. To protect ourselves we wrapped the lower half of our faces in handkerchiefs. A few herbaceous plants — *Cesneraceae, Solanaceae, Urticaceae, Verbenaceae, Oxalidaceae, Piperaceae* — were taking advantage of the rich soil at the mouth of the cave; farther back all plant life stopped. The floor belonged to four-inch cockroaches, and in the darkest recesses of the room a den of rattlesnakes guarded a subterranean lake at a lower level. If the visual impression of the cave was overpowering — like a stage in which some great non-human drama was soon to unfold — the deafening cacophony of shrieks, cackles, and raucous clucks emitted by the literally thousands of animals who hung or swooped from its ceiling was even more so. There were bats, swallows, and small green parrots, but the noisiest and most numerous were gray-brown birds with large eyes whom the natives mistakenly call owls. In fact they were oilbirds — *Caprimulgiformes* and bizarre relatives of the nightjar. The squabs are very plump, and for centuries the Indians have boiled their fat for oil — hence their name.

That afternoon I had tea again with Ruth and Lorenzo on the porch of her chalet. My Amazon adventure was drawing to a close, and I was already starting to feel bereft. What was the experience going to do to me, I wondered. I desperately wanted to take the experience with me, to "collect" it, as the Frenchman was collecting his butterflies. Instead of swinging a net I had taken notes and pictures; but it was the same impulse. I often wondered what the Menkranoti had thought I was doing in their village; they had been too polite to ask. But on a primary level they knew. I was reminded that, like many "primitive" people, they had been reluctant to let us take their picture because they sensed that we were "stealing their souls."

I already knew that the trip had profoundly shaken my cultural foundations, not only through the experience of undisturbed nature and of people living in the wilderness, but through the constant sight of poverty. I thought of all the wonderfully kind and openhearted people I had met who had so little in the way of material goods and who lived completely in the moment, because that was all there was. These people did not worry about documenting their existence, about proving that they had been there and died having accomplished such-and-such. They hid nothing, proved nothing, needed nothing, just were. I never met a poor South American who was not at ease with his place in life, no matter how difficult or depressing it may have been. There is great personal strength in these people, and their example had been one of the great lessons of the trip. Surrounded by their outlook one's sense of the importance of what one was doing, one's ambitions to make a name for oneself among the small circle of like-minded on another continent, to be accepted by the vogue of that particular moment, had been hard to keep up. I knew it would be hard to return.

Ruth listened to my ramblings with rare understanding. She had left our civilization twenty years before, and nothing had happened since to make her regret the decision. "Civilization doesn't give enough of a return," she said, pouring me another cup of tea. "The people who live here and die here, in these mountains, are better off." The tea was brewed from a delicious lemon-scented grass called *Yerba louisa* that grew in the garden. Below the porch the lavendar tongues of tall terrestrial Japanese orchids were giving themselves to the light, and a light rain was sifting down on the lawn. Behind the lawn, a hundred feet away, the furious muddy brown Huallaga was racing around a rocky gray sandbar, and behind the river the view stretched for miles up the gap of the Monson River valley, where the Cueva de las Lechuzas was: one mountain side coming down from the right, one from the left, another from the right, another from the left, each panel a different shade of green, and the final ridge pure blue.

But my appreciation of the view was shadowed by the knowledge that it would not be as it was now much longer. Tingo Maria, and indeed all of Amazonia that civilization has reached, is disappearing before one's very eyes. All commercial products of nature are being extracted, harvested, hunted, or collected without *"um pingo de vergonha,"* without a drop of shame, as a Brazilian had put it. The natural world in itself has no value to most men; as Ruth phrased it, *"el humano no estima."*

Two months later I was back in the United States. My bizarre collection of spears and blowguns, and the ragged remnants of my tropical kit evoked no response from the weary commuters with whom I boarded the train at New York City. The man who sold newspapers and cigarettes at my hometown station looked and looked, and when he finally realized who I was he asked, "So how was Africa?"

Bibliography

Agassiz, Louis, *A Journey in Brazil,* Boston, Ticknor and Fields, 1968.

Amadon, Dean, "The Nocturnal Curassow," *Animal Kingdom,* August/September, 1975.

Arnaud, E., and Alves, A. R., "A Extincao dos Indios Kararao, Baixo Xingu, Para," *Boletim do Museu Paraense Emilio Goeldi,* No. 53, June 26, 1974.

Arnaud, Expedito, "O servico de protecao aos Indios," O Museum Goeldi Ano do Sesquicentenario, Publicacoes Avulsas, 20, Belém, 1973.

Avila-Pires, F. D. de, "The Floating Community of Amazonas," *Natural History,* October, 1965.

Baekeland, G. B., and Gimbel, P. R., "Para-explorers Challenge Peru's Unknown Vilcabamba," *National Geographic,* August, 1964.

Bailey, R. C., "Progress of a Breeding Project for Non-human Primates in Colombia," *Nature,* Vol. 248, No. 5447.

————, "Social Structure and Ecology of New World Primates," unpublished manuscript, 1977.

Bates, Henry Walter, *The Naturalist on the River Amazons,* New York, Dover Publications, 1975.

Bates, Marston, *The Forest and the Sea,* New York, Vintage Books, 1960.

————, *South America,* New York, Time-Life Books, 1964.

Beebe, William, *Jungle Peace,* London, Witherby & Co., 1919.

————, *Tropical Wild Life,* New York, New York Zoological Society, 1917.

233

Beltrao, L., *O Indio, um mito Brasileiro,* Petropolis, Editora Vozes, 1972.

Benson, W. W., et al., "Co-evolution of Plants and Herbivores: Passion-flowers Butterflies," *Evolution,* Vol. 29, No. 4, December, 1975.

Bingham, Hiram, "The Story of Machu Picchu," *National Geographic,* February, 1915.

Bodard, Lucien, *Green Hell,* New York, E.P. Dutton, 1971.

Bowman, Isaiah, *The Andes of Southern Peru,* New York, Henry Holt and Co., 1916.

Booth, Margaret, *An Amazon Andes Tour,* London, Edward Arnold, 1910.

Branston, Brian, *The Last Great Journey on Earth,* New York, Weybright and Talley, 1970.

Bratt, Lars C., *Opportunities for Forest Industry Development in the Amazon Region,* New York, Development and Resources Corp., 1973.

Breeden, Robert L., ed., *Primitive Worlds,* Washington, The National Geographic Society, 1973.

Brinkmann, W. L. F., and do Nascimento, J. C., "The Effect of Slash and Burn Agriculture on Plant Nutrients in the Tertiary Region of Central Amazonia," *Acta Amazonica,* Vol. 3, No. 1, 1968.

Brooks, Edwin, et al, *Tribes of the Amazon Basin in Brazil 1972,* London, Charles Knight & Co., 1973.

Brooks, John, *The South American Handbook,* London, Mendip Press, 1974.

Brown, John, *Two Against the Amazon,* London, Hodder & Stoughton, 1952.

Brown, K. S., "Geographical patterns of evolution in neotropical Lepidoptera," *Journal of Entomological Biology,* Vol. 44, 1975.

——, and Turner, J. R. G., "Quarternary Refugia in Tropical America: Evidence from Race Formation in *Heliconius* Butterflies," *Proceedings of the Royal Society,* B.187, 1974.

Brown, Rose and Bob, *Amazing Amazon,* London, Rich & Cowan, 1943.

Brush, Stephen B., "Farming at the Edge of the Andes," *Natural History,* May, 1977.

Calder, Nigel, *The Restless Earth,* New York, The Viking Press, 1972.

Campbell, R., "A Timely Reprieve or a Death Sentence for the Amazon," *Smithsonian Magazine,* October, 1977.

Carneiro, Robert, "Extra-marital Sex Freedom Among the Kuikuru Indians of Mato Grosso," *Revista do Museo Paulista,* São Paulo, Vol. X, 1956/58.

Cavalcante, Paulo B., *Frutas Comestivais da Amazonia,* Manaus, INPA, 1976.

Chagnon, Napoleon, "The Feast," *Natural History,* April, 1968.

————, *Studying the Yanomamo,* New York, Holt, Rinehart, and Winston, 1974.

————, *Yanomamo, The Fierce People,* New York, Holt, Rinehart, and Winston, 1968.

————, "Yanomamo — The Fierce People," *Natural History,* January, 1967.

Churchward, Robert, *Wilderness of Fools,* London, George Routledge & Sons, 1936.

Clark, Leonard, *The Rivers Ran East,* London, Hutchinson, 1954.

Collier, Richard, *The River That God Forgot,* New York, E.P. Dutton, 1968.

Cotlow, Lewis, *Amazon Head-Hunters,* New York, Henry Holt and Co., 1953.

Cowell, Adrian, *The Heart of the Forest,* London, Victor Gollancz Ltd., 1960.

————, *The Tribe That Hides From Man,* London, The Bodley Head, 1973.

Davis, S., and Mathews, R. O., "The Geological Imperative," Cambridge, *Report of the Anthropology Resource Center,* November, 1976.

de Castro and Reis, A. F., "Food Problems in the Amazon Area," *Symposium on the World Food Supply,* Washington, 1952.

De Graff, F. W. U., *Head-hunters of the Amazon,* London, Herbert Jenkins, 1923.

De Schauensee, R. M., *A Guide for the Birds of South America,* Wynnewood, Livingston Publishing Co., 1970.

Domville-Fife, Charles W., *Among Wild Tribes of the Amazons,* London, Seeley, Service, and Co., 1924.

Dozier, C. L., *Land Development and Colonization in Latin America: Case Studies of Peru, Bolivia, and Mexico,* New York, Praeger Publishers, 1969.

Ducke, A., and Black, G. E., "Notes sobre a fitogeographia da Amazonia Brasileira," *Boletim Tecnico do Instituto Agronomico do Norte,* Belém, 1954.

Duguid, Julian, *Green Hell,* New York, The Century Co., 1931.

————, *Tiger-Man,* London, Victor Gollancz, Ltd., 1932.

Eidt, R.C., "Pioneer Settlement in Eastern Peru," *Annals of the Association of American Geographers,* Vol. 52, No. 3, 1967.

Eiten, George, "The *Cerrado* Vegetation of Brazil," *New York Botanical Garden Review,* April/June, 1972.

Eiten, George, "An Outline of the Vegetation of South America," *International Primate Society,* Symp. 5th Cong., 1974.

Emmel, Thomas C., "Adaptation on the Wing," *Natural History,* October, 1975.

————, *Butterflies,* New York, Alfred A. Knopf, 1975.

Fawcett, Col. P. H., *Exploration Fawcett,* London, Hutchinson, 1953.

Fejos, Paul, *Ethnography of the Yagua,* New York, The Viking Fund, 1943.

Ferreira, Marcio, "Estudo sobre o comportamento de quelonios na Regiao Amazonica," *Comunicacao Tecnica,* No. 15, PRODEPEF, Brasília, April 17, 1977.

Ferris, Harry, "The Indians of Cuzco and the Apurimac," *American Anthropological Association,* Memoir No. 14, 1916.

Fittkau, E. J., et al., ed., *Biogeography and Ecology in South America,* Amsterdam, The Hague, Dr. W. Junk, 1968–9, two vols.

Fidalgo, O., and Prance, G. T., "The Ethnomycology of the Sanama Indians," *Mycologia,* January/February, 1976.

Fleming, Peter, *Brazilian Adventure,* New York, Charles Scribner's Sons, 1934.

Flowers, Nancy, "The Royal Fleece of the Andes," *Natural History,* May, 1969.

Franck, Harry A., *Vagabonding Down the Andes,* New York, The Century Co., 1917.

————, *Working North From Patagonia,* New York, Grosset & Dunlap, 1921.

FUNAI, Brasília, "Susypaua: the Brazilian Indian Legislacao," *Boletim Informativo,* Nos. 9/10, 11/12, 14, 15/16, 17, 1970–77.

Furneaux, Robin, *The Amazon, the Story of a Great River,* New York, G. P. Putnam's Sons, 1970.

George, W. G., "Rarely Seen Songbirds of Peru's High Andes," *Natural History,* October, 1964.

Gery, J., and Junk, W., *The Fresh-water Fishes of South America,* Amsterdam, The Hague, 1969.

Gill, Richard C., *White Water and Black Magic,* New York, Henry Holt & Co., 1940.

Goodland, R. J. A., and Irwin, H. S., *Amazon Jungle: Green Hell to Red Desert?,* Amsterdam, Elsevier Scientific Publishing Company, 1975.

Goodman, E. J., *The Explorers of South America,* New York, Macmillan, 1972.

Grant, Verne, *The Origin of Adaptations,* New York, Columbia University Press, 1963.

Greenewalt, C. H., "Marvelous Hummingbird Rediscovered," *National Geographic,* July, 1966.

Gross, Daniel R., *Peoples and Cultures of Native South America,* New York, The Natural History Press, 1973.

Haffer, J., "Speciation in Amazonian Forest Birds," *Science,* July 11, 1969.

Hamilton, Lawrence S., "Tropical Rainforest Use and Preservation," *Special Publication of the Sierra,* International Series No. 4, March, 1976.

Hanson, Earl Parker, *Journey to Manaos,* London, Victor Gollancz, Ltd., 1938.

Harner, M. J., *The Jivaro,* New York, Anchor Press, 1973.

———, "The Sound of Rushing Water," *Natural History,* June/July, 1968.

Haskins, Cary P., *The Amazon —The Life History of a Mighty River,* Garden City, Doubleday, Doran & Co., 1943.

Heeks, Richard H., unpublished report on the Kreen-akroare, FUNAI, 1976.

Herndon, Wm. Lewis and Gibbon, Lardner, *Exploration of the Valley of the Amazon,* Washington, Robert Armstrong, 1853.

Hewett, Edgar L., *Ancient Andean Life,* New York, Biblo and Tannen, 1968.

Hill, Albert F., *Economic Botany,* New York, McGraw-Hill, 1937.

Holtum, R. E., "Evolutionary Trends in an Equatorial Climate," *Symposia of the Society of Experimental Biology,* No. 7, 1953.

Huxley, Francis, *Affable Savages,* London, The Travel Book Club, 1956.

Huxley, Matthew, and Capa, Cornell, *Farewell to Eden,* New York, Harper and Row, 1964.

Irwin, H. S., "Coming to Terms with the Rain Forest," *Garden,* May/June, 1977.

Jahoda, J., and O'Hearn, Donna L., "The Reluctant Amazon Basin," *Environment,* October, 1975.

James, D. E., "The Evolution of the Andes," *Scientific American,* August, 1973.

Janzen, Daniel H., "Herbivores and the Number of Tree Species in Tropical Forests," *The American Naturalist,* November/December, 1970.

———, "Tropical Black Water Rivers, Animals, and Mast Fruiting by *Dipterocarpaceae,*" *Biotropica* Vol. 6, No. 2, 1975.

————, "Why Mountain Passes Are Higher in the Tropics," *The American Naturalist,* May/June, 1967.

Joly, Aylthon Brandao, *Botanica,* São Paulo, Editora Nacional, 1976.

Junqueira, Carmen, "The Brazilian Indigenous Problem and Policy: The Example of the Xingu National Park," AMAZIND/IWCIA document, Copenhagen/Geneva, 1973.

Kandell, Jonathan, "Brazilian Squatters' Inroads in Amazon Provoke Indians," *New York Times,* September 8, 1976.

————, "Violence in the Amazon: Brazil Echoes U.S. West," *New York Times,* July 20, 1976.

Knowles, O. H., *Investment and Business Opportunities in Forest Industrial Development of the Brazilian Amazon,* Rome, FAO, 1969.

Lamb, F. Bruce, *Wizard of the Upper Amazon,* Boston, Houghton Mifflin Co., 1975.

Lazar, Alan, *Anthology of Central and South American Indian Music,* Folkways Records, Album No. FE 4542.

Leacock, Seth and Ruth, *Spirits of the Deep,* New York, Anchor Press, 1975.

Lovejoy, Thomas J., "Bird Diversity and Abundance in Amazon Forest Communities," *The Living Bird,* Thirteenth Annual, 1974.

Lovejoy, Thomas E., *Brasil Trip Report,* World Wildlife Fund, Washington, 1976.

————, "Refugia, Refuges, and Minimum Critical Size: Problems in the Conservation of the Neotropical Herpetofauna," unpublished manuscript.

————, "The Transamazonica: Highway to Extinction?," *Frontiers,* Academy of Natural Science of Philadelphia, Spring, 1973.

MacNamara, M. C., "The Bald Uakari," *Animal Kingdom,* August/September, 1975.

MacNeish, Richard S., "The Peopling of the New World," *American Scientist,* May/June, 1976.

Maguire, B. "Two Decades of Exploration in the American Tropics," *The Garden Journal,* July/August, 1964.

Matthiessen, Peter, *At Play in the Fields of the Lord,* New York, Random House, 1965.

———, *The Cloud Forest,* New York, Ballantine Books, 1961.

Maybury-Lewis, David, *Akwe-Shavante Society,* London, Oxford University Press, 1967.

———, *The Savage and the Innocent,* London, Evans Bros., 1965.

McGahan, Jerry and Libby, "The Condor, Soaring Spirit of the Andes," *National Geographic,* May, 1971.

McIntyre, Loren, "The Amazon — Mightiest of Rivers," *National Geographic,* October, 1972.

———, "Lost Empire of the Incas," *National Geographic,* December, 1973.

Meggers, Betty J., *Amazonia,* Chicago, Aldine Publishing Co., 1971.

——— and Evans, Clifford, *Archealogical Investigations at the Mouth of the Amazon,* Washington, Government Printing Office, 1957.

———, "Vegetational Fluctuation and Prehistorical Cultural Adaptations in Amazonia," unpublished manuscript, 1976.

———, Ayensu, E. S., and Duckworth, W. D., eds., *Tropical Forest Ecosystems in Africa and South America,* Washington, Smithsonian Institution Press, 1973.

Merrill, Elmer D., *Plant Life of the Pacific World,* Washington, Infantry Journal, 1945.

Mittermeier, R., "Mystery Monkey," *Animal Kingdom,* June/July, 1975.

———, "A Turtle in Every Pot," *Animal Kingdom,* April/May, 1975.

———, and Coimbra-Filho, Adelmar F., "Primate Conservation in Brazilian Amazonia," unpublished manuscript.

Momsen, Richard P., *Brazil: A Giant Stirs,* Princeton, D. Van Nostrand Co., 1968.

Morrison, Tony, *Land Above the Clouds,* London, Andre Deutsch, Ltd., 1974.

Moseley, M. E., et al., "Peru's Ancient City of Kings," *National Geographic,* March, 1973.

Murphy, Robert F., *Headhunter's Heritage,* Berkeley, University of California Press, 1960.

Myers, G. S., "The Amazon and Its Fishes," *Aquarium Journal,* March, 1947.

Neville, M. K., "Social Relations within Troops of Red Howler Monkeys, *Folia Primat.* Vol. 18, 1972.

Oliveira, R. C. de, *O Indio e o Mundo dos Brancos,* São Paulo, Livraria Pionera Editora, 1972.

Passerinho, J. G., *Amazonia — The Challenge of the Tropics,* Rio de Janeiro, Primor, 1971.

Pereira, Nunes, *Panorama da Alimentacao Indigena,* Rio de Janeiro, Editora Livraria, 1974.

Phelps, Gilbert, *The Green Horizons,* New York, Simon and Schuster, 1964.

Pinkley, Homer Vergil, "The Ethno-ecology of the Kofan Indians," Doctoral Thesis, Harvard University, 1972.

Pope, Clifford H., "The Six Giants," *Natural History,* June/July, 1962.

Prance, G. T., *Algumas Flores da Amazonia,* Manaus, INPA, 1976.

———, "Ethnobotanical Notes from Amazonian Brazil," *Economic Botany,* Vol. 26, No. 3, 1973.

———, "An Index of Plant Collectors in Brazilian Amazonia," *Acta Amazonica,* Vol. 1, No. 1, 1972.

———, ed., "The Phytogeographic Subdivisions of Amazonia and Their Influence on the Selection of Biological Reserves," in *Extinction is Forever,* New York Botanical Garden, 1976.

———, "Phytogeographic Support for the Theory of Pleistocene Forest Refuges in the Amazon Basin," *Acta Amazonica,* Vol. 3, No. 3, 1974.

———, and Arias, J. R., "A Study of the Floral Biology of *Victoria amazonica,*" *Acta Amazonica,* Vol. 5, No. 2, 1975.

———, and Prance, Anne, "Plants of Amazonia," *Garden Journal,* February, 1970.

Prescott, W. H., *History of the Conquest of Peru,* New York, Modern Library, N.D.

Projeto RADAM, *Levantamento de Recursos Naturais,* Ministerio das Minas e Energia, Rio de Janeiro, Vols. 1–7, 1973–4.

Puttkamer, Jesco von, "Brazil's Beleaguered Indians," *National Geographic,* February, 1974.

Ramamurti, K. S., et al., *An Analysis of Spatial Variation of Precipitation over the Amazon Basin in Brazil,* CNPQ, São Paulo, 1972.

Ramos, A. R., "The Social System of the Sanuma of Northern Brazil," Doctoral Thesis, University of Wisconsin, 1972.

Raven, Peter, "Angiosperm Biogeography and Past Continental Movements, *Annals of the Missouri Botanical Garden,* Vol. 61, No. 3, 1974.

————, and Axelrod, D. I., "History of Flora and Fauna of Latin America," *American Science,* Vol. 3.

Reichel-Dolmatoff, G., *Amazonian Cosmos,* Chicago, University of Chicago Press, 1971.

————, "Cosmology as Ecological Analysis . . . A View from the Rain Forest," *Man,* Vol. 11, No. 3, September, 1976.

Ribeiro, Darcy, *Os Indios e a Civilizacao,* Petropolis, Editora Vozes, 1977.

Richards, Paul W., *The Social Insects,* New York, Harper and Row, 1961.

————, *The Tropical Rain Forest,* Cambridge, University Press, 1964.

————, "The Tropical Rain Forest," *Scientific American,* September, 1973.

Ricklefs, R. E., *Ecology,* London, Thomas Nelson Ltd., 1973.

Rondon, C. M. daS., *Indios do Brasil,* Rio de Janeiro, Conselho Nacional de Protecao aos Indios, 1953.

Roosevelt, Theodore, *Through the Brazilian Wilderness,* London, J. Murray, 1914.

Ross, E. R., "Birds That 'See' in the Dark with Their Ears," *National Geographic,* February, 1965.

Ruiz, Lopez, *Travels of Ruiz and Pavone and Domrey in Peru and Chile (1777–1788),* trans. D. E. Dahlgren, Chicago, Field Museum, 1940.

Russell, W. M. S., "The Slash-and-Burn Technique," *Natural History,* March, 1968.

Sand, Algo, *Senor Bum in the Jungle,* London, Victor Gollancz Ltd., 1932.

Savoy, Gene, *Antisuyo,* New York, Simon and Schuster, 1970.

Schery, R. W., *Plants for Man,* London, George Allen and Unwin, Ltd., 1954.

Schreider, H., and Schreider, F., *Exploring the Amazon,* Washington, National Geographic Society, 1970.

Schultes, Richard Evans, *The Botany and Chemistry of Hallucinogens,* Springfield, Charles Thomas, 1973.

————, and Swain, Tony, "The Plant Kingdom: A Virgin Field for New Biodynamic Constituents," *Proceedings of the Second Philip Morris Science Symposium,* 1976.

Schulthess, E., and Egli, E., *The Amazon,* New York, Simon and Schuster, 1960.

Schulz, Harold, "Brazil's Waura Indians," *National Geographic,* January, 1966.

Schurz, William Lytle, "The Amazon, Father of Waters," *National Geographic,* April, 1926.

————, *Brazil,* New York, E. P. Dutton, 1961.

Seeger, Anthony, "The Meaning of Body Ornament: A Suya Example," *Ethnology,* July, 1975.

Seitz, *People of the Rain-Forests,* London, William Heinemann, 1963.

Seyfert, C. K., and Sirkin, L. A., *Earth History and Plate Tectonics,* New York, Harper and Row, 1973.

Shneebaum, Tobias, *Keep the River to Your Right,* New York, Grove Press, 1974.

Simpson, B. B., "Pleistocene Changes in the Flora of the High Tropical Andes," *Paleobiology,* Vol. I, No. 3, 1975.

Siskind, J., "Special Hunt of the Sharanahua," *Natural History,* October, 1974.

Smith, Nigel J. H., "Brasil's Transamazon Highway Settlement Scheme: Agrovilas, Agropoli, and Ruropoli," *Association of American Geographical Proceedings,* Vol. 8, 1976.

————, "Destructive Exploitation of the South American River Turtle," *Yearbook of Pacific Coast Geographers,* Vol. 36, 1974.

————, "Spotted Cats and the Amazon Skin Trade," *Oryx,* July, 1976.

————, "Transamazon Highway: A Cultural-ecological Analysis of Settlement in the Lowland Tropics," Doctoral Thesis, Dept. of Geography, University of California, Berkeley, 1976.

Snow, Sebastian, *My Amazon Adventure,* London, Odhams Press, Ltd., 1952.

Sponsel, E. L., et al., "Evaluation of Squirrel Monkey Ranching on Santa Sophia Island, Amazonas, Colombia," *International Zoo Yearbook,* Vol. 14, 1974.

Spruce, Richard, *Notes of a Botanist on the Amazon and Andes,* New York, MacMillan and Co., London, 1908.

Steele, Arthur R., *Flowers for the King,* Durham, Duke University Press, 1964.

Sterling, Thomas, *The Amazon,* New York, Time Inc., 1973.

Sternberg, Hilgard O'Reilly, *The Amazon River of Brazil,* Franz Steiner Verlag, Wiesbaden, 1975.

————, *Development and Conservation,* University of California Center for Latin American Studies, Reprint No. 447.

————, "Radiocarbon Dating as Applied to a Problem of Amazonian Morphology," Centro de Pesquisas de Geografia do Brasil, Rio de Janeiro, 1960.

Stevens, Albert W., *Exploring in the Valley of the Amazon in a Hydroplane,* National Geographic Society, April, 1926.

Steward, Julian H., *Handbook of South American Indians,* Vols. 1–7, Washington, Government Printing Office, 1946–1959.

————, and Faron, L. C., *The Native Peoples of South America,* New York, McGraw-Hill, 1959.

Superintendency for the Development of Amazonia (SUDAM), Annual Report, Belém, 1970.

Sullivan, Walter, *Continents in Motion,* New York, McGraw-Hill, 1974.

"The Three Brazils," *The Economist,* Survey 7, July 31, 1976.

Todd, Millicent, *Peru, A Land of Contrasts,* Boston, Little, Brown and Co., 1914.

Tomlinson, H. M., *The Sea and the Jungle,* Barre, The Imprint Society, 1971.

Turner, John R. G., "Mimicry: A Study in Behavior, Genetics, Ecology, and Biochemistry," *Scientific Progress,* Vol. 58, 1970.

————, "Muellerian Mimicry," in *Population Genetics and Ecology,* ed. Samuel Karlin, New York, Academic Press, 1976.

————, "A Tale of Two Butterflies," *Natural History,* February, 1975.

Turner, Terence S., "The Northern Kayapo of Central Brazil," unpublished manuscript, 1967.

————, "Social Structure and Political Organization Among the Northern Kayapo," Doctoral Thesis, Harvard University, 1966.

van der Slooten, et al., "Especies florestais da Amazonia," PNUD/FAO/IBDF, *Serie technica* No. 6, Brasília, 1976.

Vanzolini, P. E., "Notes on Nesting Behavior of *Podocnemis expansa* in the Amazon Valley," *Avulsos de Zoologia,* Vol. II. No. vii, 1967.

Verne, Jules, *The Giant Raft,* New York, Charles Scribner's Sons, 1900.

Villas Boas, Claudio and Orlando, *Xingu: The Indians, Their Myths,* New York, Farrar, Strauss & Giroux, 1973.

von Hagen, Wolfgang, ed., *The Green World of the Naturalists; Five Centuries Of Natural History in South America,* New York, Greenberg, 1948.

von Humboldt, Alexander, *The Travels and Researches of Alexander von Humboldt,* Edinburgh, Oliver and Boyd, 1836.

Von Ihering, Rodolpho, *Dicionario dos Animais do Brasil,* São Paulo, Editora Universidade de Brasília, 1968.

Wadia, A. S. N., *A Thousand Miles up the Amazon,* London, J. M. Dent and Sons, 1936.

Wagley, Charles, *Amazon Town,* New York, Knopf, 1964.

————, ed., *Man in the Amazon,* Gainesville, University of Florida Press, 1973.

Wallace, Alfred Russel, *A Narrative of Travels on the Amazon and Rio Negro,* London, Ward, Lock, and Bowden Ltd., 1895.

Walle, Paul, *Bolivia,* London, T. Fisher Unwin, 1914.

Weaver, K., and Littlehales, B., "The Five Worlds of Peru," *National Geographic,* February, 1964.

Weberbauer, A., *Die Pflanzenwelt der Peruanischen Anden in Ihren Grundzugen Dargestellt,* Leipzig, W. Englemann, 1911.

Werder, Ulrich, "General Aspects of Fish Culture in the Amazon Area," unpublished manuscript, 1977.

Wetterberg, G. B., "Uma analise de prioridades em conservacao da natureza na Amazonia," PNUD/FAO/BRA, *Serie technica,* No. 8, Brasília, 1976.

White, Peter T., and Parks, Winfield, "Giant Brazil," *National Geographic,* September, 1962.

Whitmore, T. C., *Tropical Rain Forests of the Far East,* Oxford, University Press, 1975.

Williams, E., "Key and Description of Living Species of Genus *Podocnemis," Bulletin of the Museum of Comparative Zoology,* June, 1954.

Wilson, Edward O., *The Insect Societies,* Cambridge, the Belknap Press, Harvard, 1971.

——, "Slavery in Ants," *Scientific American,* June, 1975.

Woodwell, George M., "The Carbon Dioxide Question," *Scientific American,* January, 1978.

Wurdack, J. J., "Botanical Exploration of the Marañon Rain Forests," *The Garden Journal,* July/August, 1964.

Zahl, Paul A., "Seeking the Truth about the Piranha," *National Geographic,* November, 1970.

——, *To the Lost World,* New York, Alfred A. Knopf, 1939.

Zarur, G., *Parentesco, Ritual, e Economia no Alto Zingu,* FUNAI, Brasília, 1975.

Zikmund, Miroslav, and Hanzelka, Jiri, *Amazon Headhunters,* Prague, Artia, 1963.

Selected
Index

Acre, 11, 20n, 36, 48
Acuticordes mosquito, 18. *See also*
    Mosquitoes
Adrianchiti, 208–212 *passim*
Affable Savages, 27
Africa, 111, 112
African river blindness, 17, 168
Agassiz, Louis, 125
Agua Boa, 141, 143, 159
Aika, 142, 144–145, 159,
    166–172, 178
Air Force, Brazilian, 159
Alalau River, 48
Alligators, 138, 172
Alpaca wool, 200
Altiplano, 219
Amahuaca, 48, 200
Amapó, 11
Amazon: first European descent
    of, 40; reversed direction of,
    12; source of, 203–204
Amazonas, 11, 48
Amazonia: prehistory of, 111–113;
    mentioned *passim. See also*
    individual states and rivers by
    name
Amazonia Legal, 11
Amazon Park, 124
Amazon Town, 106
Amoebas, 17, 103
Anaconda, 155–156
Ancilostomiasis, 17
Andes, 39–40; mentioned, 12, 36,
    198

Andujar, Claudia, 180
Angel, Timmy, 9
Angiosperms, 111
Ango, Mikanon, 208
Animals, 112, 149; endangered,
    187–201; export of, 196;
    laboratory, 188, 196; skin
    traffic in, 187, 188, 189,
    199–200; *See also*
    individually by name
Animism, 40
Anonaceae, 121
Anopheles mosquito, 16. *See also*
    Mosquitoes
Anta, 139, 148
Antapallpa, 220–221
Anthropologists, 45
Ants, 7, 118, 170–171
Approach posts, 44, 46, 115
Apurimac River, 198, 200, 204, 208
Araceae, 13, 228
Araguaçema, 57
Araguaya River, 30, 34, 58, 59
Arana, Julio Cesar, 42
Arapaima gigas, 126
Ararayas, 149
Arborviruses, 18
Arequipa, 204, 205
Arkata silver mine, 209
Arias, Jorge, 104–105
Arraras amarelhos, 149
Aruak, 40
Aruana, 126
Asheshov, Nicholas, 198, 204

247

Asia, 111, 112, 113
Augutero, 197
Auka, 197, 198
Ayacucho, Peru, 39

Bailey, Bob, 189–191, 196, 201
Balanophoraceae, 79
Bananas, 80, 115
Barra (former name of Manaus),
    99
Bates, Henry Walter, 15–16, 20,
    41–42, 120, 126, 138, 145,
    171, 175; mentioned, 2, 133
Bates, Marston, 67
Bats, 66, 67, 149, 229
Bau, 68
Bebgogti, 63, 66, 68, 73
Bees, 86, 102, 120
Beetles, 17, 102, 120, 228
Bela Terra, 96
Belém, 7–18, 19, mentioned, 1,
    17, 99
Belém-Brasília highway, 8, 19, 21,
    57
Belhausia, 17
Benavides, Felipe, 199–201, 204
Benmoti, 62
Berhinouilh, 212
Beriberi, 17
Bertholletia excelsa, 15
Bichus de pe, 18
Big-foot, 158
Birds, 2, 7–8, 13, 23, 34–35, 116,
    120, 121, 149–151, 229. *See
    also individually by name*
Bitterns, 151
Bixa orellana, 71, 176, 213
Blackwater fever, 18
Boa Ilha, 158
Bôa Vista, 114, 141, 185
Bolivia, 200
Bombaceae, 13
Bonifacio, 216, 217

Botany of Amazon. *See* Plants
Botfly, 18
Bôte, 126
Boza, Hernan, 219
Brasília, 33, 45, 49
Brazilian Shield, 60, 112, 113, 118
Brazil-nut trees, 15, 20n, 86, 150
Bridge Over San Luis Rey, The, 204
Brown Keith, 123
Bubonic plague, 17
Burseraceae, 15
Buterpa oleracea, 14n
Butterflies, 7–8, 13, 34, 118–126
    passim, 177, 228–230

Caatinga, 37
Cabeça-Seca, 48
Caboclos, 12, 20–21, 44
Cacao tree, 72
Cachimbo, 49
Cailloma, 205, 208
Caleri, Jean, 48, 159–160, 185
Campina, 37
Candirus, 127, 154
Caprimulgiformes, 229
Capybara, 151
Caracaraí, 113, 141
Caraipa grandiflora, 14n
Carajas Mountains, 12
Carapa guianensis, 14n
Caribbean pine, 27
Carlos (Peruvian gatekeeper),
    205–207
Carpenter, Clarence R., 67, 190
Carvajal, Gaspar de, 41
Carville, La., 107
Castanha Creek, 160
Castro, José de, 20
Catfish, 127, 148, 154
Catholic missionaries, 43, 185
Catrimani River, 142, 143–161,
    187
Cattle ranching, 19, 30

Caxão, 172
Cayapo, 41, 48, 56, 57, 59–60,
    86–87. *See also* Menkranoti
Caymans, 138, 150, 197
Cecropias, 150
Cerrado, 36
Chagas (acting chief of the Aika),
    164, 167–168
Chagas (pilot), 133–134
Chagas' disease, 17, 105
Chagas Institute, 24
Chagnon, Napoleon, 179
Chiclayo, 2
Chiggers, 18
Childbirth, 79–80, 183–184
Children, 71
Chocecoroa, Mount, 204
Cholera, 17
Chumbivillcas, 217, 218
Chivray, 207–208
CIA, 43
Cintas-Largas, 48
Civilizados, Indian clashes with,
    44–45
Cloroquine, 225
Cobra grande, 158
Coca, 205, 210, 227
Coca-Cola Company, 227
Cocaine, 187, 188
Colombia, 43, 53, 118
Congress, Brazilian, 45
Condors, 200–201
Conquistadores, 39–40
Conservation, 197, 199. *See also*
    Park system; Refugia
Contraceptive plants, 40, 73, 74, 75
Cordillera, 198, 200, 204
Corhausanta, 204
Corn, 40
Corythophora, 122
Costus, 115
Cowell, Adrian, 50, 184, 185
Cowfish, 129–130
Crops, 80, 98, 106, 156, 168
Crotalidae, 177

Cryobalanaceae, 121
Cueva de las Lechuzas, 229
Cuiabá-Santarém highway, 51, 92
Cuílha fruit, 153
Cuiu-cuiu, 127
Cujubim Falls, 159
Culex mosquito, 22
Cunha, Tristao de, 41
Curassows, 149, 170

Darwin, Charles, 17, 99
*Darwinism: An Exposition of the
    Theory of Natural Selection*,
    121
Davilla vines, 73
Davis, John, 94
Deer, pampas, 35
Delaney, Danny, 2, 7, 32, 66, 71, 72,
    87, 92, 101; mentioned, 60, 97
Dení, 76
Dermotobia hominis, 18
Diamonds, 10, 92, 101–102
Didi, 144, 146
Dinizia excelsa, 15
Diphtheria, 17
Disease, 15–18, 66, 103–108, 209
Distrito Federal, 33
Doctrine of Signatures, 74
Dogs, 64
Dolphin, 126
Drug traffic, 187, 188, 227–228
"Dry-Heads," 48
Duarte, Paulo, 53

Ecology. *See* Animals, endangered;
    Conservation; Forest; Park
    system; Refugia
Economist, The, 27
Ectoparasites, 18
Ecuador, 118
Eiten, George, 35–36

Eketi, 73, 79–80
Electric eels, 128
Electric fish, 154
El Empresa Nacional de la Coca, 227
Elephantiasis, 17
Equine encephalitis, 18
Erythroxylaceae, 121, 228
Eschweilera, 14n
Espinar, 213
Ethnobotany of Amazon, 75–77. *See also* Medicines, herbal
Euterpe oleracea, 14n
Exploration of the Valley of the Amazon, 1
Evandro Chagas Institute, 15
Evolution, 117
Explorers, 2, 44. *See also* Bates; Spruce; Wallace

Fabaceae, 13
FABE, 159
FAO, 37
Farinha, 82, 156
Farming, 80, 98, 156, 168; of fish, 139
Fazenda Uraem. *See* King Ranch
Fazendeiros, 19–32 *passim*, 44
Febre negra de Lábrea, 18
Fer-de-lance, 177
Ferris, Tim, 78, 225
Fever. *See* Disease; Malaria
Flash floodplain forest, 37
Flowers, 115–116. *See also* Plants
Flora and Fauna II, 134, 141
Frankfurt Zoological Society, 200
Fruit trees, 72–73
Folk remedies. *See* Medicines, herbal
Food and Agricultural Organization, 37
Ford, Henry, 17, 96
Fordlândia, 17, 96

Forest, 36–38, 106, 117, 124, 174. *See also* Jungle; Trees
Fourneaux, Robin, 42–43
FUNAI, 11, 27, 33, 43–49, 53–56 *passim*, 75, 180

Garimpeiros. *See* Prospectors
Gastroenteritis, 94
Gause's Law, 194
Gavião, 45
Geiba pentandra, 13
Geology of Amazonia, 12
Germany, 187
Gerridae, 146
Gery, Jacques, 125, 127
Gibbons, 191
Gilberto, Dr., 15–16, 18
Gill-net, 130
Glander, Kenneth, 190
Gmelina, 27
Goiás, 34, 41, 57
Gondwanaland, 111, 113
Gonorrhea, 66
Goupia glabra, 14n
Grant, Verne, 122
Grass, on ranch, 29
Green Hell Tours, 53
Guan, 173, 176
Guanaco, 212
Guitar lessons, 77–78, 222
Gum, 142, 147
Gurupi River, 27, 31
Guyana Shield, 112, 113, 118, 148

Haffer, J., 123
Hallucinogens, 169, 173, 174, 187, 188
Handbook of South American Indians, 168
Hansen's disease, 107
Harvard, 76, 121, 170
Hawks, 150

Heelas, Richard, 52
Heliconia, 115
Heliconius, 118–119
Hepatitis, 16
Herndon, William, 1
Herons, 150
Highways, 19
Hissing beetle, 17
Hoatzins, 149
Hospital for Tropical Diseases, 16
Howler monkeys, 67
Huallaga Valley, 227
Humboldt, Alexander von, 7, 42, 117, 133
Hummingbirds, 149
Huts, Cayapo, 82, 85
Huxley, Francis, 27

IBDF, 133, 148
Ibis, 150, 176
Igapó, 14, 36
Igarapé Putada, 158
Iguanas, 150
Inambu, 172
Incas, 39–40, 205, 218
INCRA, 93–94
Indian Protection Service, 44
Indians, 2, 11, 12, 20, 39–89. *See also individual tribes:* Aikas; Amahuaca; Cabeça-Seca; Caxão; Cayapo; Cintas-Largas; Dení; Gavião; Inambu; Jivaro; Jauari; Kreen-Akroare; Kyabi; Machiguenga; Macu; Mayaruna; Mayoluno; Menkranoti; Mundurucu; Mura; Omagua; Opikteri; Parahori; Paumari; Pouari; Quechua; Surui; Suya; Ticuna; Trumai; Tucano; Txucurramai; Umutina; Urubú; Waimiri-Atroaris; Waura; Xavantes; Xinguano; Yagua; Yanomamo; Yurimagua

Influenza, 16
INPA, 102–106 *passim;* 128, 130; mentioned, 111, 121, 125, 173, 178
Insects, 67, 83, 102–103, 145, 146, 152, 170–171. *See also* Butterflies
Iquitos, 52, 197
Iriri River, 61, 63
Ishkariani, 43
ISL (Summer Institute of Linguistics), 198
Ismarth, General, 52, 53–54, 160
Itaituba, 92
Itaúba wood, 147

Jacaretingas, 138, 172
Jacú, 173
Jaguar, 1, 151, 187, 188, 189, 196–197
Jamanxim River, 92
Jandia, 154
Japanese mining enterprise, 215
Japís, 150
Japòs, 150
Jararaca, 177
Jauari, 160, 173, 183
Javier, 220–221
Jê linguistic group, 40, 56
Jesuits, 42–43
Jivaro, 48, 53, 198, 225
Jungle, 13–15; Andean, 226–227, 228; clearing of, 27–31, 115–123. *See also* Forest; Trees
Jupiter, 78
Jurua River, 131
Justicia pectoralis, 173

Kandell, Jonathan, 37
Kaolin, 27
Karekra, 73

Karib, 40
Katanga silver mine, 214, 215
Kayangung, 43
Kerr, Warwick, 102, 105
Kingfishers, 149
King Ranch, the, 19– 32
Koti, 73
Krakiêro, 73
Kreen-akroare, 48, 49– 52, 73
Kubitschek, Joscelino, 33
Kyabi, 51

Laguna McIntyre, 204
Lanternaria, 152
Land Above the Clouds, 217
Laterization, 29
Laurichocha, Lake, 203
Lecythidaceae, 15, 121, 123, 150
Leguminosae, 118
Leishmaniasis, 16, 104– 105
Leonça, 169– 175 *passim*
Leprosy, 16, 107– 108
Leticia, 53, 168, 187– 189
Light, quest for, 116– 117
Lima, 197– 198, 204, 228
Livitaca, 214, 217– 218
Llamas, 200, 210, 211– 212
Lovejoy, Tom, 38, 124
Lucena, Paulo, 53
Lucia Maria, 98
Ludwig, Daniel K., 26
Lungfish, 128

Macacos de cheiro, 8
Macaws, 149
Macheteiros, 23– 30 *passim*
Machiguenga, 48, 199, 200
McGahan, Gerry and Libby, 201
McIntyre, 204
MacNeish, Richard, 39
Macu, 48
Madagascar, 112, 131

Madeira River, 44
Madre de Dios River, 200
Mafia, 227
Magnolia, 118
Magnolidae, 111
Malaria, 15– 16, 24– 26, 105, 113,
    143, 225; mentioned, 94
Maloccas, 48
Manatees, 129– 130, 188
Manaus, 16, 98, 99– 109, 128;
    mentioned, 11, 48, 187
Maned wolf, 34
Mangroves, 37
Manioc, 40, 52, 82, 156, 164
Manoel, 163– 170 *passim*
Manu Park, 199, 200
Mapinguari, 158
Marajó Island, 9, 12, 19, 37, 40
Maranhão, 11, 25, 41
Marañon River, 203, 204
Marantaceae, 13, 115
Maria, 145, 146, 152– 154, 157
Mariscadors, 130– 131
Marmosets. *See* Monkeys
Marquez, Luis, 218– 219
Mason, Richard, 50
Mata, 36, 37
Mata de cipó, 36
Matari, 41– 42
Mateiros, 15
Mato Grosso, 11, 36, 41, 48, 50
Matos, Antonio, 109
Matrincha, 128
Matthiessen, Peter, 198– 199
Maukayachta, 212
Mayaruna, 48, 53, 198
Mayoluno, 48
Measles, 16
Medicine men, 73
Medicines, 3, 15– 18, 104– 105,
    178, 205; herbal, 72– 77
    passim, 109, 209, 213
Meggers, Betty, 21, 123
Melastomaceae, 112
Menibiok, 66, 68, 82
Menkranoti, 49, 61– 91

Menkranoti village, 56–89 *passim*
Mestizos, 198
Metals, discovery of, 12
Miiasis, 18
Mimicry, 119–121
Mimosa pudica, 7
Minaspata, Mount, 204
Minguartia guyanensis, 121
Ministry of the Interior, 45
Mira Norte, 57
Missao Cristao Evangelico, 78
Missionaries, 42–43, 80
Misti, Mount, 204, 207
Mittermeier, Russell, 191, 192, 197
Mohawk, 166
Monkeys: *Cairara,* 192; capuchin, 192; endangered, 189; howler, 67–68, 152, 189–190, 191; marmoset, 190–191, 195; and medical research, 188; night, 195; saki, 194–195; spider, 192–193; squirrel, 8, 193–194; tamarin, 195; titi, 194; uakari, 194; woolly, 192, 193
Monson River, 230
Montane forest, 36
Montrichardia arborescens, 150
Morrison, Tony, 198, 199, 217
Mosquitoes, 16, 18, 22, 25–26, 145; mentioned, 18. *See also* Malaria
Moto, Captain de, 41
Mountain sickness, 204, 205, 209
Muir, John, 1
Mundurucu, 31, 92
Mura, 41–42
Mureles, Chico, 63
Murelles, Apuena, 51
Museo Goeldi, 14
Music, Quechua, 219–220
Mutuca, 18
My Amazon Adventure, 203
Mycchorizhae, 20
Myths, Aika, 172; Cayapo, 84–85; Yanomamo, 182

"Nam" boots, 166
Napalm, 160
Napo River, 40
National Foundation for the Indians, 11
National Geographic Society, 151, 204
National Institute for Colonization of Agrarian Reform, 93–94
National Research Institute of Amazonia, 102–106 *passim*
Naturalist-explorers, 2. *See also* Bates; Spruce; Wallace
Neto, Paolo N., 37
Netto, Otto B., 11
Neves, Luis, 44
New York Botanical Garden, 75
New York Times, 37
New York Zoological Society, 197
Nhàk-ba, 70
Niche-partitioning, 122
Nichols, Bob, 199, 200
Nile, the, 204
Norbert, Brother, 96
Nordestino migration, 94
Notes of a Botanist in the Amazon and the Andes, The, 175–176
Numbers, Cayapo, 87
Nut gatherers, 45–46. *See also* Brazil-nut gatherers

Ocelots, 196
O Globo, 51
Oil, 12
Oilbirds, 229
Oil companies, 198, 200
Oliveira, Ismarth A. de, 48
Omagua, 40–41
Onchocerciasis, 17, 168
Opikteri, 184
Orbygnia martiana, 64
Orellana, Francisco de, 40
Origin of species, theory of, 117
Origins of Adaptations, 122

Orinoco geese, 149–150
Orinoco River, 40, 133
Orioles, 150
Oripush fever, 18
Oropendulas, 150
Otters, 1, 151, 187, 188, 197
Oxygen and rain forest, 37–38
Owls, 35, 229

Pacú, 178
Pacú River, 160, 176–177
Painting, body, 70–71
Paititi, 199
Pakux, 73
Palm trees, 20n, 36, 150
Pampas deer, 35
Pampas Galeras, 199, 200
Papagaios, 149
Papaova snake, 149
Pará (former name of Belém), 1
Pará, history of Indians in, 41;
    mentioned, 11, 12, 15, 48, 49;
    ranching in, 19–32
Paracas, 199, 200
Paragominas, 21
Parahori, 160
Pará River, 131
Parque Nacional do Brasília, 34
Paranoa, Lake, 35
Parkia pendula, 121
Park system, 123–124, 199–200
Parrish, Skip, 57
Paruro, 205
Passion-flower vines, 118–119
Paumari, 132
Pava de tombes, 2
Peasants. *See Caboclos*
Pedrinho, 163–167 *passim*
Peixe-boi, 129–130
Pentaclethra macroloba, 14n
Perenatomine, 15
Perimetral Norte, 180
Peru, 43; author's travels in,
    197–231; mentioned, 52, 118

Peruano, José, 141–165, 179
Pharmacology of Amazon, 75–77.
    See also Medicines, herbal
Phoebis philea, 66
Pia, 116
Pigs, wild, 159
Pillpinto, 221, 223
Pinga, 58
Pinto, Gilberto, 48–49, 114
Piracatinga, 127
Piranhas, 10, 128–129, 151, 154
Piraiba, 127, 154
Pirarara, 127
Pirarucú, 126
Pires, João Murça, 14–15, 36, 76n,
    111
Piulis d'agua, 146
Pium mosquitoes, 145
Paragominas, 31
Planalto, the, 33–38
Plants, 72, 75–77, 115–123
    passim, 228–230 *passim. See
    also individual plants by
    name;* Medicines, herbal
Platyrrhines, 189. *See also*
    Monkeys
Plenopid snails, 17
Plowman, Tim, 228
"Plucking of the virgin's hair," 53
Pneumonia, 16
Podocnemidae, 133
Podocnemis, 131
Poison, arrow, 173
Pongo de Mainique, 198, 225
Porpoise, 126
Porto Velho, 101
Portugal, King of, 43
Portuguese colonizers, 42–43, 99
Posto de atracao, 46. *See also*
    Approach posts
Postos indigenos, 44. *See also*
    Approach posts
Pouari, 160
Pourouma trees, 73, 79, 170
Pouraquê, 154
Prance, Ghillean, 75, 111–115

passim, 121, 150
Pregnancy and plants, 79– 80
PRODENA, 199
Projeto RADAM, 10– 12
Prospectors, 44, 92, 101
Protestant missionaries, 43, 57
Pterocarpus officinalis, 14n
Pukatire, 72– 73
Purseglove, T. W., 80
Purus River, 131
Putumayo River, 40, 42

Quechua, 200, 205– 222
Quechua language, 40, 206– 207
Quechualand, 203– 231
Queixada, 159
Quinine, 15

Racial makeup of Brazil, 136n
RADAM, 10– 12, 20n
Radio Cuba, 152
Rainfall and Amazon Valley, 38
Raitaushiteris, 184
Ranchers, 19– 32 *passim,* 44
Rane, 58– 59
Rasgado River, 61, 66
Rats, 152
Reductions, 42
Refugia, 123– 124
Reichert family, 96
Remedies, folk. *See* Medicines,
    herbal
Remrare, 73– 74
Reis, Arthur Fereira, 20
Reiss, Rangell, 52
Restinga, 37
Rhea, 34
Rice, 27
Richards, P. W., 117
Rio Alalalu, 159
Rio Auaris, 179

Rio Branco, 19, 130– 134 *passim,*
    141
Rio Cunhuá, 76
Rio das Mortes, 41
Rio Fresco, 61
Rio Negro, 37, 98, 134
Rio Roosevelt, 44
Rio Tapajós, 17, 92, 95– 98;
    mentioned, 12, 124
Rio. *See* River
River. *See rivers by name:* Agua
    Boa; Alalau; Apurimac;
    Araguaya; Auaris; Branco;
    Catrimani; Cunhá; Das
    Mortes; Fresco; Iriri;
    Jamanxim; Jurua, Madeira;
    Madre de Dios; Marañon;
    Napo; Negro; Orinoco; Pacú;
    Pará; Purus; Putumayo;
    Rasgado; Roosevelt;
    Sepotouba; Solimoes; Tapajós;
    Tocantins; Trombetas; Ucayali;
    Urubamba; Xixê; Xingú
"River of Doubt", 44
Roberto, José, 78
Roberts, Tyson R., 127n
Rodriguez, William, 173
Rondon, Candido M. da S., 44, 46
Rondônia, 11, 45; mentioned, 12,
    36, 48
Roosevelt, Theodore, 44,
    128– 129, 138, 147, 177
Roraima, 10, 11, 19, 114;
    mentioned, 12, 36, 101, 141
Rowcliff, Charles, 24, 26– 31
Rubber, 96, 99, 141
Ruby, 163– 170 *passim*
Ruth, 228
Rylands, Anthony, 191, 195

Saffirio, Giovanni, 160
Salesians, 43
Sandflies, 18
Santarém, 19, 92, 96– 97

Santa Sophia Island, 189
São João, 23
São Paulo, 54, 102
São Sebastião, 158
Saporo, 128
Sawfish, 126
Scabies, 18
Schaller, George, 197
Schimper, A. F. W., 117
Schistosomiasis, 17
Schneider family, 78
Schultes, Richard E., 76, 118
Scientific American, 37
Scorpions, 82
Selaginella, 13
Selva, 36
Sepotouba River, 47
Serra de Carajas, 36
Serra do Cachimbo, 59
Serra do Gradaos, 60
Serra do Matao, 60
Serra Tabatinga, 164, 165
Sertanistas, 11, 46–51
Shamans, 74, 79, 169
Shaves, Johnny, 9–10, 24, 204
SIL, 43, 78, 198
Siskins, 34
Sixth Battalion of Construction
       Engineers, 113–114
Sizoens, 16
Smallpox, 17
Smith, Nigel, 94, 95, 196–197
Snakes, 120, 149, 177–178
Snow, Sebastian, 203, 209
Soccer, 65
Soil problems, 19–21
Solimoes River, 127, 130, 204
Spanish colonizers, 41–42
SPI, 44
Spruce, Richard, 2, 5, 111, 134,
       157, 175, 226
Stars, 78–79, 215
Sterling, Thomas, 174
Sternburg, Hilgard O., 95
Sting-rays, 126, 148
Storks, 82, 150

Strongiloidiasis, 17
SUCAM, 18
Sulfa drugs, 15
Summer Institute of Linguistics,
       43, 78, 198
Superintendency for Public Health
       Campaigns, 18
Surinam, 102
Surui, 45, 48
Suya, 52
Swift-Armour Company, 21, 27
Symphonia globulifera, 14n

Tachigalia, 118
Tachi trees, 150
Taida, 170
Talauma, 118
Tambaqui, 127–128
Tambés, 27
Tapirira guianensis, 14n
Tapajós, 132
Tape recording, 68
Tartarugas, 131, 132–133
Taxapuh, 54
Tea, 158, 230
Teatro do Amazonas, 100
Téfé, 187
Terra firme, 14, 20n, 150
Tetragastris trifoliata, 14n
Tewet, 71, 73, 88
Theobroma subincanum, 14n
Through the Brazilian Wilderness,
       138
Ticks, 18
Ticuna, 168, 188
Tingo Maria, 227–237
Tocandeira ants, 7
Tocantins River, 12, 34
Tomeasu, 9
Tortoise, 171–172
Tototobi, 18, 169
Toucans, 149
Townsend, Cameron, 43
Traira, 128, 154
Tralhoto, 128

Transamazonica, 92– 95
Trees, 13– 15, 111– 113, 118, *See also* Forest; Jungle
"Tribe That Hides From Man, The," 50, 184
Trichocephaliasis, 17
Triponozoma crusii, 17
Trombetas River, 131
Tropical Crops, 80
Trumai, 40
Tsalickis, Mike, 187– 189, 200
Tuberculosis, 16, 167
Tucano, 53
Tucunaré, 127– 128
Tucuxi, 126
Tullis, Jimmie R., 24– 26
Tunga penetrans, 18
Tupi-Guarani, 40
Turtles, 130– 139, 148; mentioned, 2, 107
Twain, Mark, 1
Txucurramai, 52, 60, 63
Typhoid, 16
Ucayali River, 203
Umutina, 47
Unevangelized Fields Service, 57
United States Air Force, 11
Universidad de la Selva, 227
Uri, 93
Urubamba River, 198, 204, 227
Urubú, 27, 31, 150
Urucú, 176, 213
Uyama, 168

Vanzolini, Paolo, 123, 178
Varig, 96
Várzea, 14, 20n, 36, 150
Vaughan family, 96
Vellozia flavicans, 35
Venereal diseases, 16
Venezuela, 48, 142
Verrugas, 209
Verswijver, Gustaaf, 54, 59– 70 *passim,* 83, 91, 197

Vicuna, 199, 200, 212
Vilafro, Lake, 204, 209
Villas-Boas, Claudio, 50– 52, 63
Villas-Boas, Orlando, 50– 51
Vines, mimicry of, 120
Virola elongata, 173
Virola surinamensis, 14n
Voice of America, 152
Volkswagen Company, 21, 30
Vouacapoua americana, 14n
Vultures, 9, 201

Wagley, Charles, 106
Waika, 183
Waimiri-Atroari, 48– 49, 113, 114, 115, 159
Wakatau, 180
Wakatauteri, 180, 184
Wallace, Alfred R., 2, 99, 116, 117, 121, 129– 130
Warari caves, 216, 218
Washaharua, 169, 173
Washington Post, 187, 226
Waura, 54
Wetterburg, Gary, 124
Wheatley, Jim, 43
Whittaker's method, 35
Wickham, Henry, 99
Wilder, Thornton, 204
Wilson, Edward O., 166, 170, 171
Witchcraft, 182– 183. *See also* Shamans
Wolves, 34
Women, Indian, 64, 68– 71 *passim,* 183– 184
Woodwell, George, 37
World Wildlife Fund, 38, 124, 199, 200
Worms, intestinal, 17, 103

Xavante, 41, 51
Xingú, 52
Xingú, the Indians, their Myths, 54

Xinguano, 51, 52, 56
Xingú National Park, 50, 55–56, 60
Xingú River, 12, 30, 61
Xirima, 167
Xixê, 61

Yagua, 168, 187
Yanomamo, 17–18, 40, 47–48, 169, 173, 179–185

Yauri, 213, 215
Yellow fever, 17
Yerba louisa, 230
Yurimagua, 127

Zaquini, Carlo, 180–185 *passim*
Zarur, George, 45–46

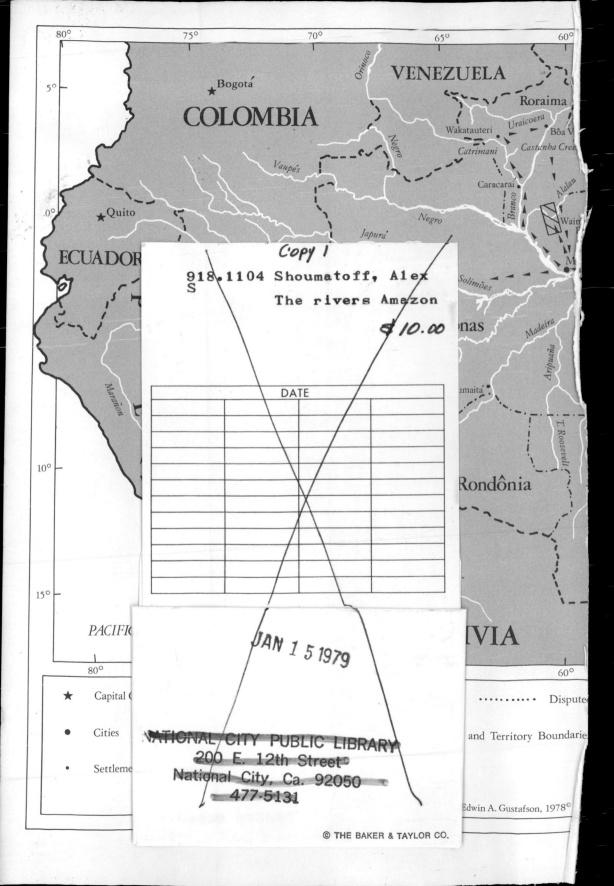